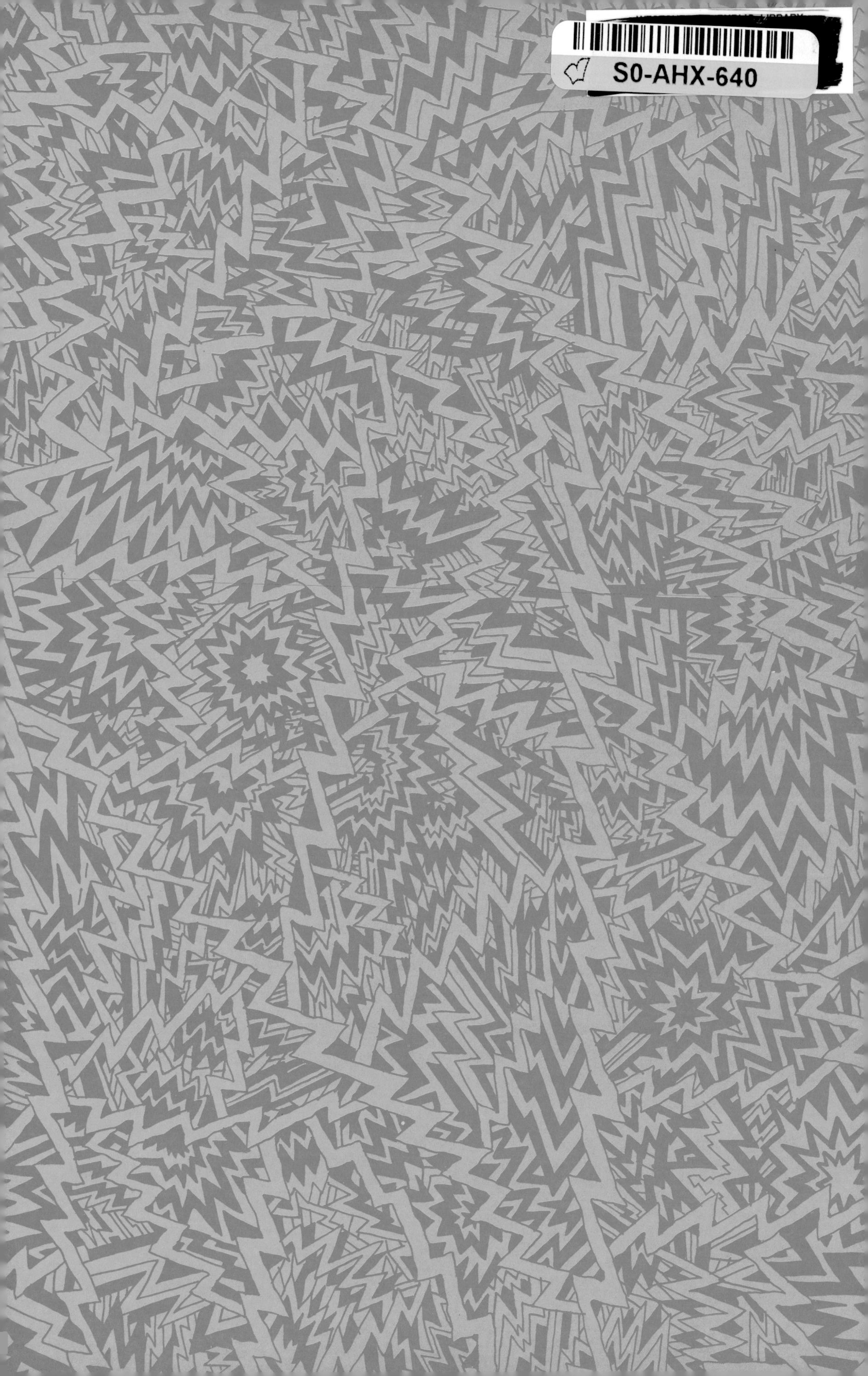

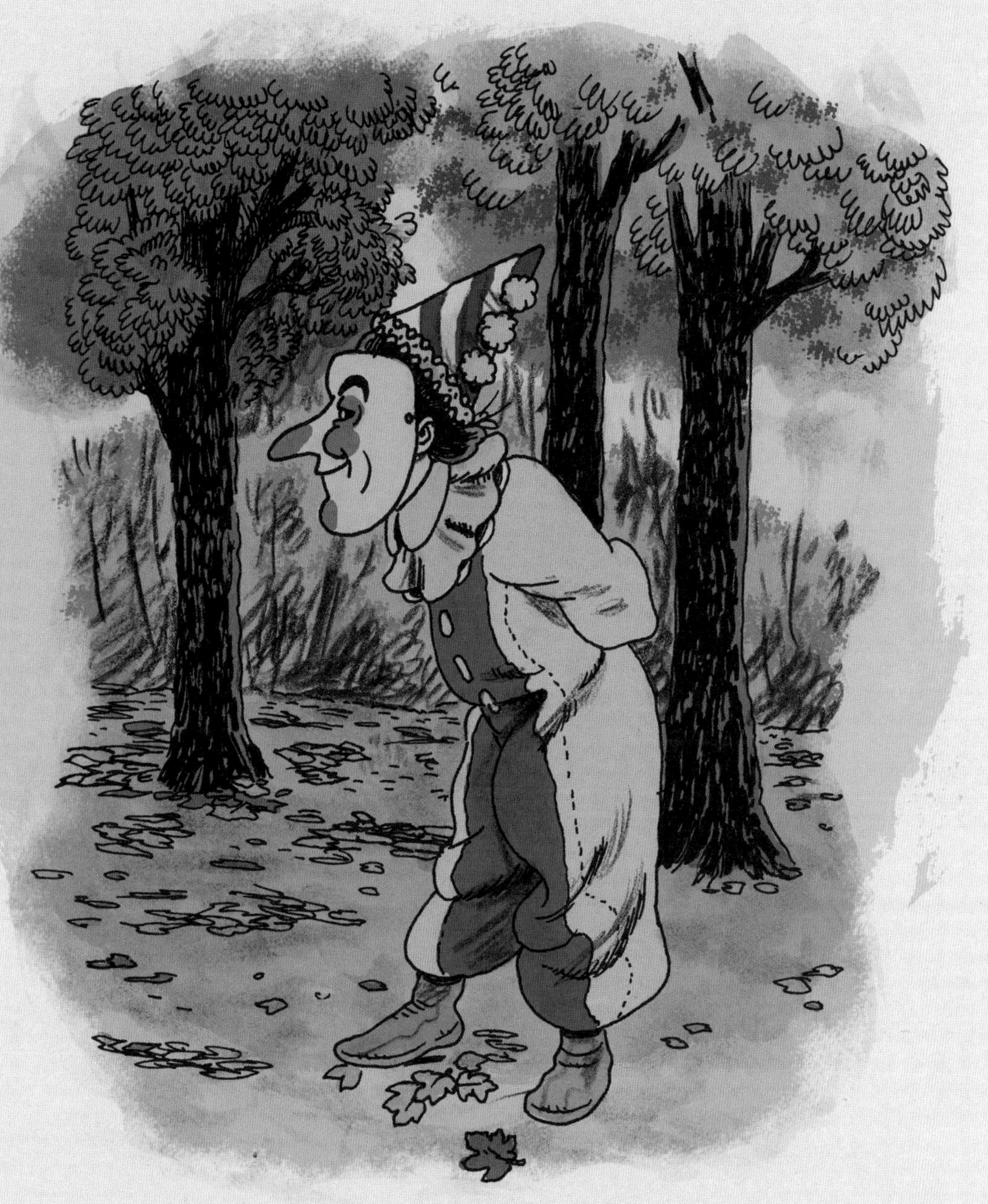

Disquiet

NOAH VAN SCIVER

FANTAGRAPHICS BOOKS INC.
7563 Lake City Way NE
Seattle, Washington, 98115

Editor and associate publisher: Eric Reynolds
Book design: Keeli McCarthy
Production: Paul Baresh
Publisher: Gary Groth

ISBN 978-1-60699-928-8
Library of Congress Control Number: 2016930125
First printing: May 2016
Printed in China

*For John Porcellino.
Best cartoonist, better friend.*

Foreword

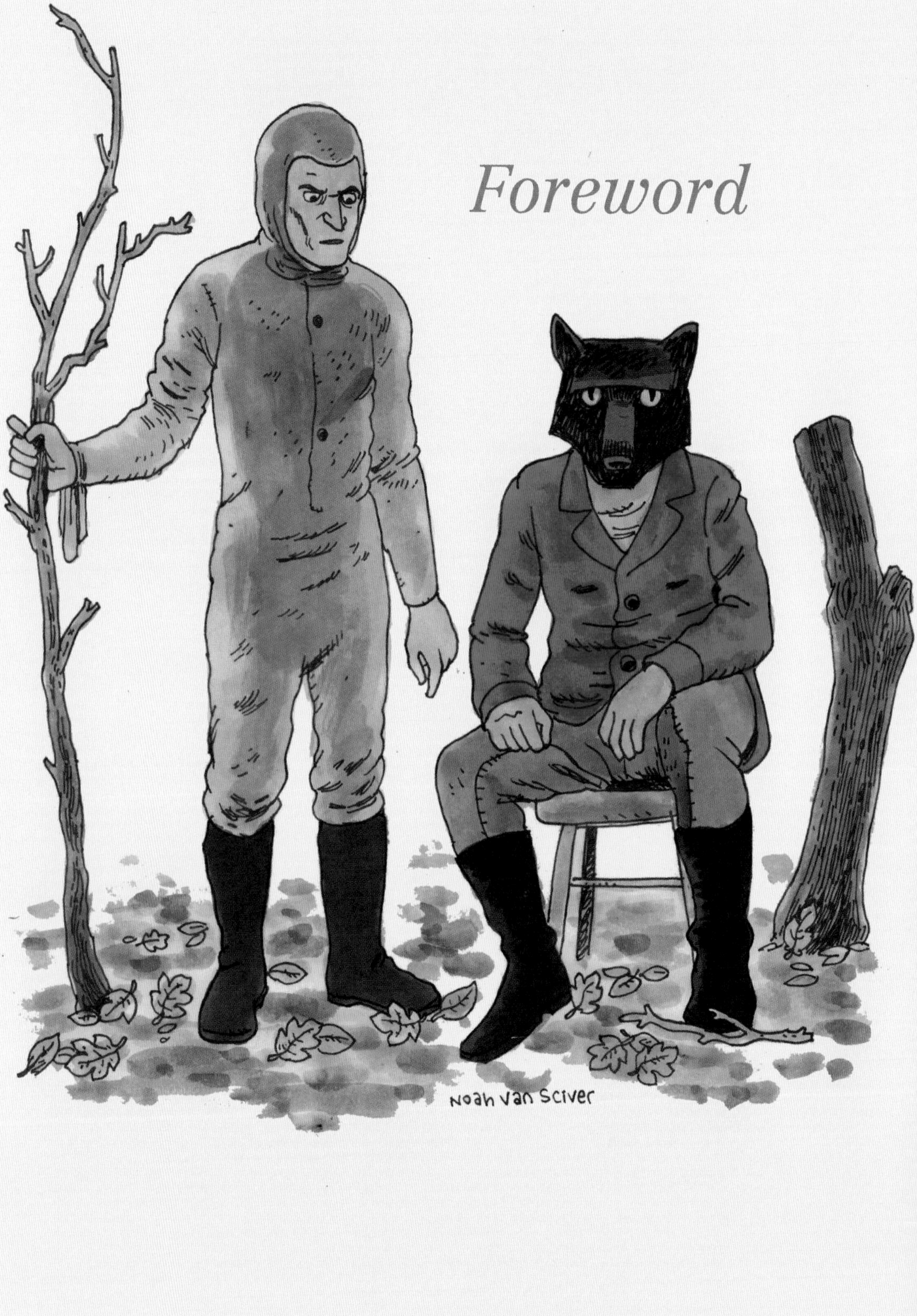
Noah Van Sciver

Noah is always drawing. "It's a personality flaw," he once told me.

When I met him, we were both underpaid employees at a corporate bagel shop. I was working on graduating from high school and he was working on his painting movement, dubbed "Noahism," which consisted of a series of impressionistic oil paintings he'd work on in his suburban apartment while eating cookies baked with stolen dough from the shop. I introduced him to Elliott Smith and he introduced me to Belle and Sebastian.

I had never been so in love.

By the time we started dating, Noah had moved on to comics, and much of our time together was spent in coffee shops and at Kinko's—he obsessively making zines to leave around Denver, and I working on some article for my college newspaper or copying flyers for my band. His work ethic was (and is) never-ending. I watched him mail out comics to everyone he admired over and over again, reacting to rejection with more and more art. It worked.

Reading Noah's comics now feels both achingly familiar and foreign. The easy chair his coat hangs on in "An Evening Alone" is the chair I bought on Craigslist for the Denver apartment we lived in (and later sold when we moved out). The blue of the walls in the breakup comic on page 88 is the exact shade that we had to paint over with white to get our deposit back. The hairpins he draws are mine, but the light switch covers are not.

I can so clearly see the specific details from Noah's life that he uses to populate the fictional world of his comics, and the new ones he invents. The deadbeat father in "The Lizard Laughs" shares a name and striking resemblance to Noah's own dad, but the scenario is imagined. Like the character in "It's Over," Noah really did have an ex who joined the Navy after they broke up. He places that truth in a new story that confronts the relationship between personal and universal tragedy. It's these biographical details that add an intimacy and veracity to his storytelling, grounding his fiction in a deeply personal reality.

The stories in this book run all over the place: from the historical comic "The Death of Elijah Lovejoy" (which I remember Noah drawing in bed; it was originally intended to be a part of his book *The Hypo*); to the quietly anticlimactic slice-of-life Christmas comic; to the bizarre "Down In A Hole" (which feels like it has loose *Simpsons* references, or maybe I think that because I remember borrowing entire seasons from our down-the-hall neighbor); to the *Tank Girl*-like silly sci-fi of "Punks V. Lizards." What comes through is wholeheartedly Noah: anxious and funny and depressed and weird and brilliant.

Noah and I were together for nearly five years, and then we weren't. The great thing about dating an artist is the ability to flip through his work and remember details long forgotten. I'd forgotten about the fake red roses in our apartment that he draws in "An Evening Alone"—that image conjures up a former life. I've always loved Noah's mind. I'm endlessly fascinated with the filter through which he sees the world, with the stories he tells, and the art he creates.

Disquiet is a glimpse into the mind of one of my favorite artists and people. And thanks to his personality flaw—I'd say gift—it's just a small portion of his vast body of work that exists and is still yet to come.

—Robin Edwards
Writer, Musician (Lisa Prank)

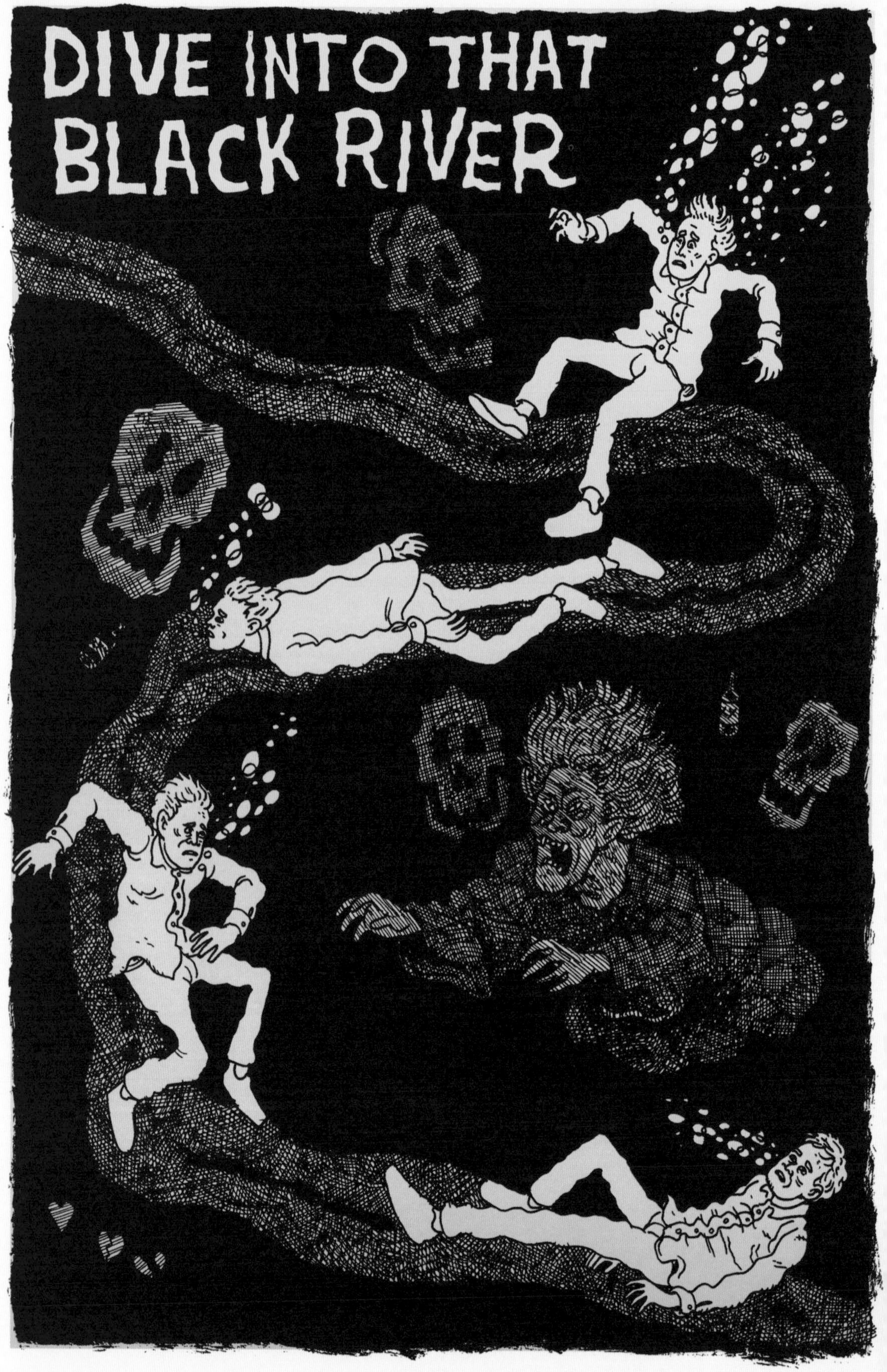
DIVE INTO THAT BLACK RIVER

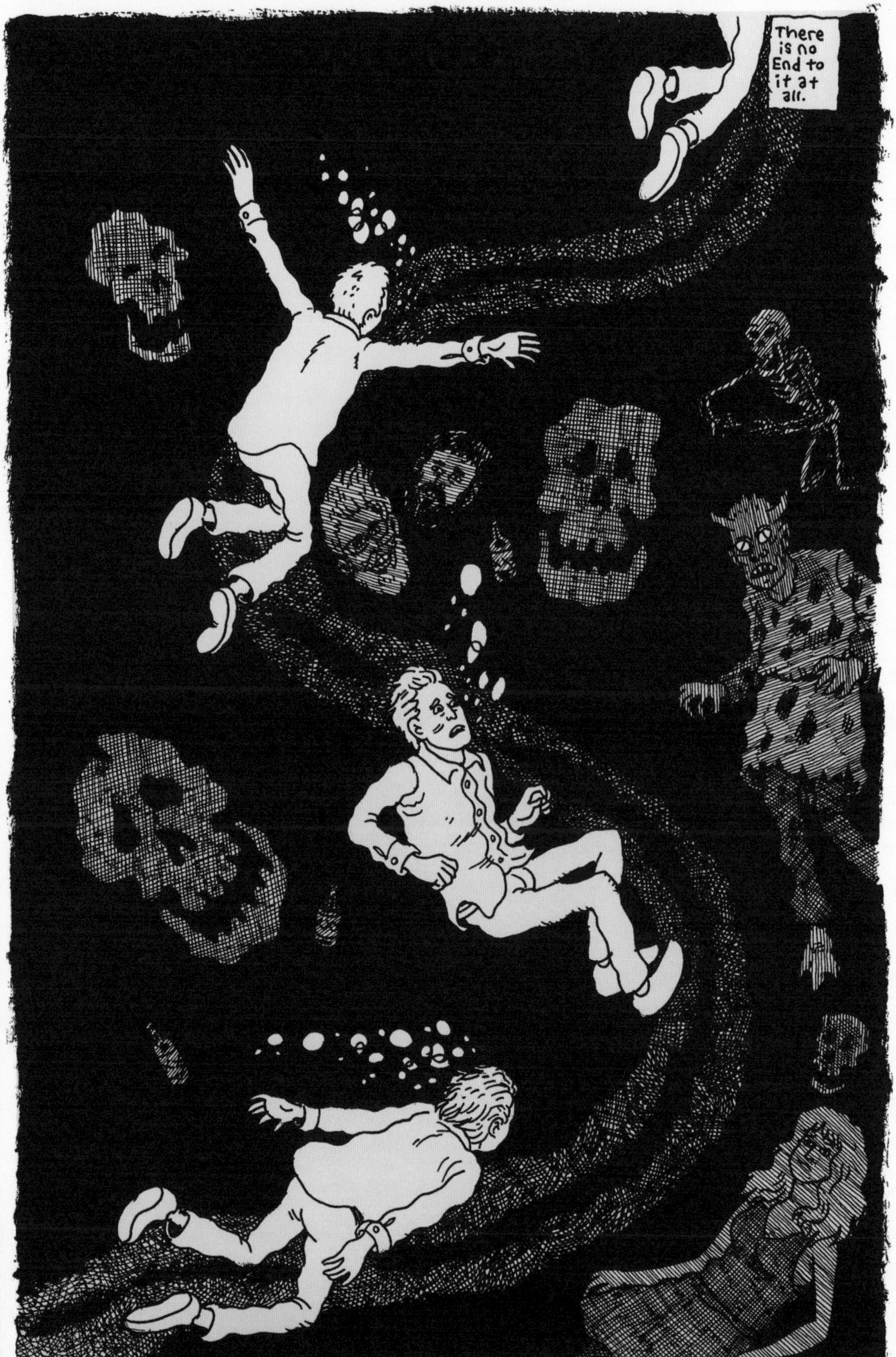
There is no End to it at all.

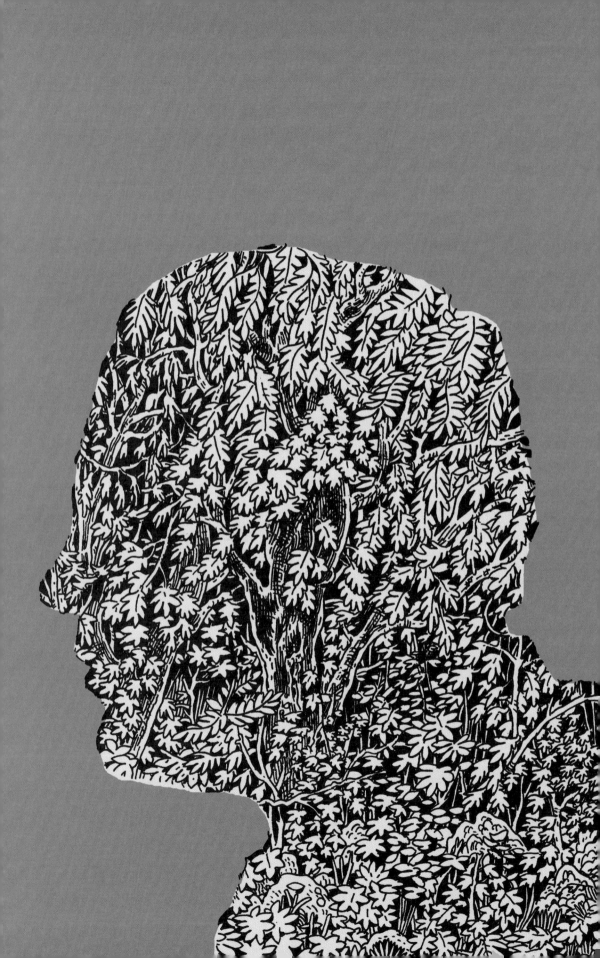

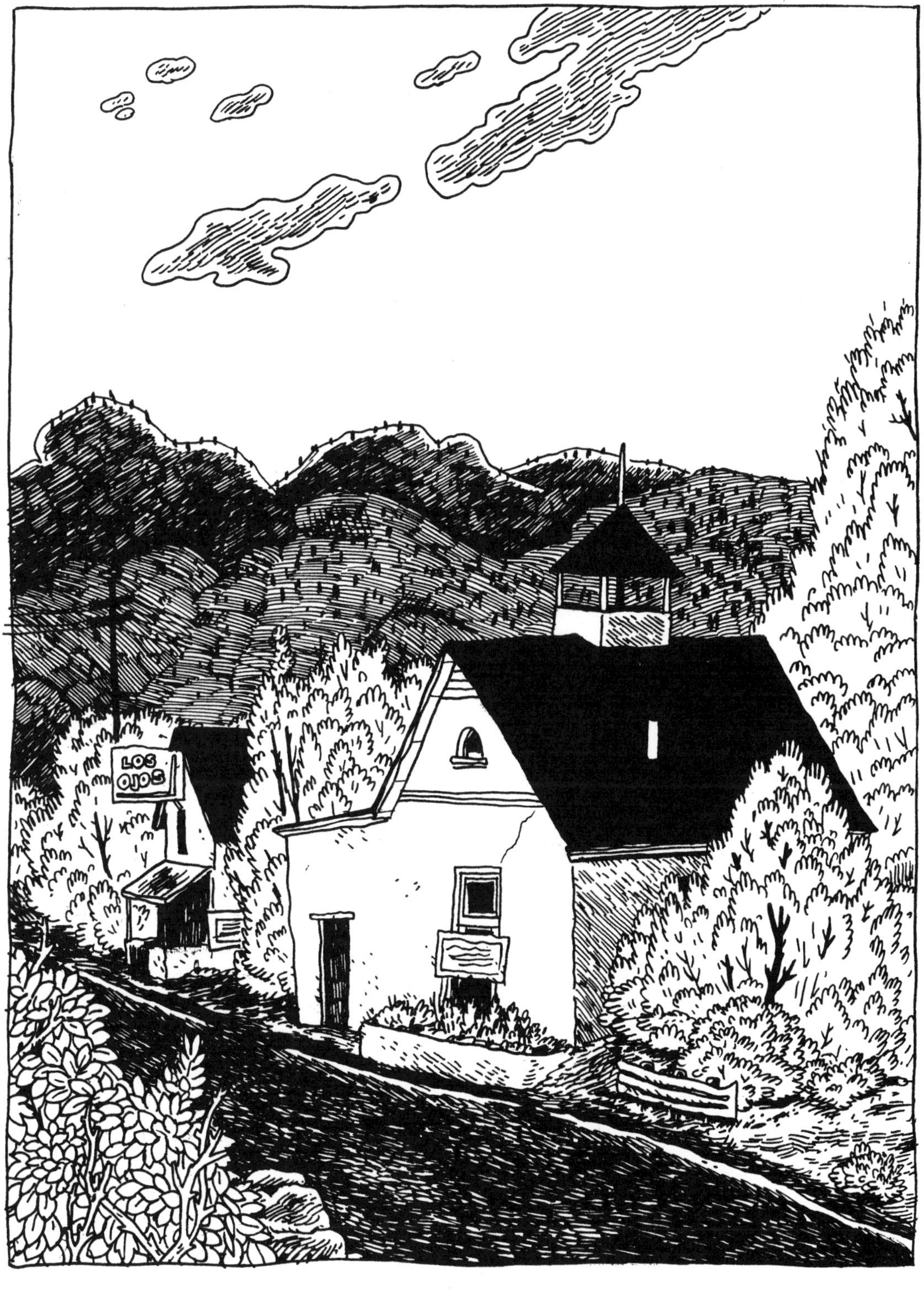
LOS OJOS

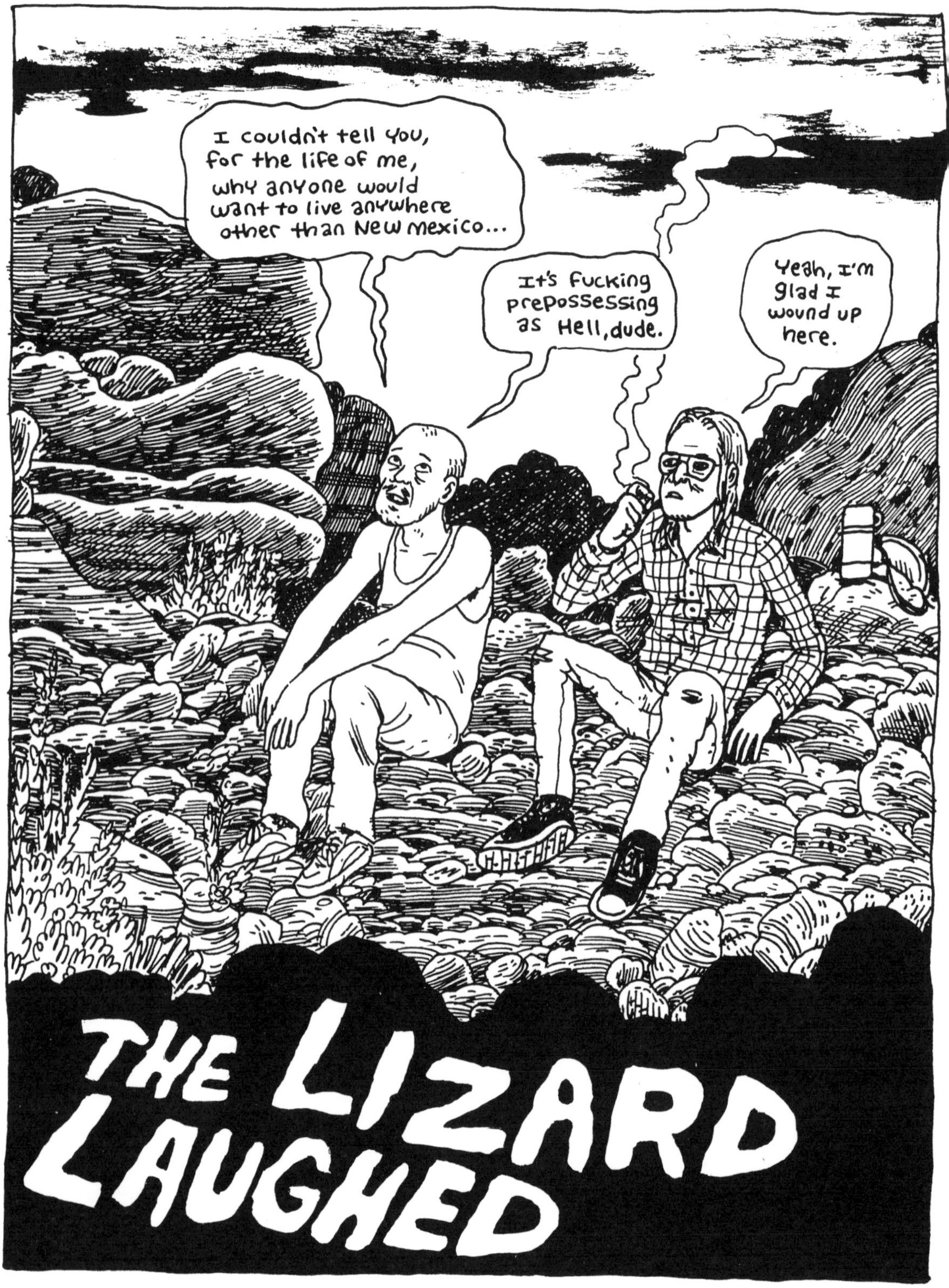
I couldn't tell you, for the life of me, why anyone would want to live anywhere other than New Mexico...
It's fucking prepossessing as Hell, dude.
Yeah, I'm glad I wound up here.
THE LIZARD LAUGHED

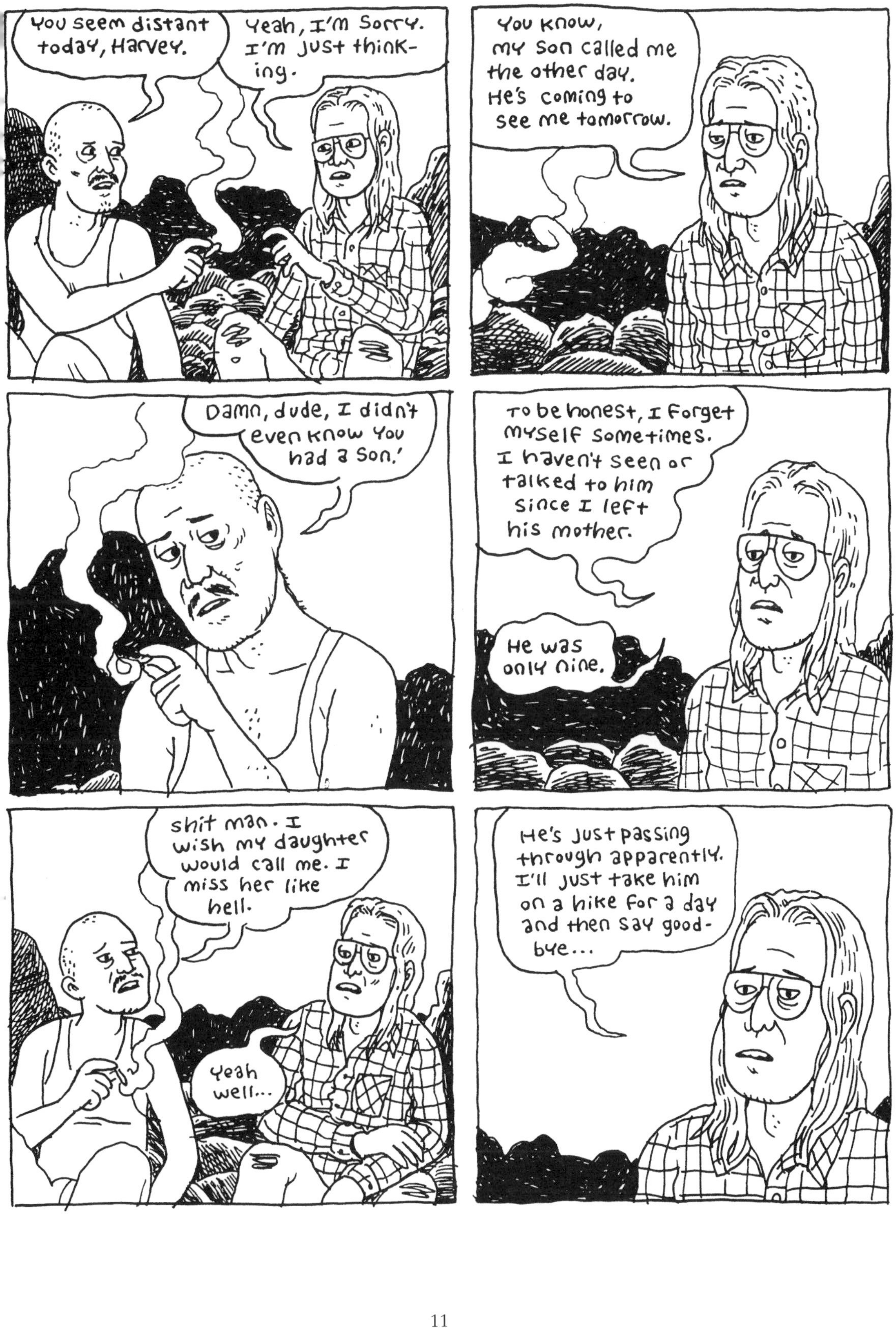
You seem distant today, Harvey.
Yeah, I'm sorry. I'm just think-ing.
You know, my son called me the other day. He's coming to see me tomorrow.
Damn, dude, I didn't even know you had a son.'
To be honest, I forget myself sometimes. I haven't seen or talked to him since I left his mother.
He was only nine.
shit man. I wish my daughter would call me. I miss her like hell.
Yeah well...
He's just passing through apparently. I'll just take him on a hike for a day and then say good-bye...

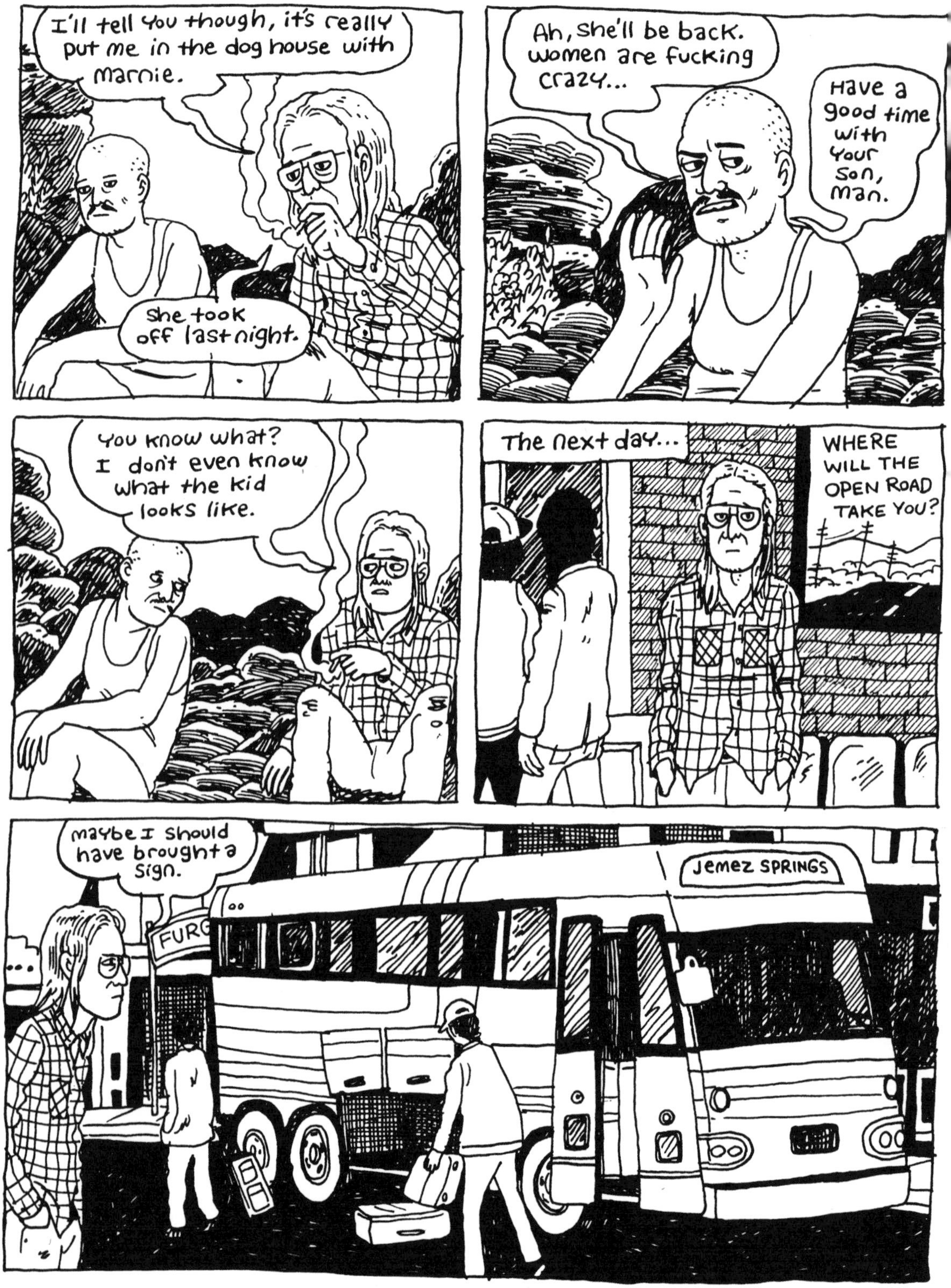
I'll tell you though, it's really put me in the dog house with marnie.
she took off last night.
Ah, she'll be back. women are fucking crazy...
Have a good time with your son, man.
you know what? I don't even know what the kid looks like.
The next day...
WHERE WILL THE OPEN ROAD TAKE YOU?
maybe I should have brought a sign.
JEMEZ SPRINGS
FURG

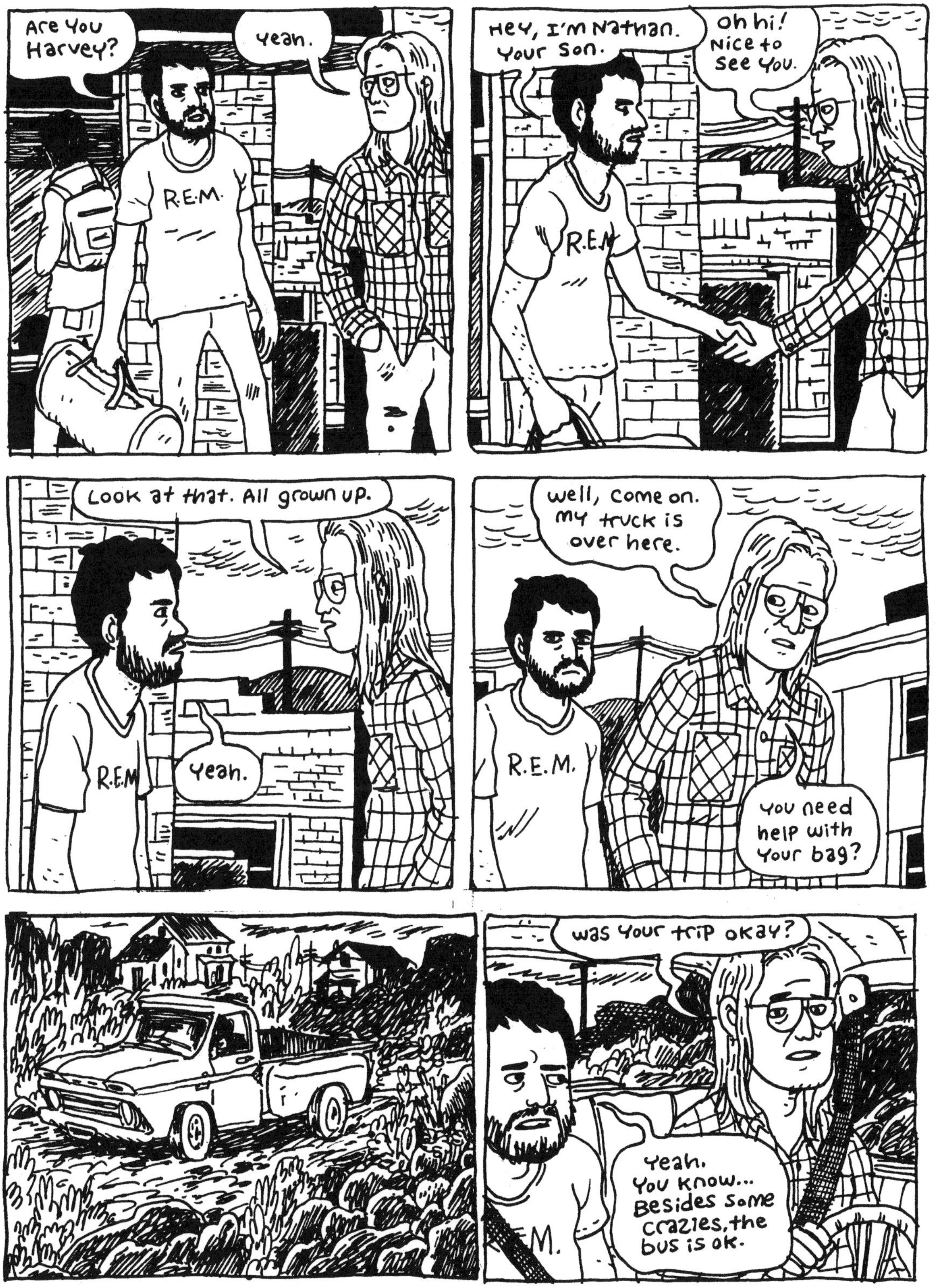
Are You Harvey?
Yeah.
Hey, I'm Nathan. Your son.
Oh hi! Nice to see You.
Look at that. All grown up.
Yeah.
Well, come on. My truck is over here.
You need help with Your bag?
Was your trip okay?
Yeah. You know... Besides some crazies, the bus is ok.

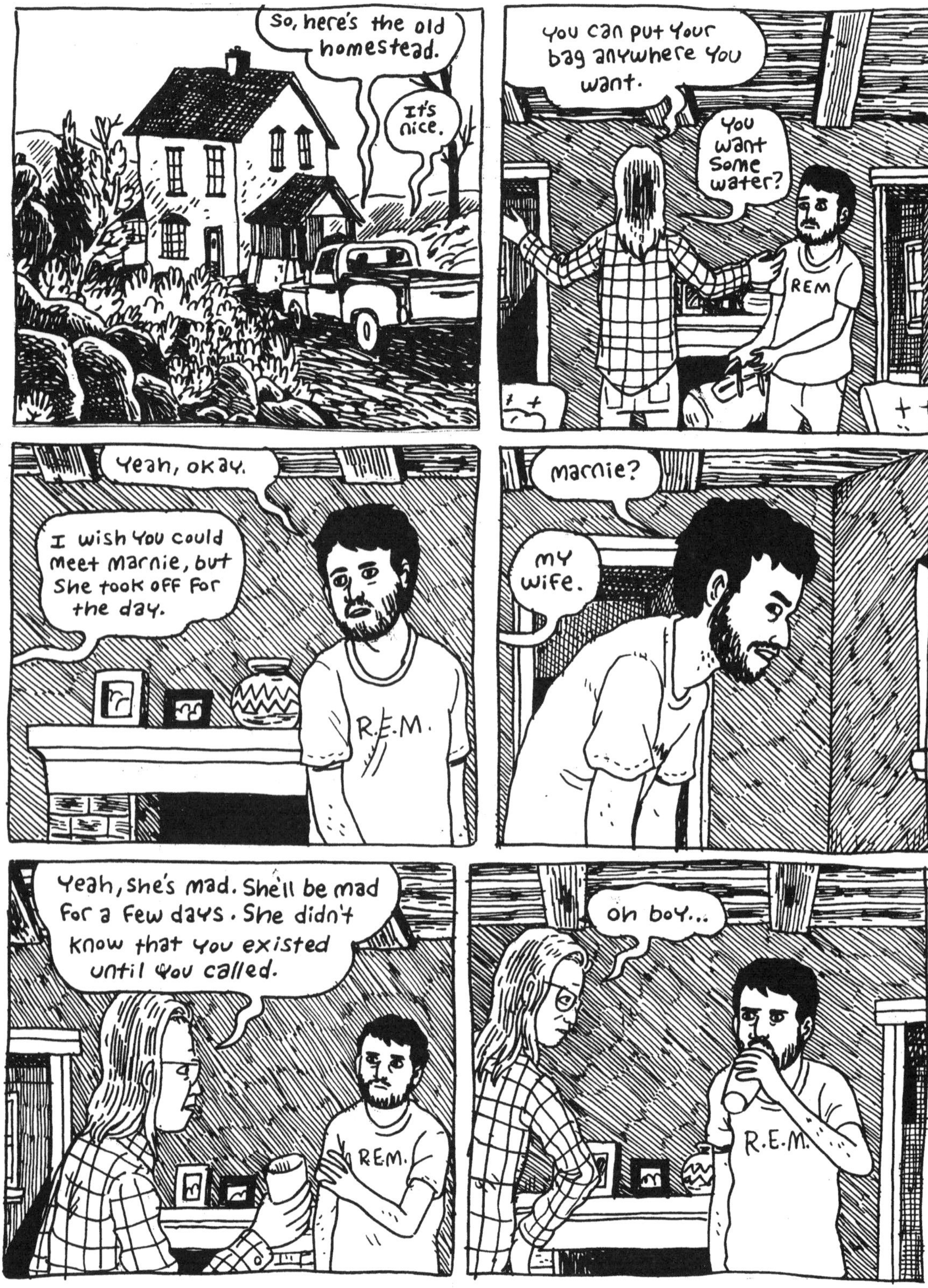
So, here's the old homestead.
It's nice.
You can put your bag anywhere you want.
You want some water?
Yeah, okay.
I wish you could meet Marnie, but she took off for the day.
REM
R.E.M.
Marnie?
My wife.
Yeah, she's mad. She'll be mad for a few days. She didn't know that you existed until you called.
R.E.M.
Oh boy...
R.E.M.

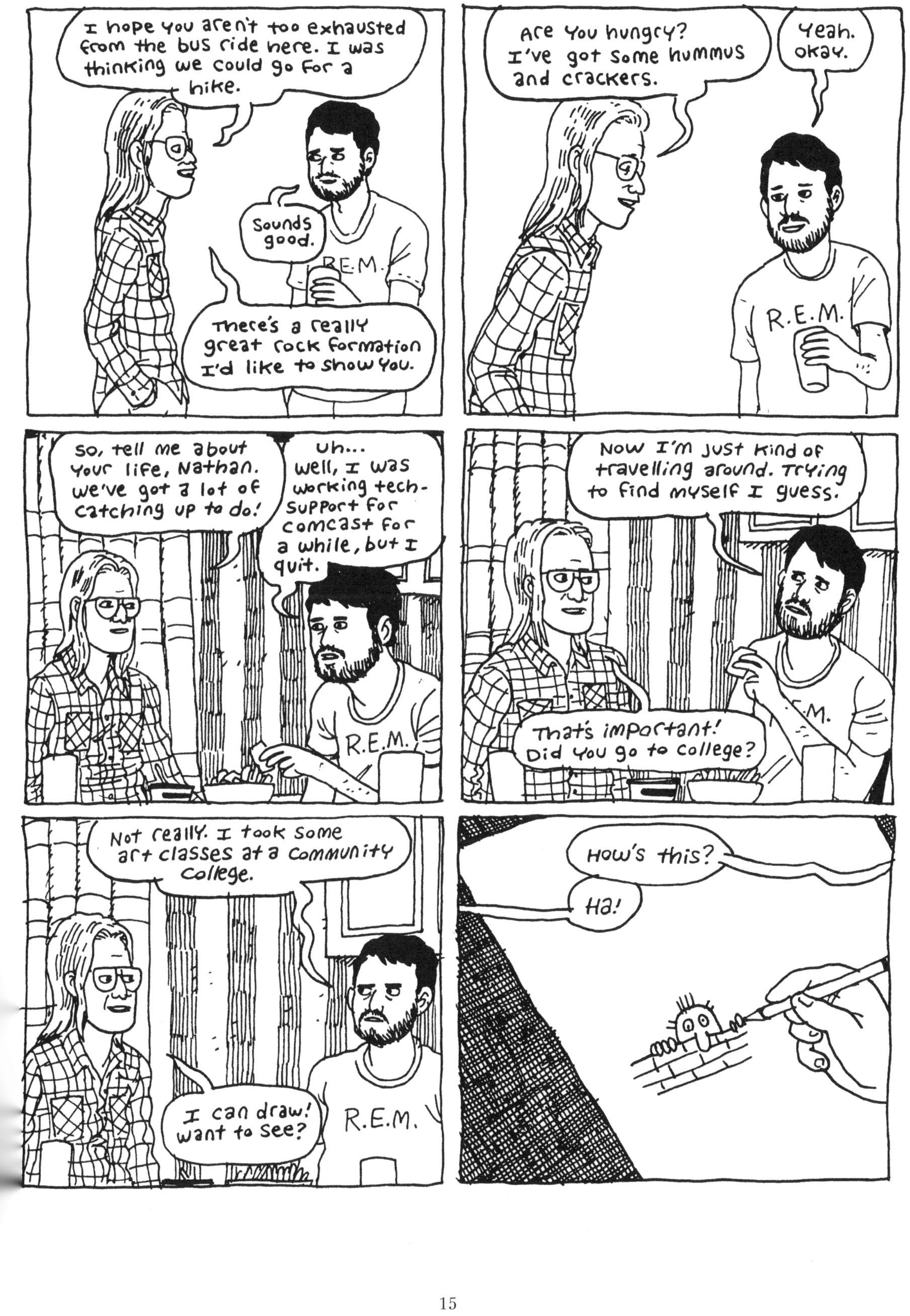
I hope you aren't too exhausted from the bus ride here. I was thinking we could go for a hike.
Sounds good.
There's a really great rock formation I'd like to show you.
R.E.M.
Are you hungry? I've got some hummus and crackers.
Yeah. okay.
R.E.M.
So, tell me about your life, Nathan. we've got a lot of catching up to do!
uh... well, I was working tech-support for comcast for a while, but I quit.
R.E.M.
Now I'm just kind of travelling around. Trying to find myself I guess.
That's important! Did you go to college?
Not really. I took some art classes at a community college.
I can draw! want to see?
R.E.M.
How's this?
Ha!

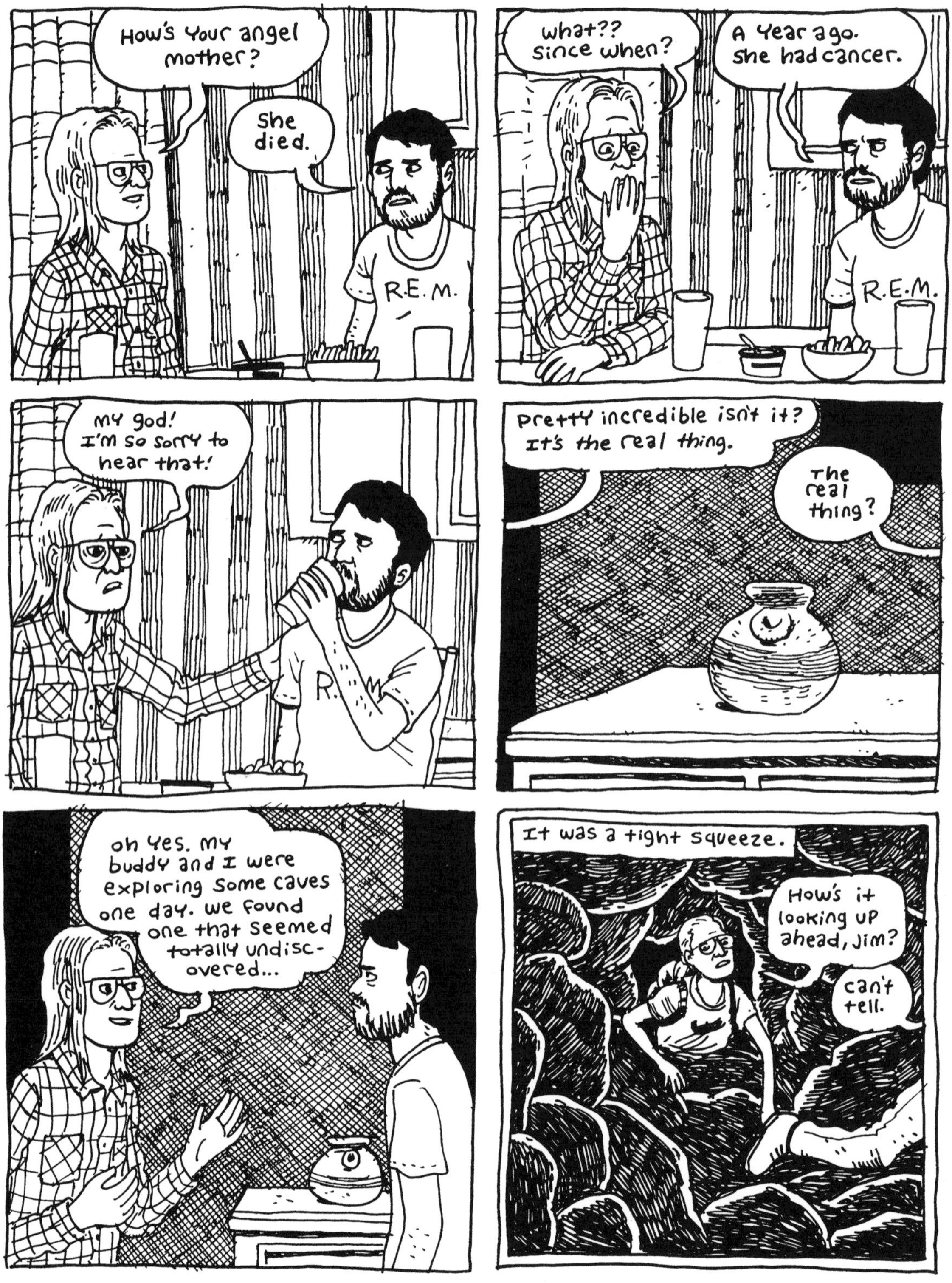
How's your angel mother?
She died.
what?? since when?
A year ago. she had cancer.
My god! I'm so sorry to hear that!
Pretty incredible isn't it? It's the real thing.
The real thing?
oh yes. my buddy and I were exploring some caves one day. we found one that seemed totally undisc-overed...
It was a tight squeeze.
How's it looking up ahead, Jim?
can't tell.
R.E.M.

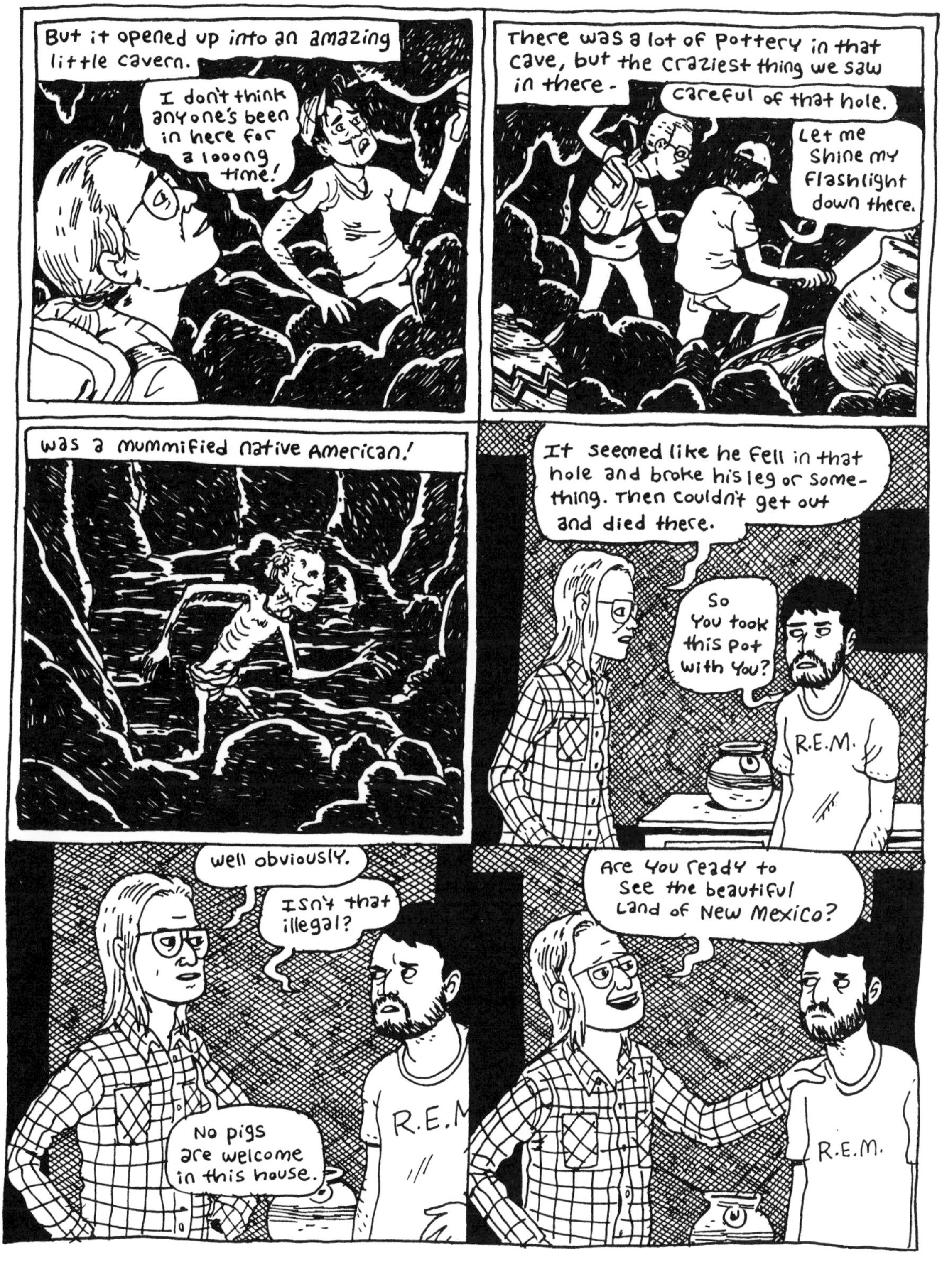

But it opened up into an amazing little cavern.
I don't think anyone's been in here for a loooong time!
There was a lot of pottery in that cave, but the craziest thing we saw in there -
careful of that hole.
Let me shine my flashlight down there.
was a mummified native American!
It seemed like he fell in that hole and broke his leg or some-thing. Then couldn't get out and died there.
So you took this pot with you?
R.E.M.
well obviously.
Isn't that illegal?
No pigs are welcome in this house.
R.E.M
Are you ready to see the beautiful land of New Mexico?
R.E.M.

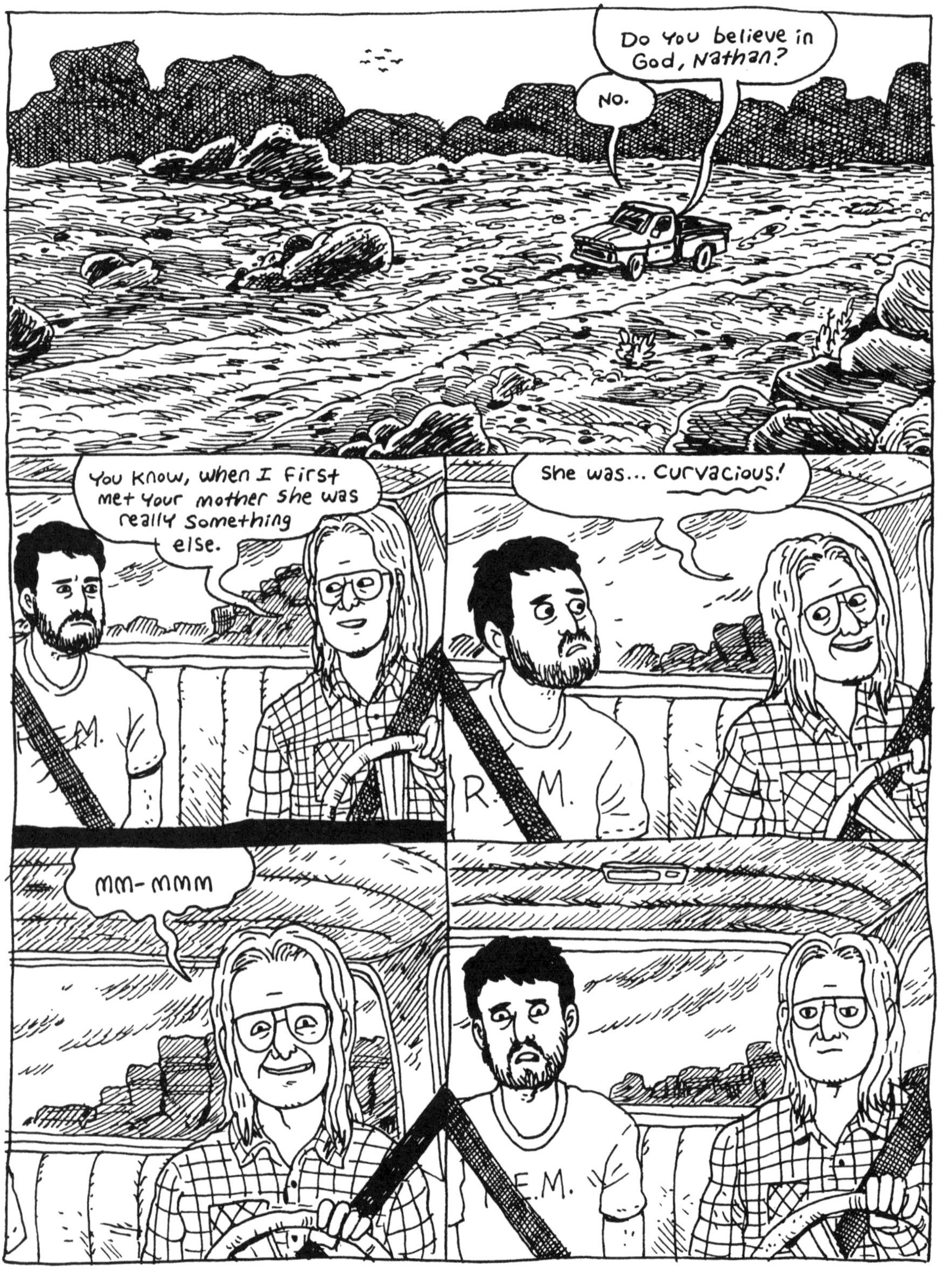
Do you believe in God, Nathan?
No.
You know, when I first met your mother she was really something else.
She was... curvacious!
MM-MMM

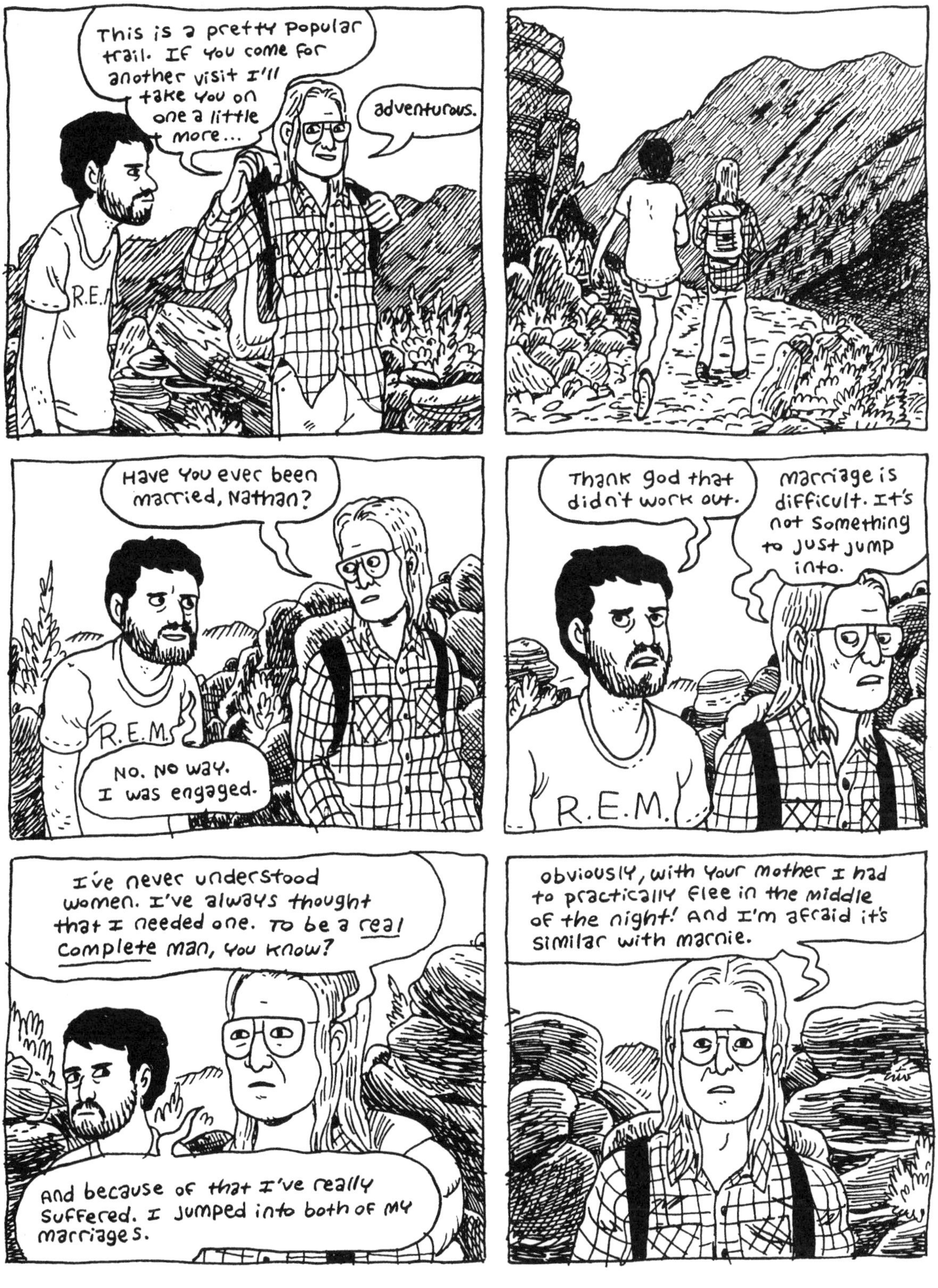
This is a pretty popular trail. If you come for another visit I'll take you on one a little more...
adventurous.
R.E.
Have you ever been married, Nathan?
R.E.M.
No. No way. I was engaged.
Thank god that didn't work out.
Marriage is difficult. It's not something to just jump into.
R.E.M.
I've never understood women. I've always thought that I needed one. To be a real complete man, you know?
And because of that I've really suffered. I jumped into both of my marriages.
Obviously, with your mother I had to practically flee in the middle of the night! And I'm afraid it's similar with Marnie.

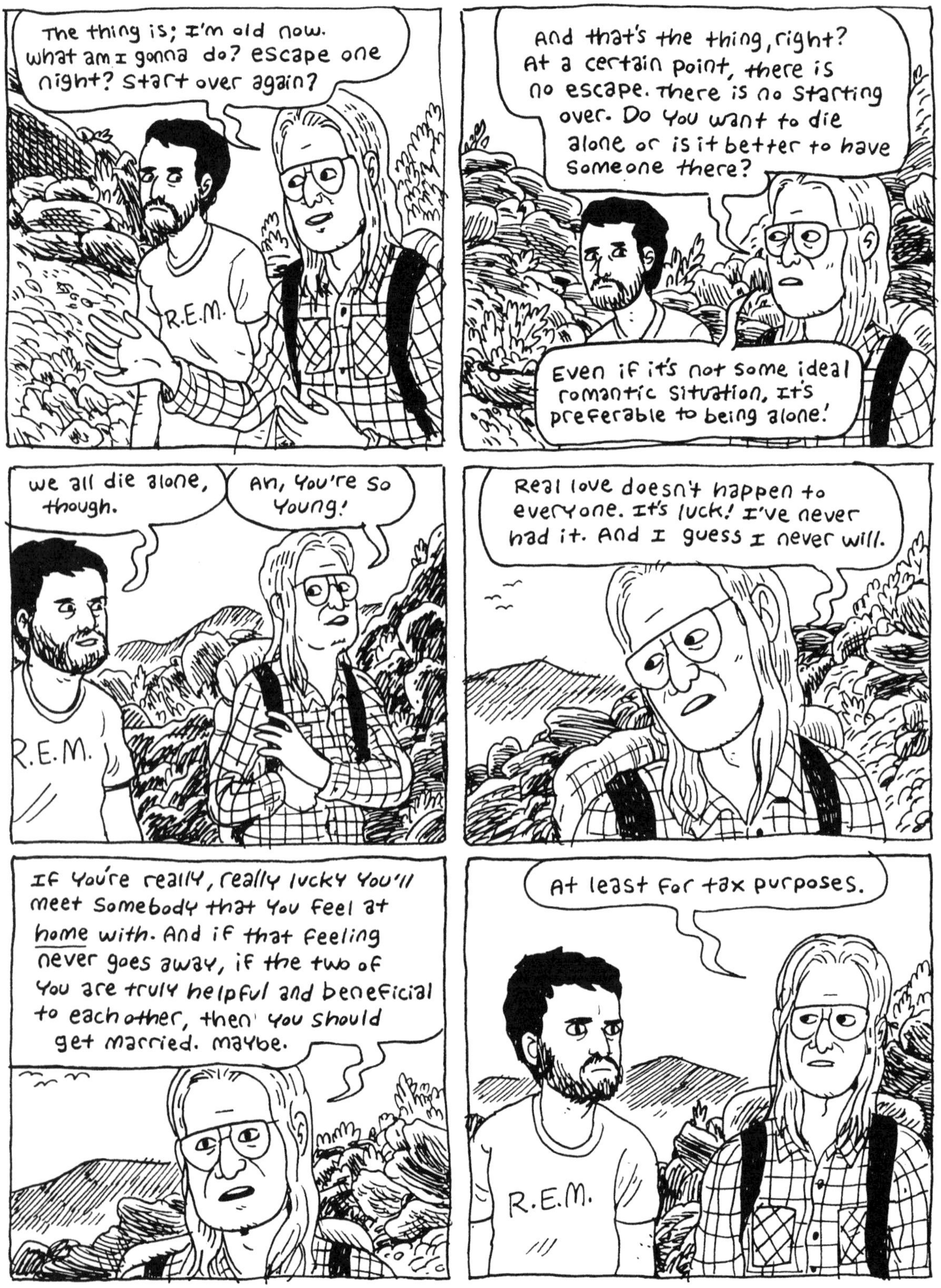
The thing is; I'm old now. what am I gonna do? escape one night? start over again?
And that's the thing, right? At a certain point, there is no escape. There is no starting over. Do you want to die alone or is it better to have someone there?
Even if it's not some ideal romantic situation, it's preferable to being alone!
we all die alone, though.
Ah, you're so young!
Real love doesn't happen to everyone. It's luck! I've never had it. And I guess I never will.
R.E.M.
If you're really, really lucky you'll meet somebody that you feel at home with. And if that feeling never goes away, if the two of you are truly helpful and beneficial to each other, then you should get married. maybe.
At least for tax purposes.

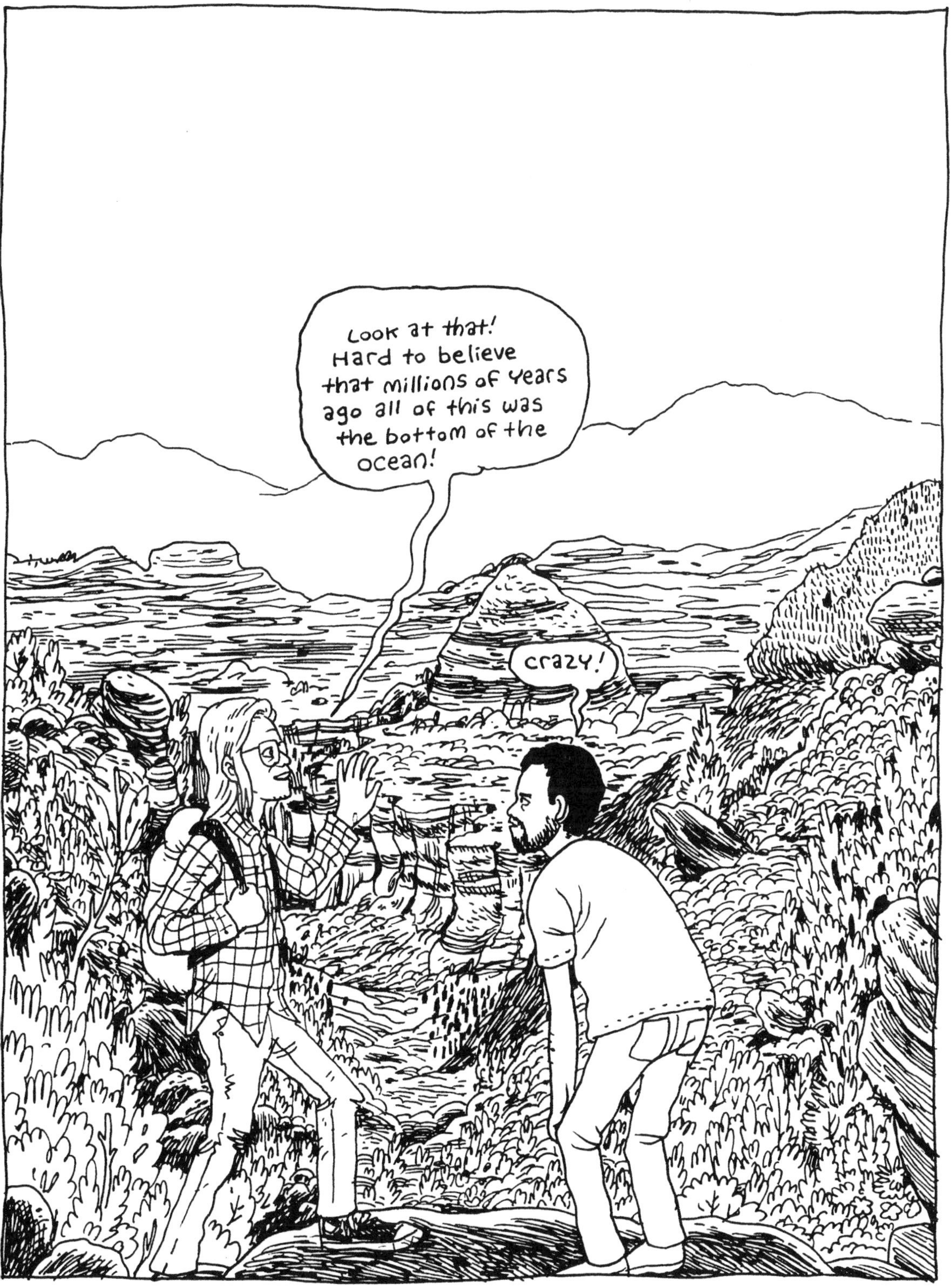
Look at that! Hard to believe that millions of years ago all of this was the bottom of the ocean!
Crazy!

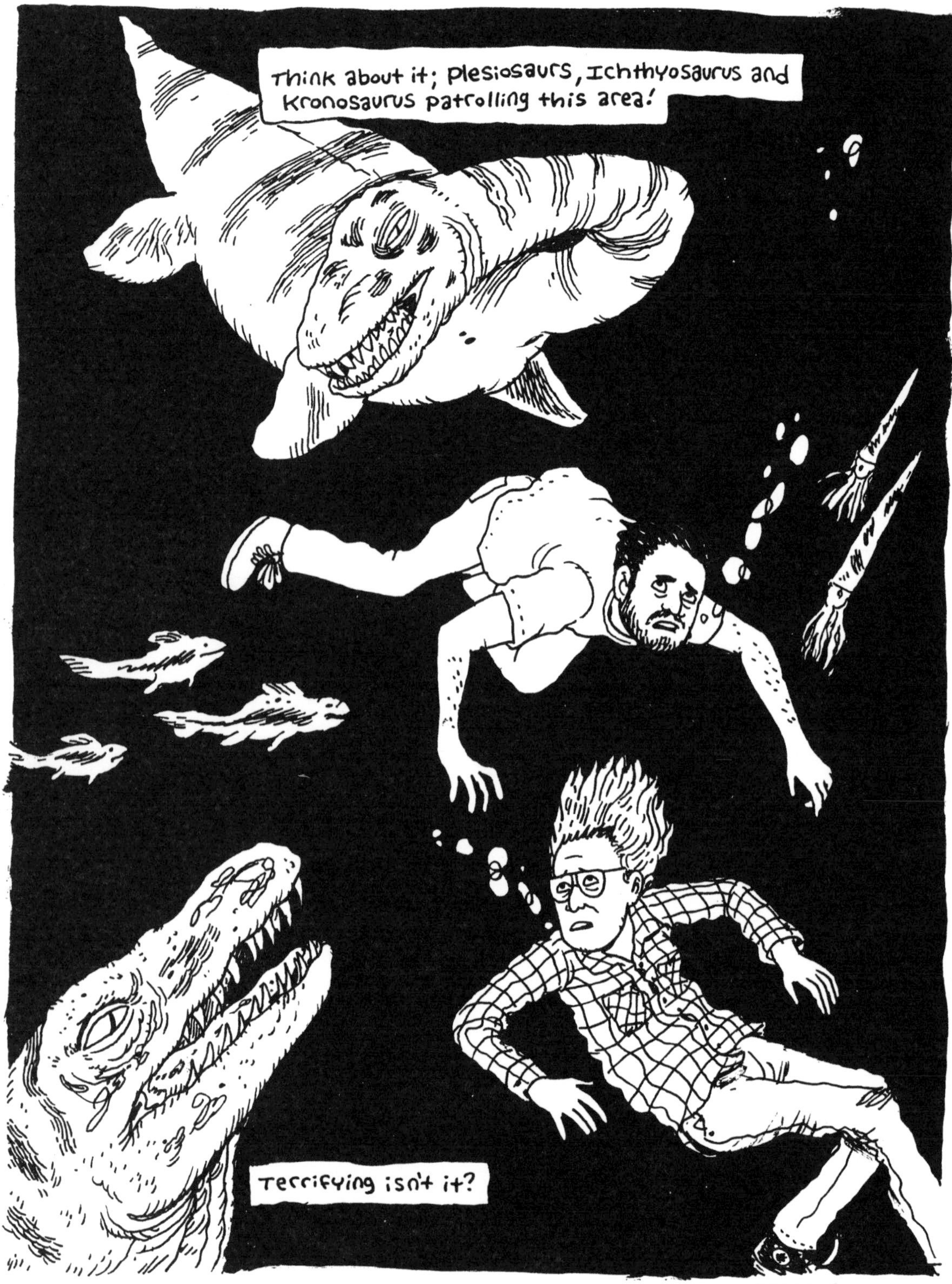
Think about it; Plesiosaurs, Ichthyosaurus and Kronosaurus patrolling this area!
Terrifying isn't it?

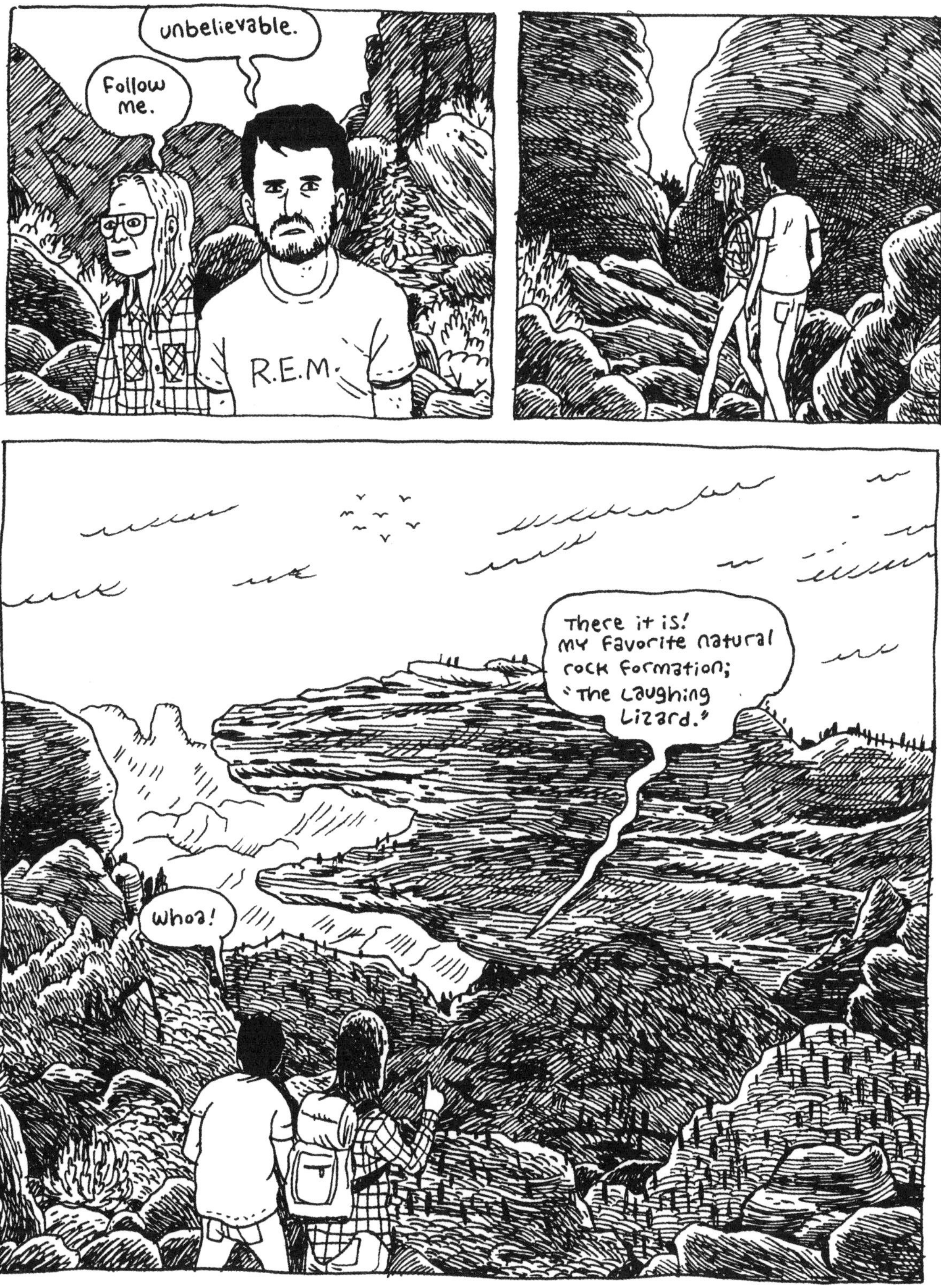
unbelievable.
Follow me.
R.E.M.
There it is! my favorite natural rock formation; "The Laughing Lizard."
Whoa!

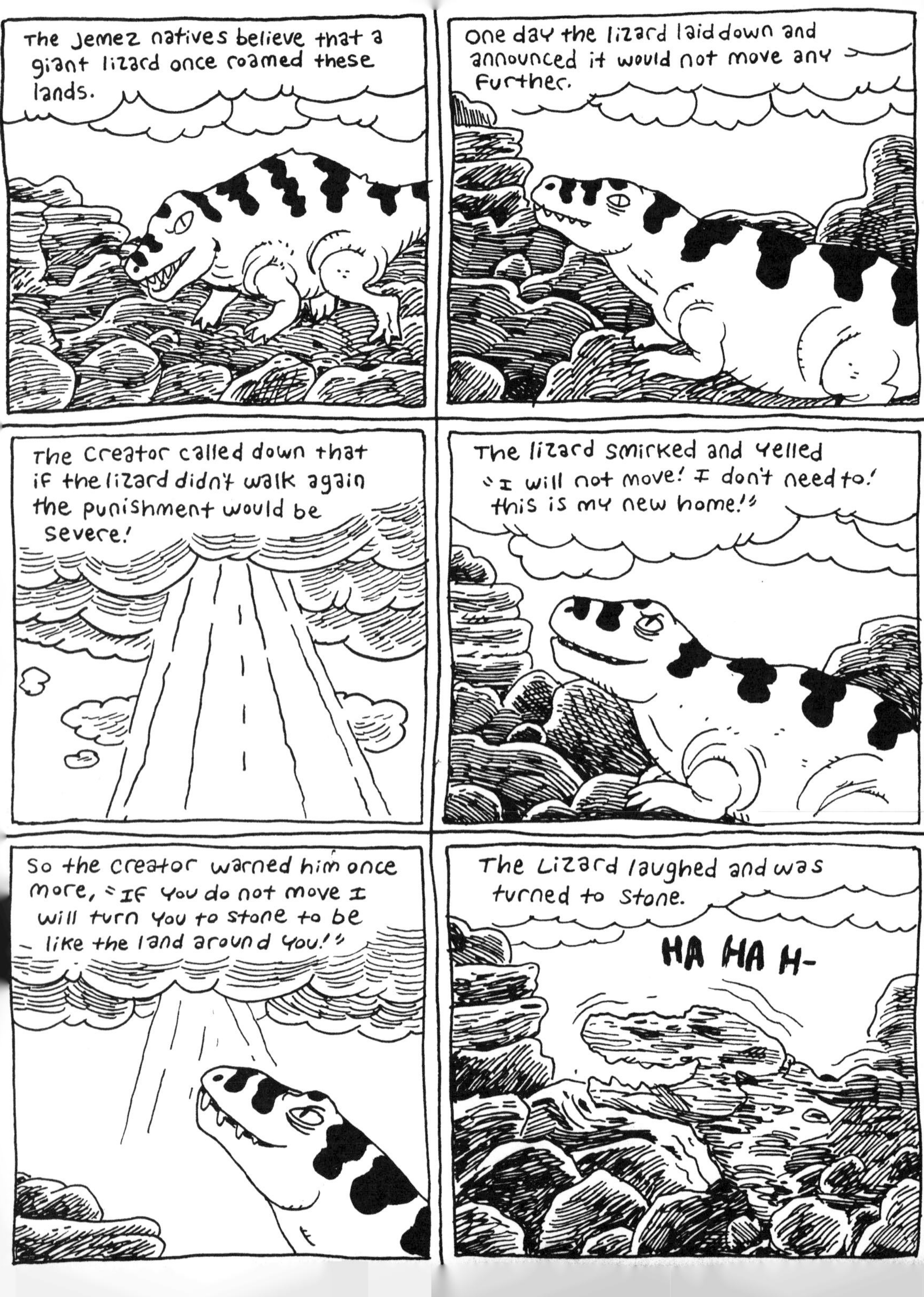
The Jemez natives believe that a giant lizard once roamed these lands.
One day the lizard laid down and announced it would not move any further.
The creator called down that if the lizard didn't walk again the punishment would be severe!
The lizard smirked and yelled "I will not move! I don't need to! this is my new home!"
So the creator warned him once more, "If you do not move I will turn you to stone to be like the land around you!"
The Lizard laughed and was turned to stone.
HA HA H-

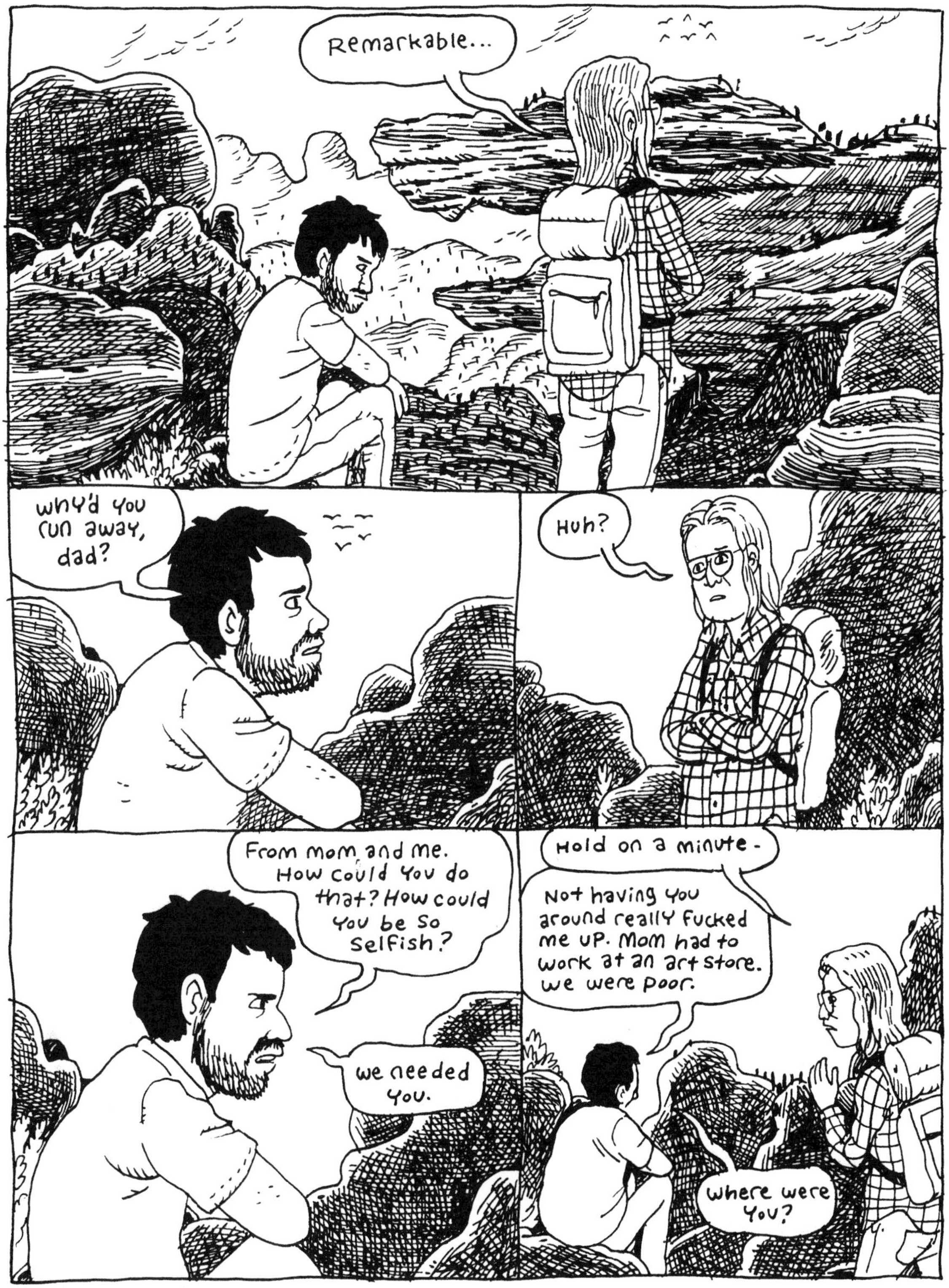
Remarkable...
why'd you run away, dad?
Huh?
From mom and me. How could you do that? How could you be so selfish?
we needed you.
Hold on a minute -
Not having you around really fucked me up. Mom had to work at an art store. we were poor.
where were you?

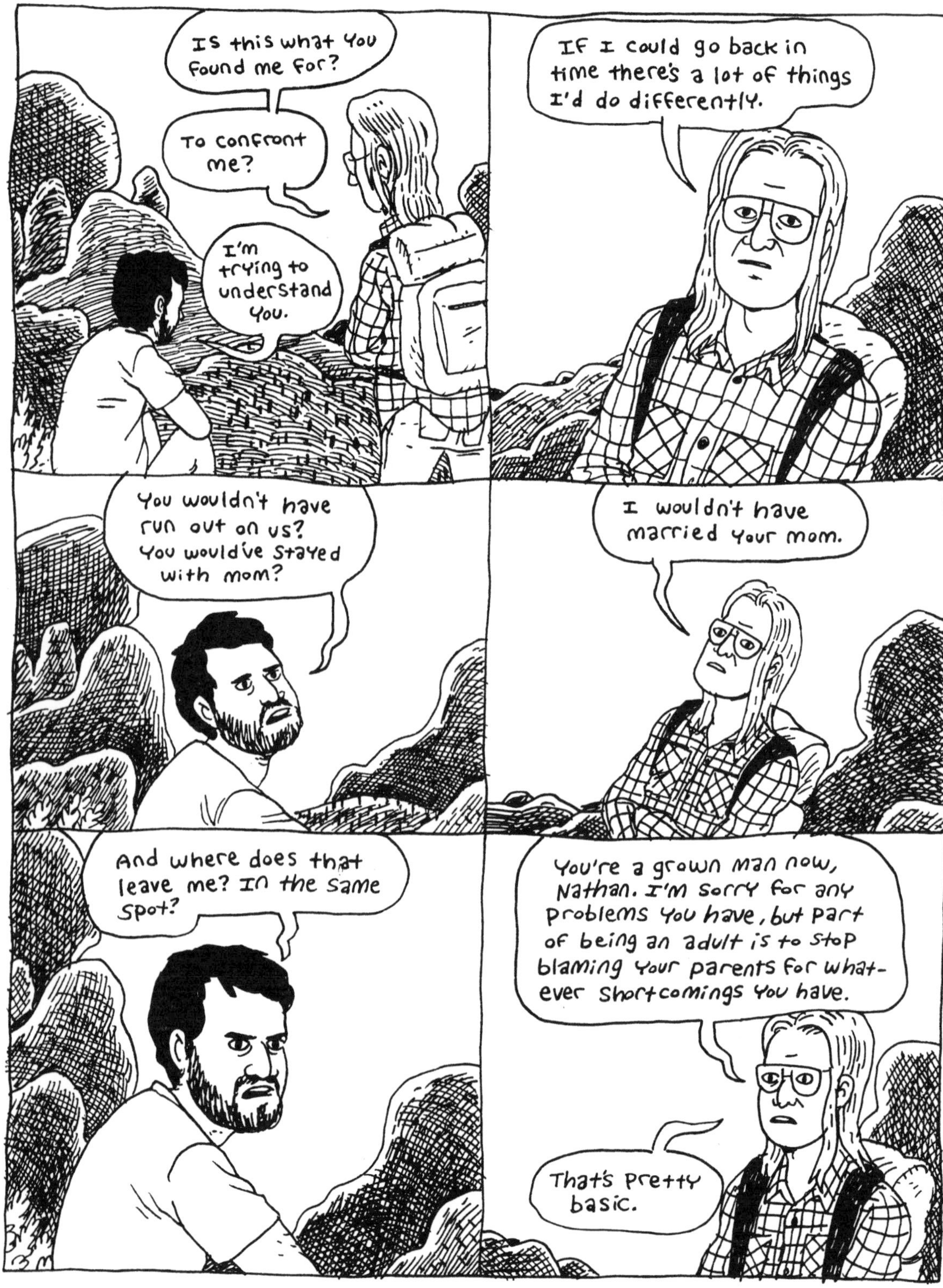
Is this what you found me for?
To confront me?
I'm trying to understand you.
If I could go back in time there's a lot of things I'd do differently.
You wouldn't have run out on us? You would've stayed with mom?
I wouldn't have married your mom.
And where does that leave me? In the same spot?
You're a grown man now, Nathan. I'm sorry for any problems you have, but part of being an adult is to stop blaming your parents for whatever shortcomings you have.
That's pretty basic.

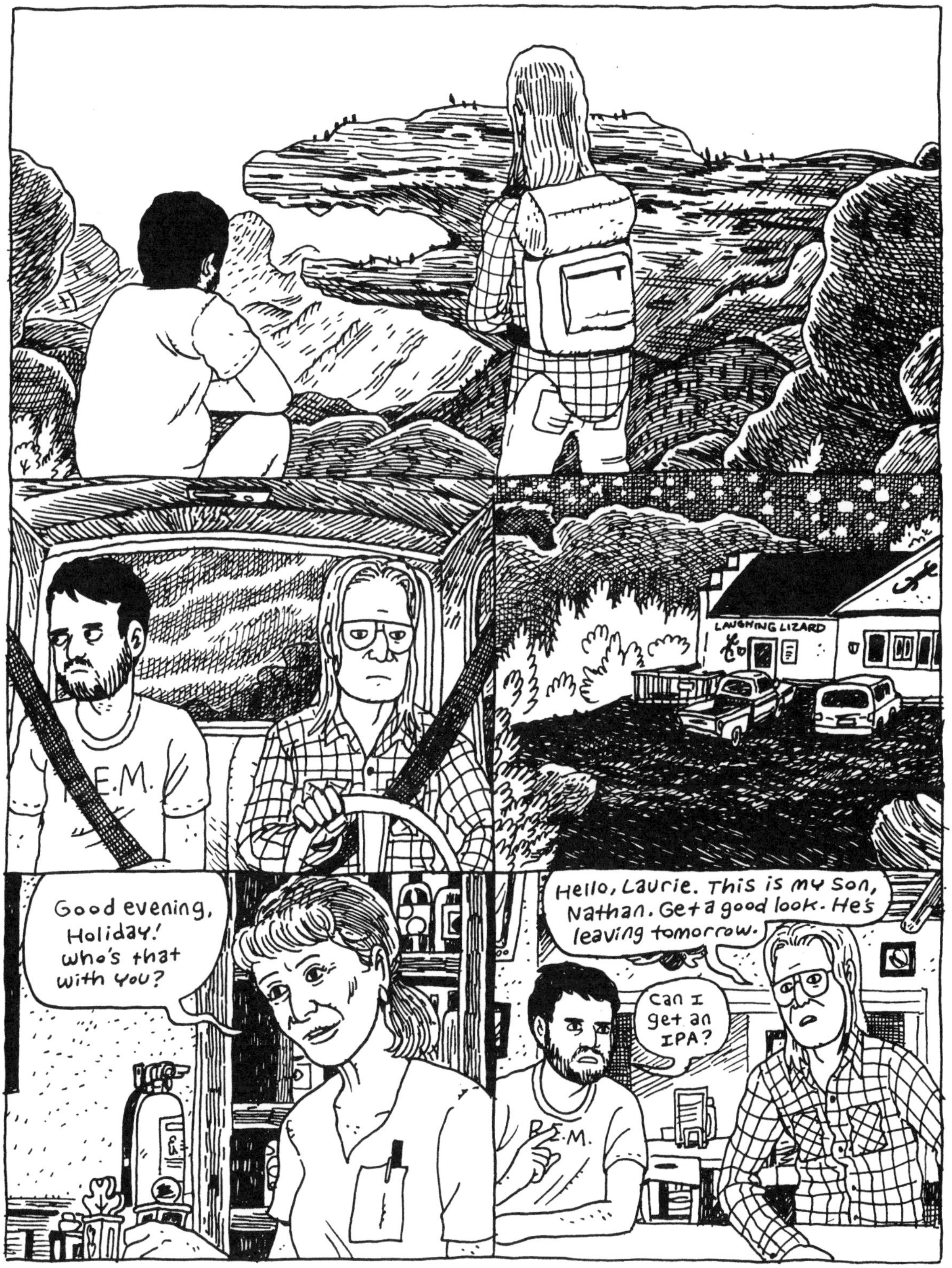
LAUGHING LIZARD
R.E.M.
Good evening, Holiday! who's that with you?
Hello, Laurie. This is my son, Nathan. Get a good look. He's leaving tomorrow.
Can I get an IPA?

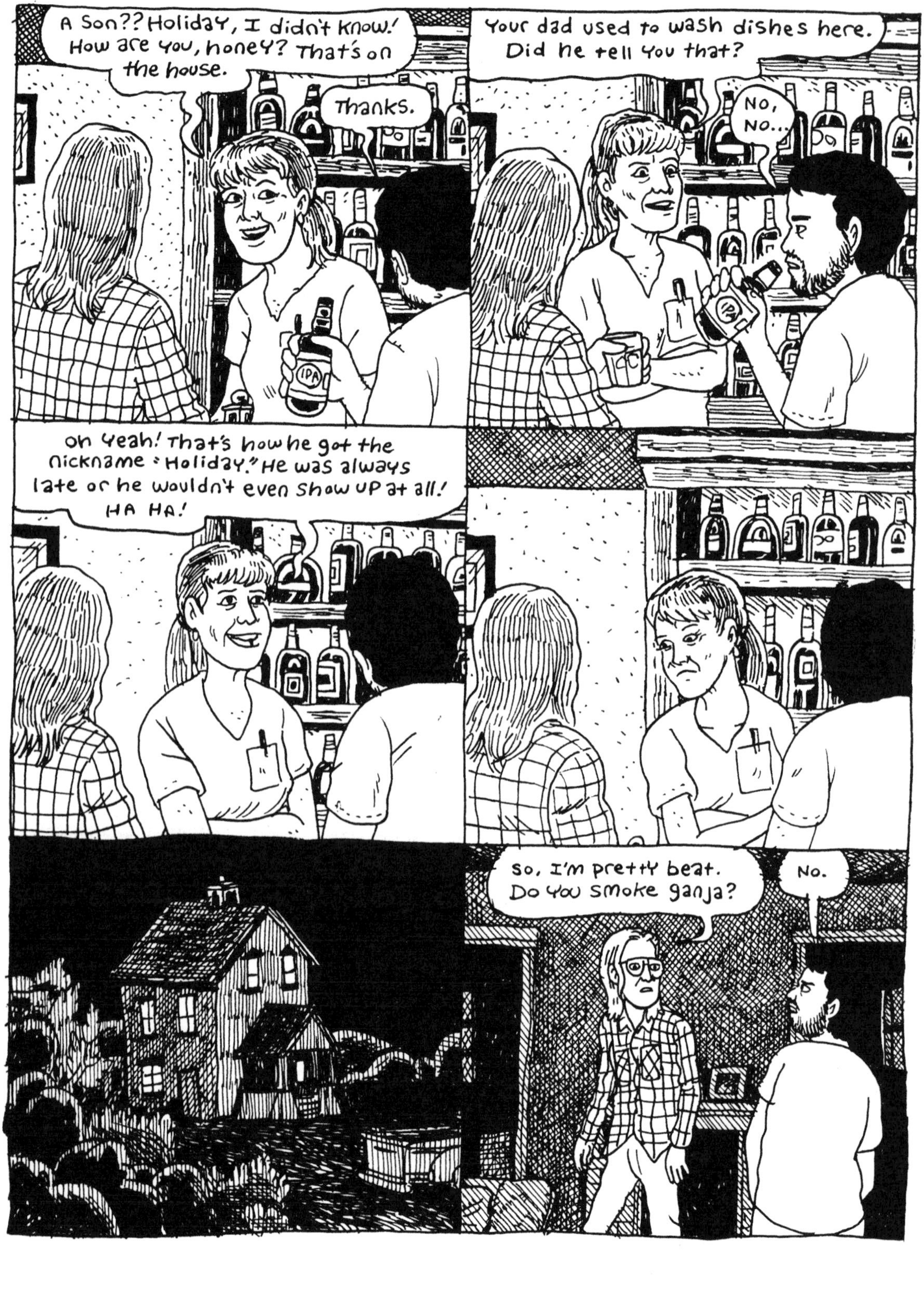
A Son?? Holiday, I didn't know! How are you, honey? That's on the house.
Thanks.
Your dad used to wash dishes here. Did he tell you that?
No, No...
Oh yeah! That's how he got the nickname "Holiday." He was always late or he wouldn't even show up at all! HA HA!
So, I'm pretty beat. Do you smoke ganja?
No.

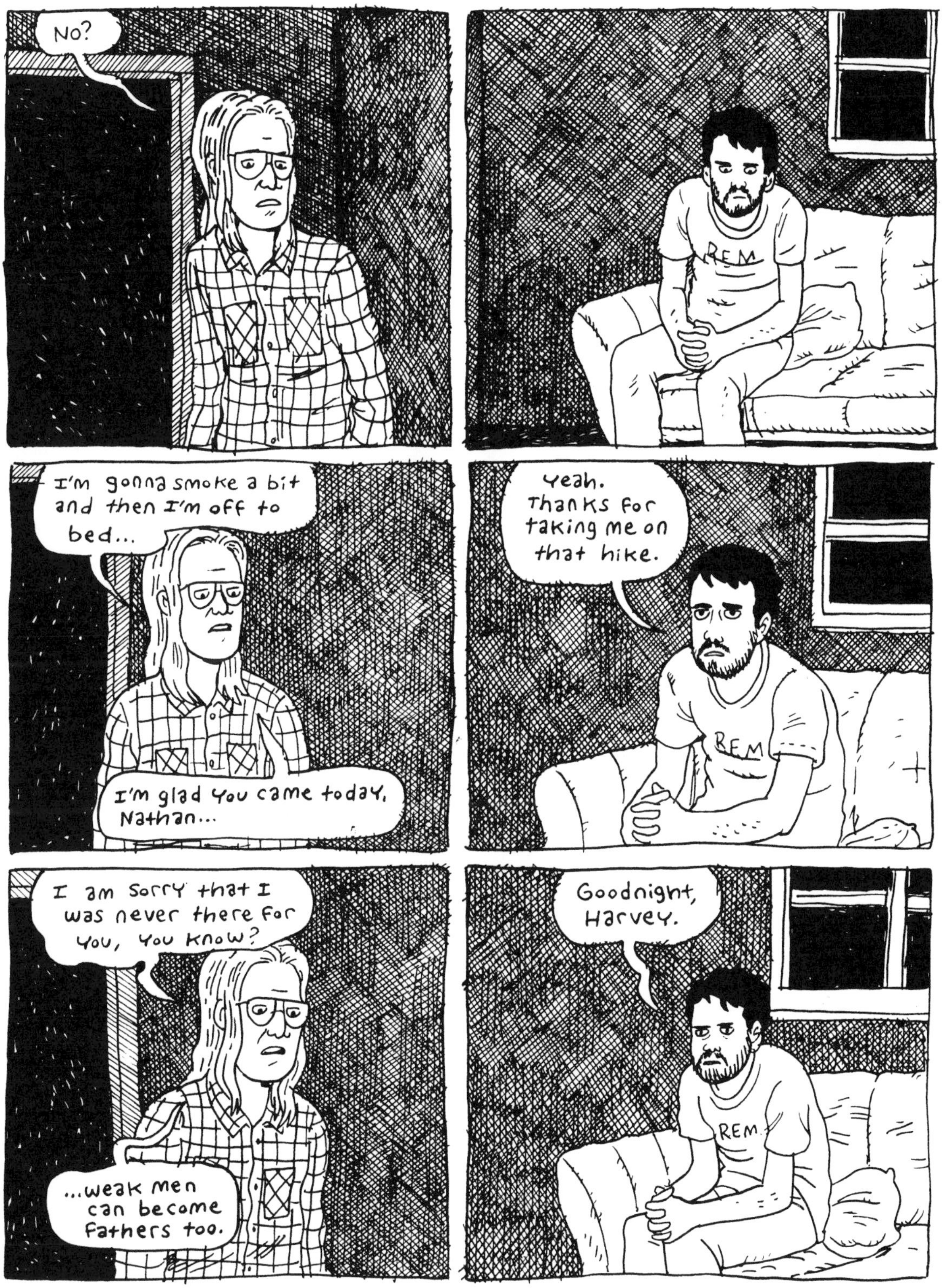
No?
I'm gonna smoke a bit and then I'm off to bed...
I'm glad you came today, Nathan...
Yeah. Thanks for taking me on that hike.
I am sorry that I was never there for you, you know?
...weak men can become fathers too.
Goodnight, Harvey.

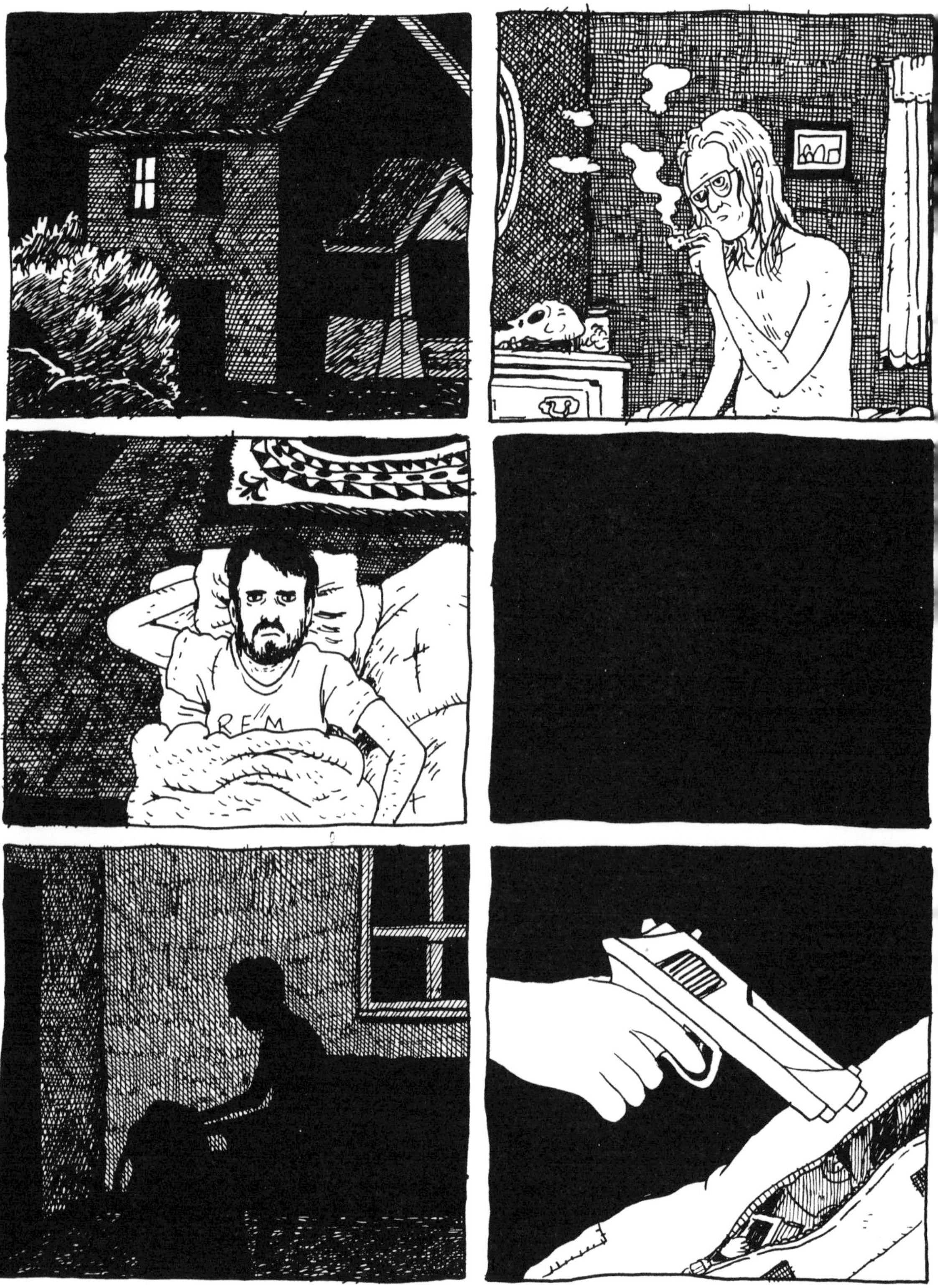
REM

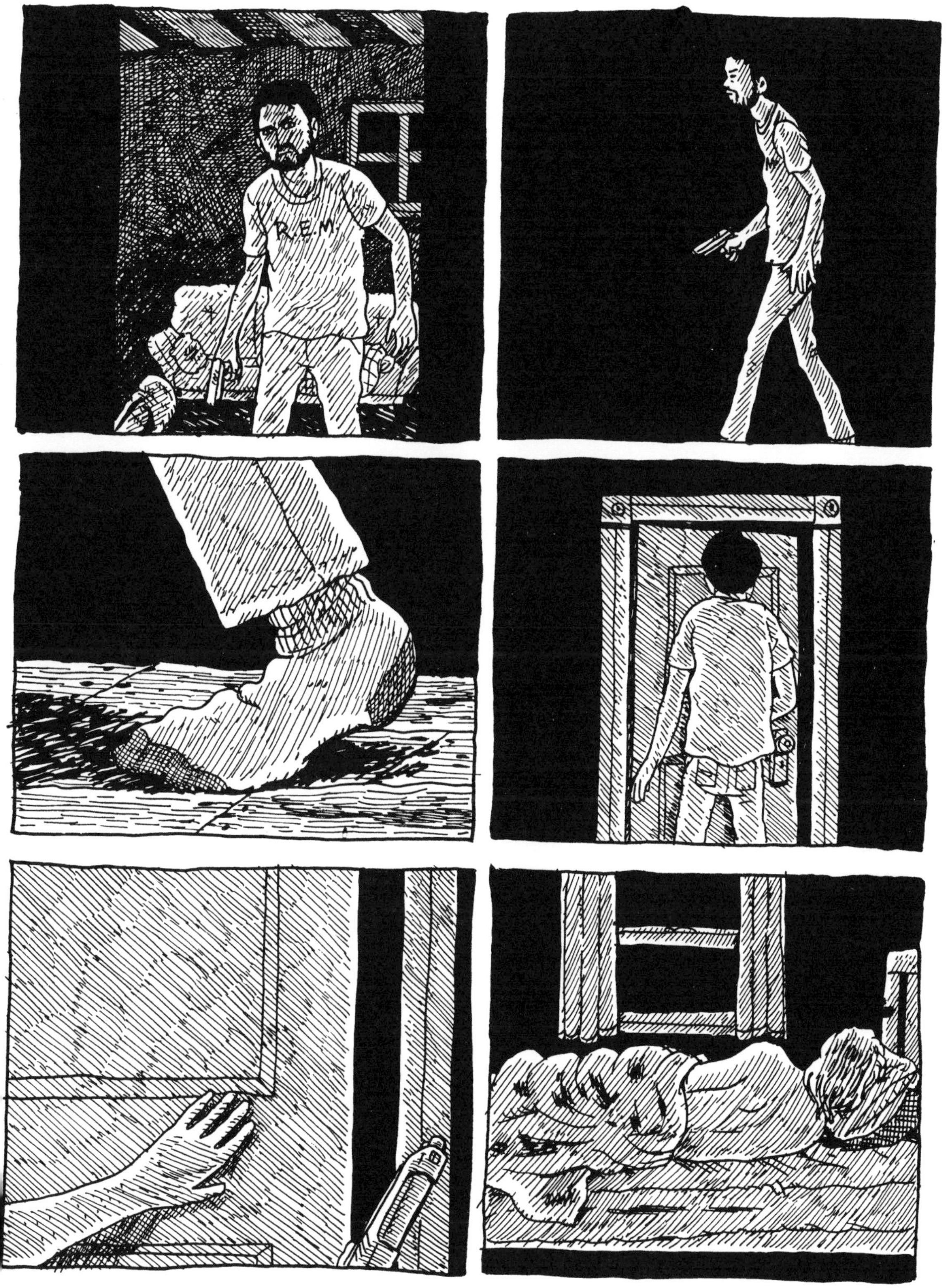
REM

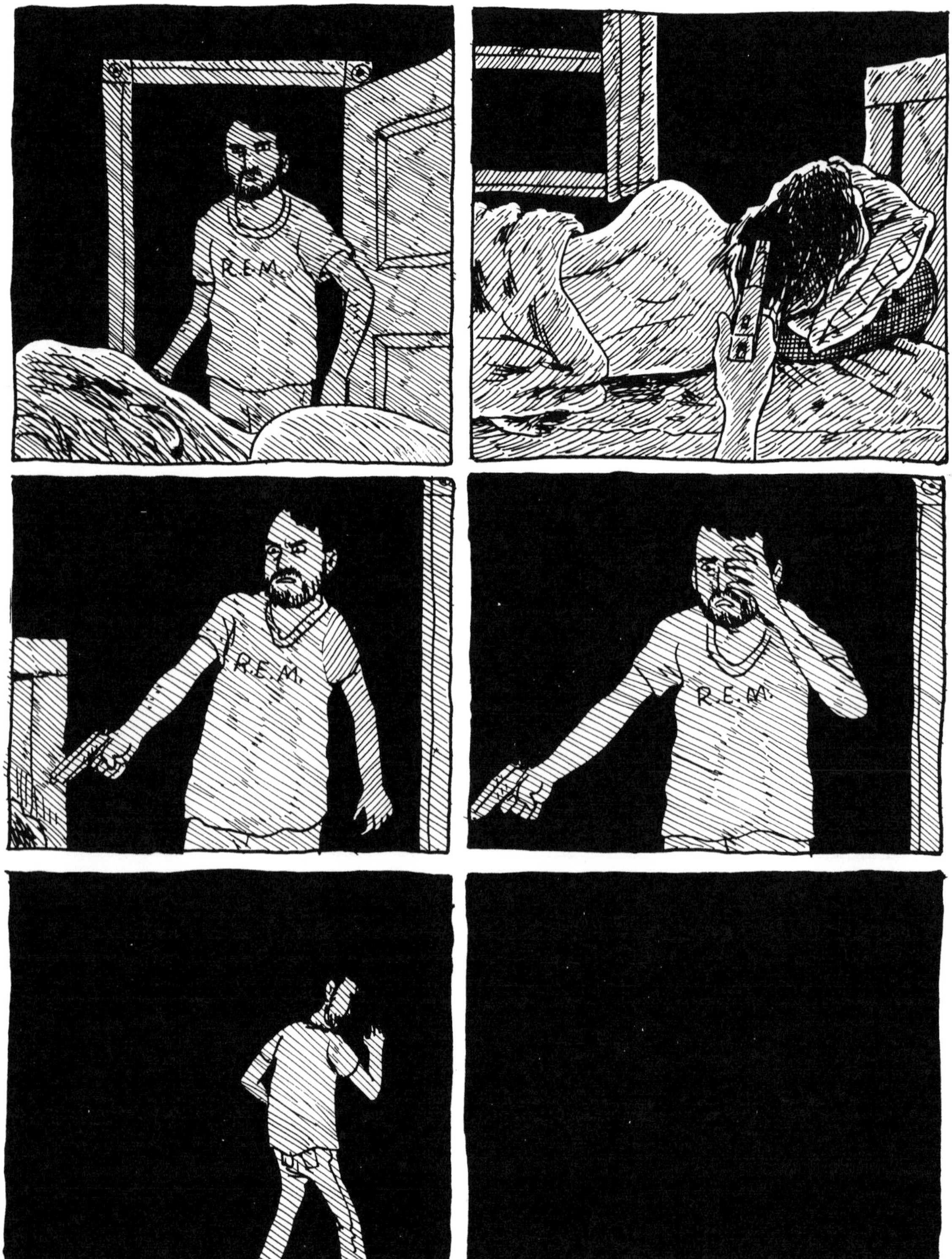
R.E.M.
R.E.M.
R.E.M.

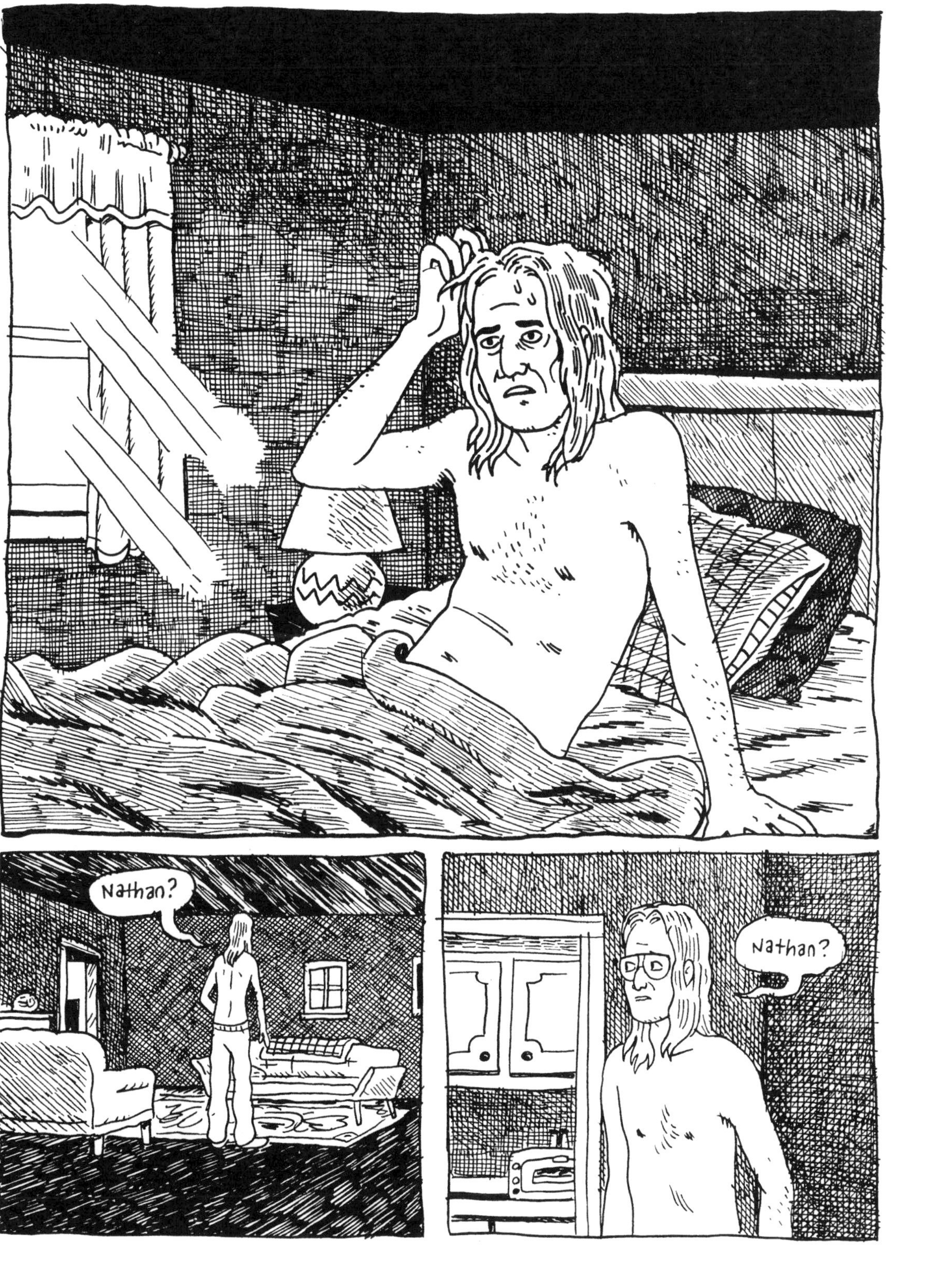
Nathan?
Nathan?

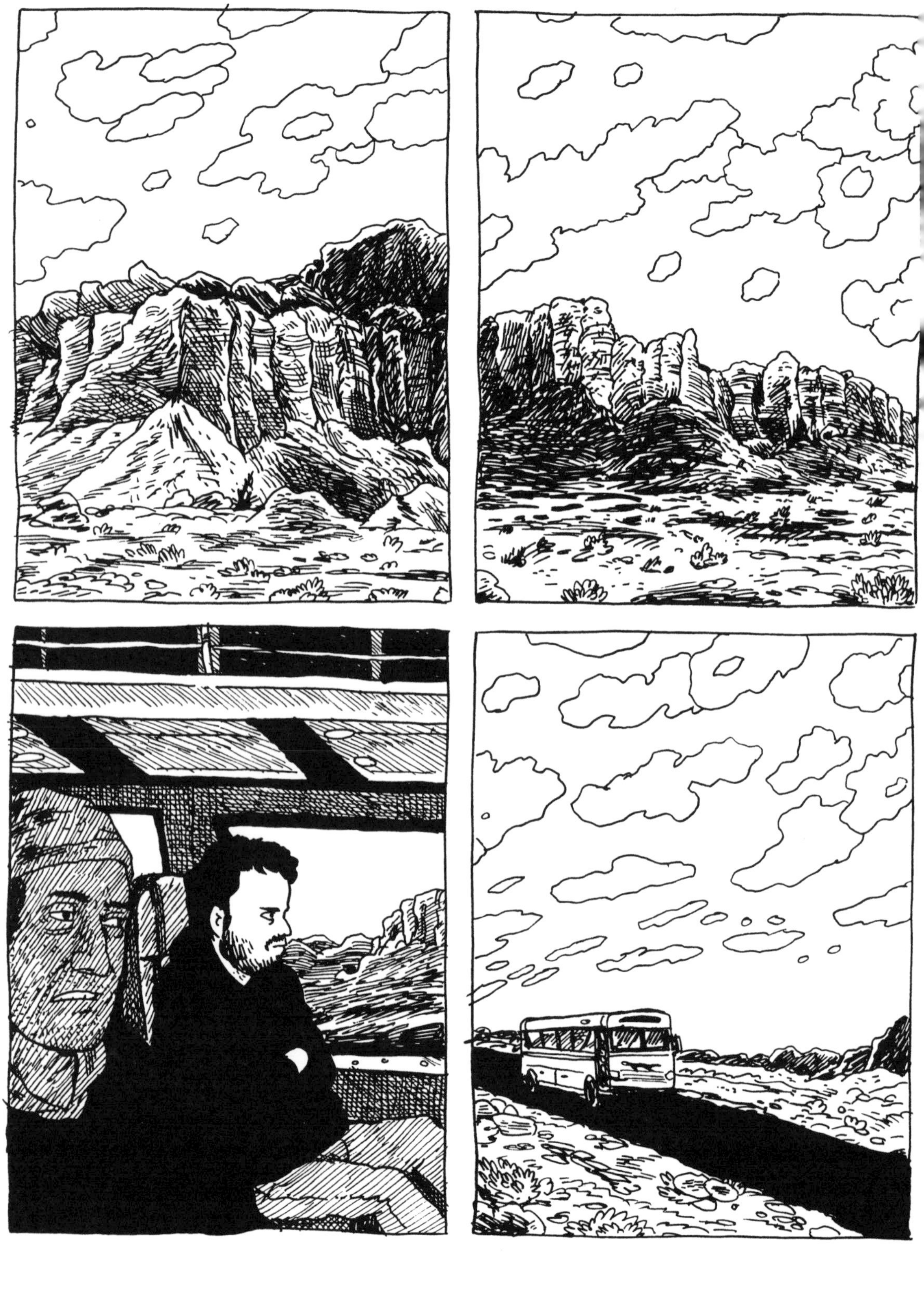

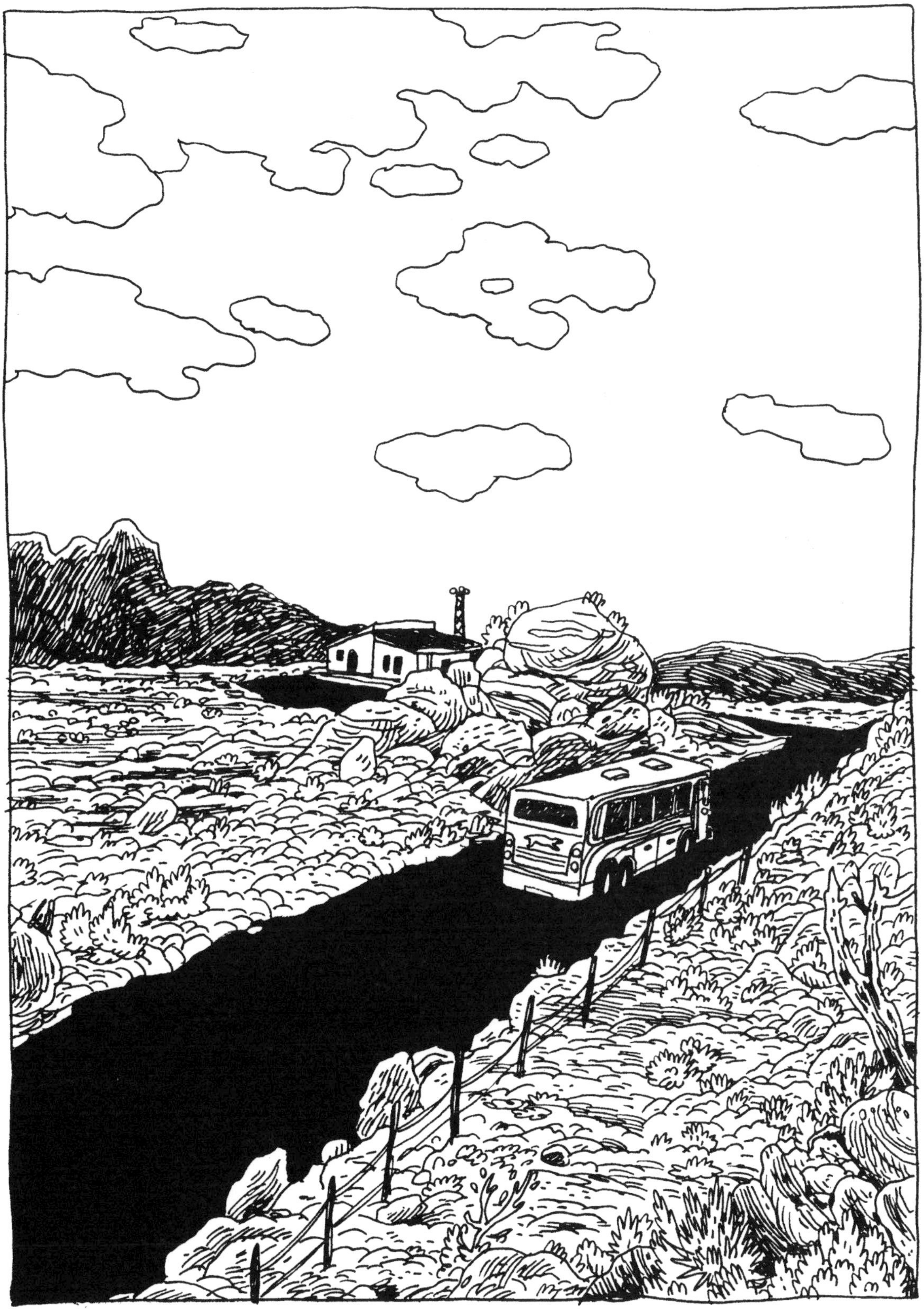

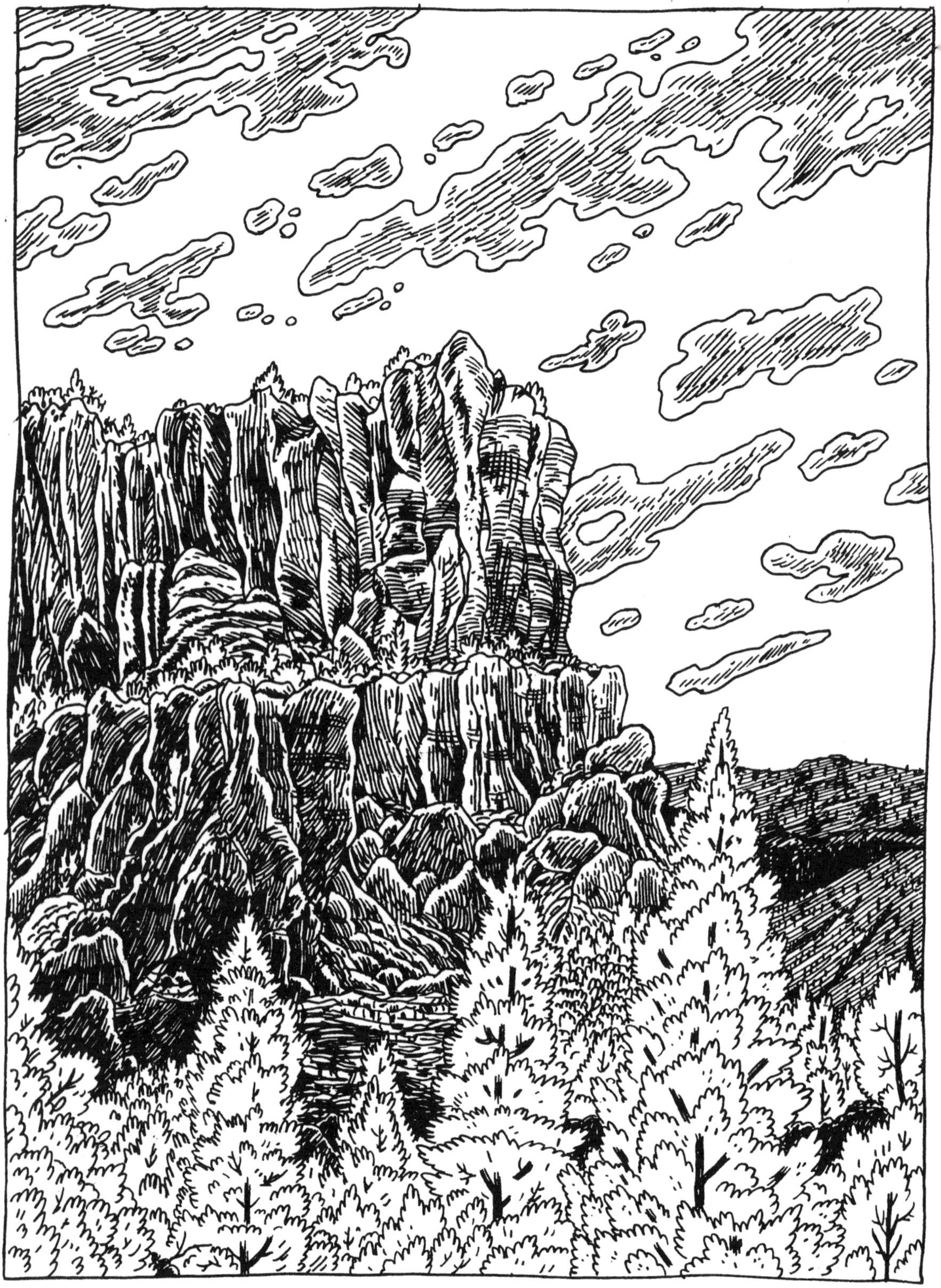

~Noah Van Sciver

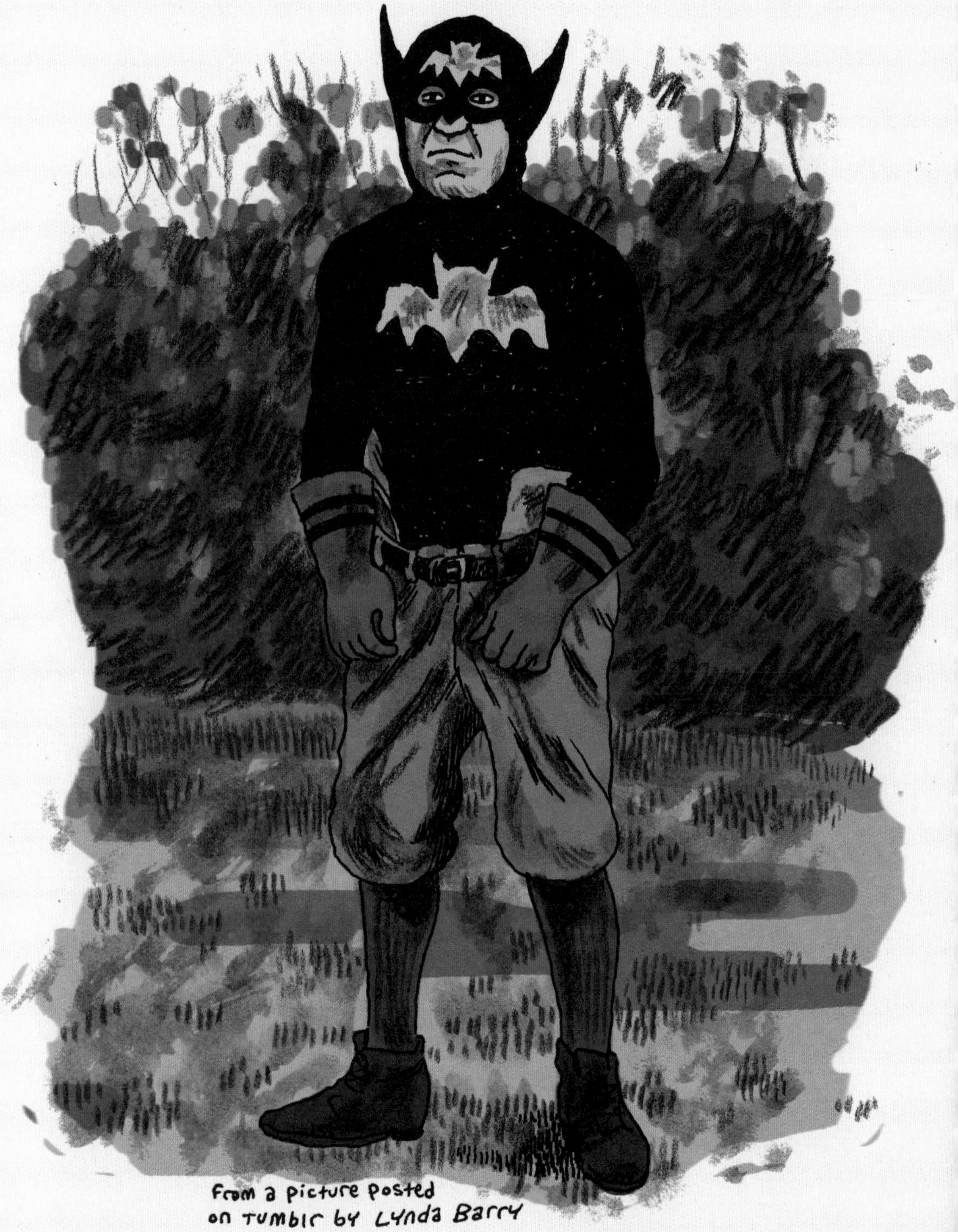
From a picture posted
on Tumblr by Lynda Barry

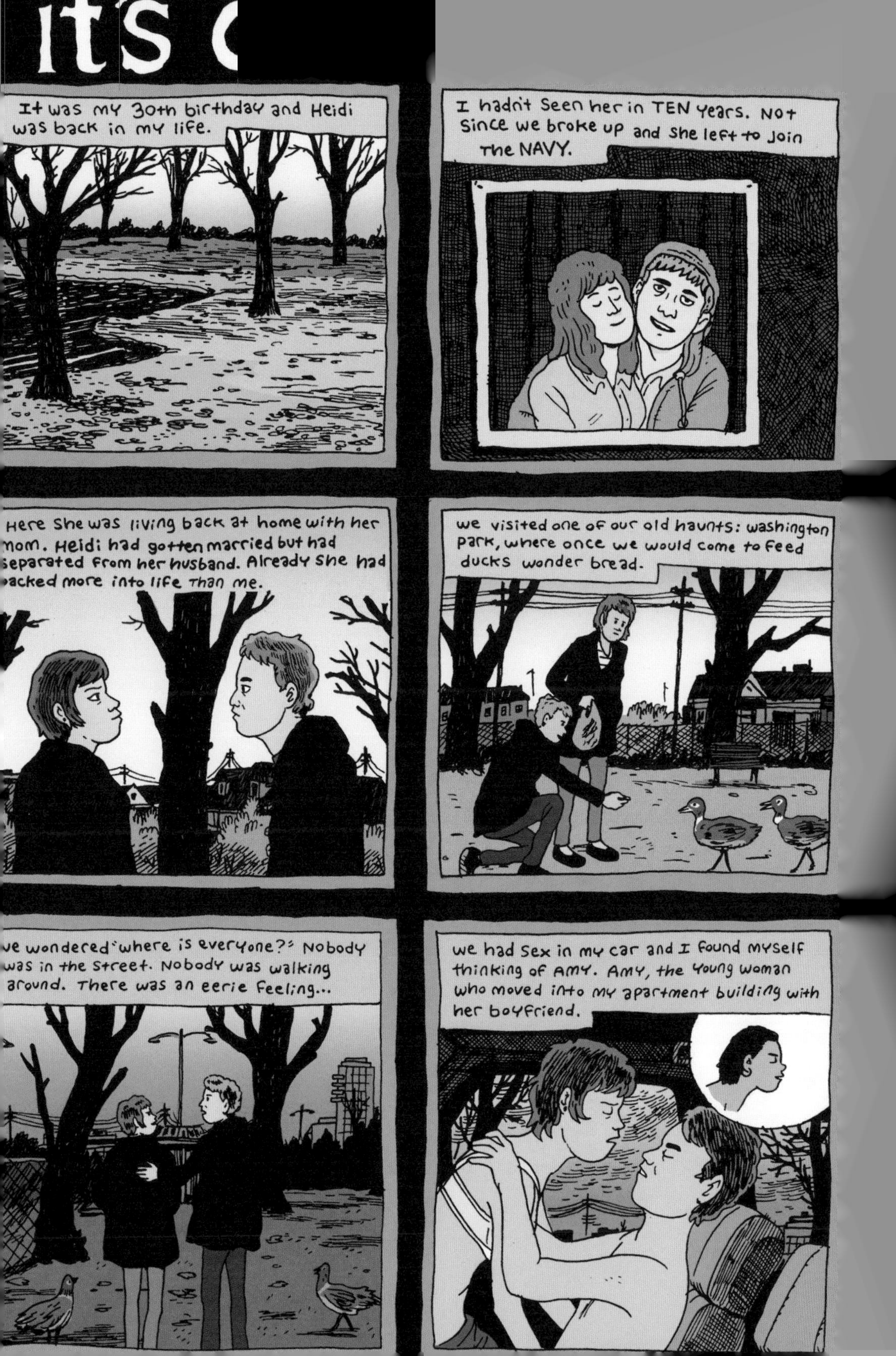
It's
It was my 30th birthday and Heidi was back in my life.
I hadn't seen her in TEN years. Not since we broke up and she left to join the NAVY.
Here she was living back at home with her mom. Heidi had gotten married but had separated from her husband. Already she had packed more into life than me.
we visited one of our old haunts: washington park, where once we would come to feed ducks wonder bread.
we wondered "where is everyone?" Nobody was in the street. Nobody was walking around. There was an eerie feeling...
we had sex in my car and I found myself thinking of AMY. AMY, the young woman who moved into my apartment building with her boyfriend.

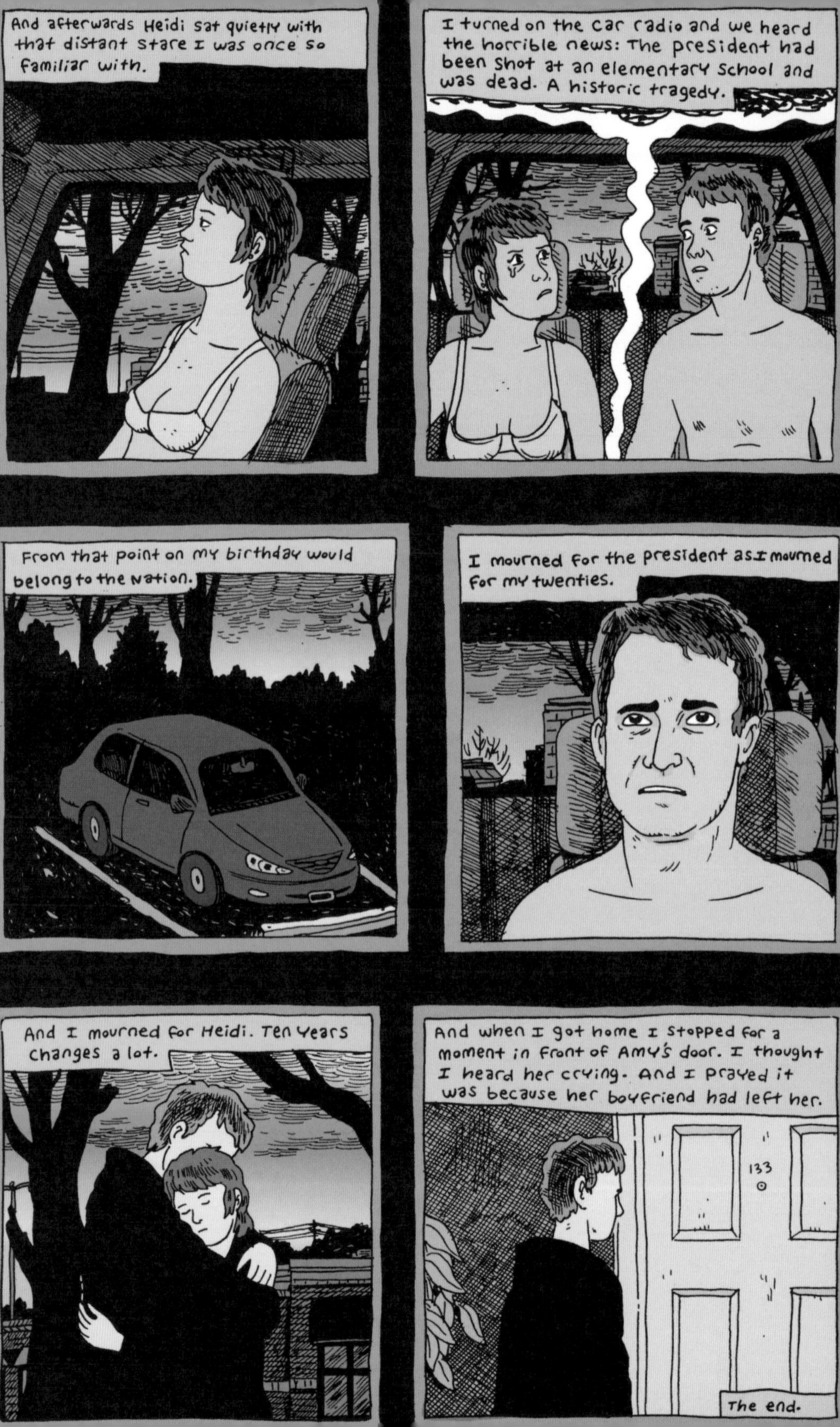
And afterwards Heidi sat quietly with that distant stare I was once so familiar with.
I turned on the car radio and we heard the horrible news: The president had been shot at an elementary school and was dead. A historic tragedy.
From that point on my birthday would belong to the Nation.
I mourned for the president as I mourned for my twenties.
And I mourned for Heidi. Ten years changes a lot.
And when I got home I stopped for a moment in front of Amy's door. I thought I heard her crying. And I prayed it was because her boyfriend had left her.
133
The end.

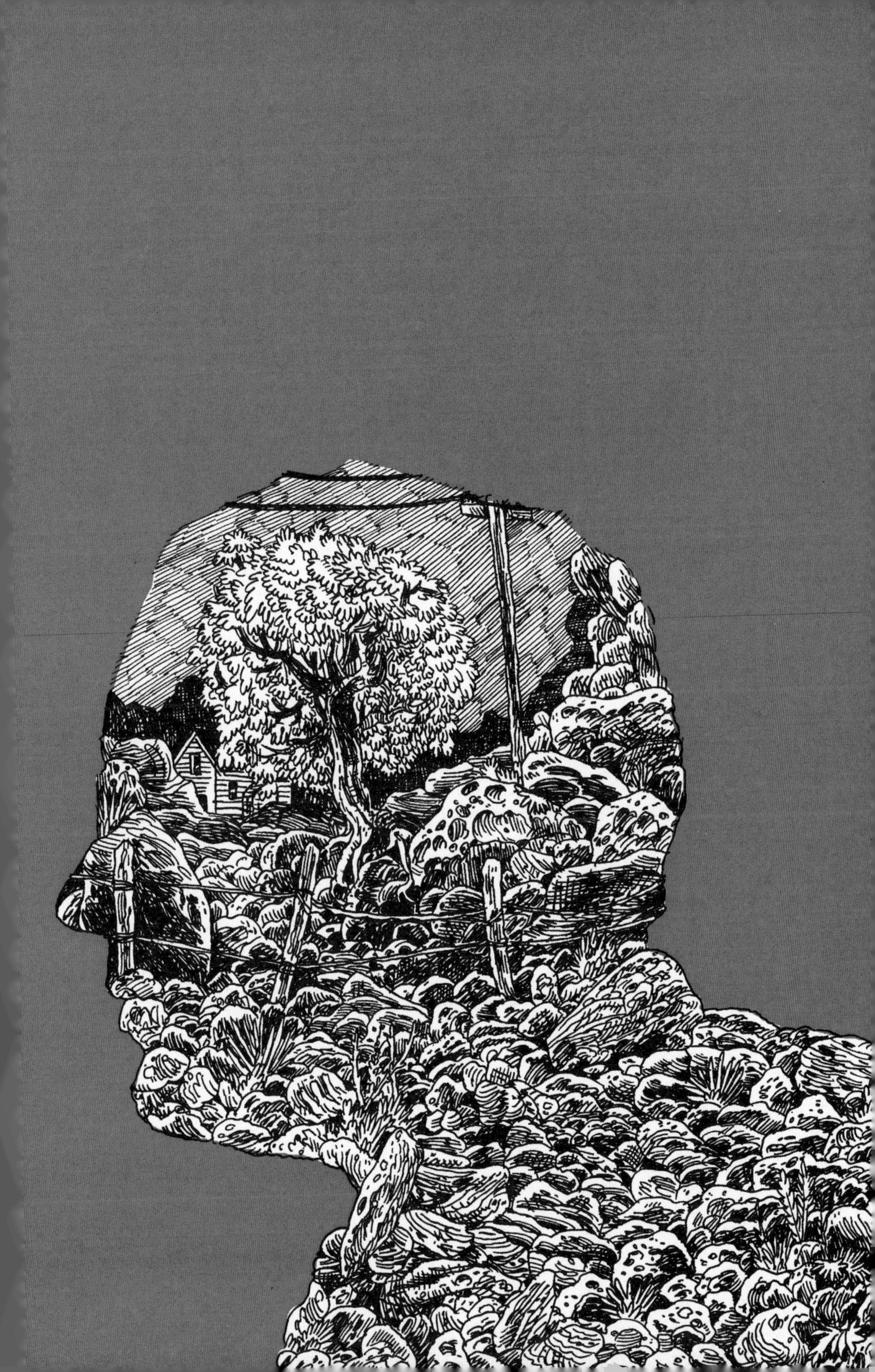

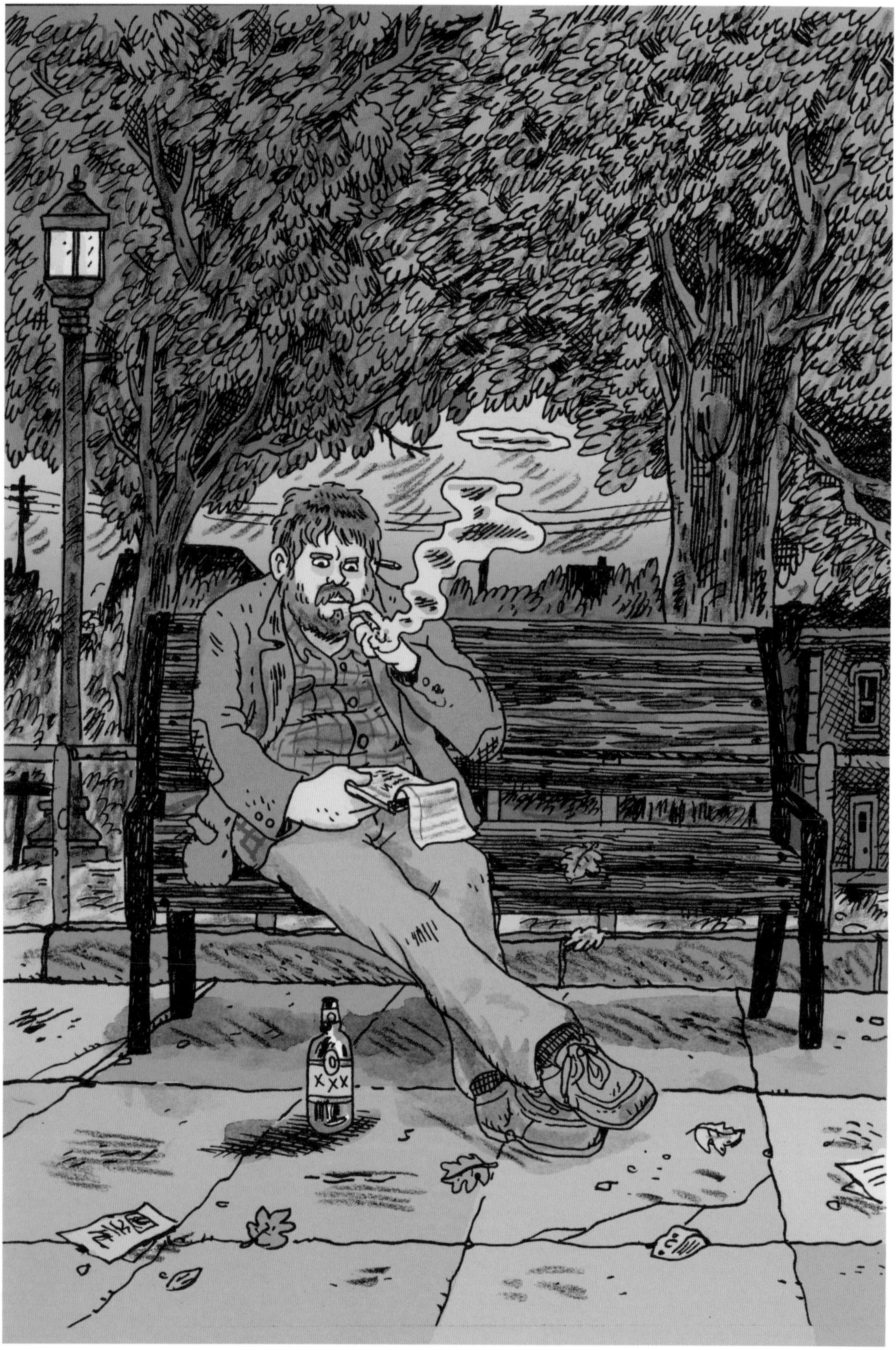

Noah Van Sciver

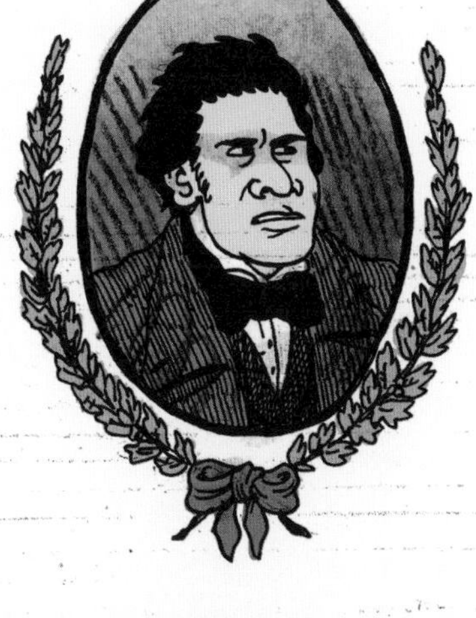

THE DEATH OF ELIJAH LOVEJOY

"As Long as I am an American Citizen and American blood runs in these Veins, I Shall hold myself at Liberty to Speak, to write and to publish whatever I please on any Subject."

— Elijah Lovejoy

Born on November 9th 1802, Lovejoy was raised in a deeply religious family. His father was a Congregational minister and his mother was a devout christian. Elijah attended Waterville College in Maine, and graduated at the top of his Class.

In 1827 he moved to St. Louis, Missouri and worked as an editor of an anti-Jacksonian newspaper and ran a school. In the next five years he became a presbyterian preacher. He Setup a church and became the editor of a weekly religious newspaper, the St. Louis observer. He wrote a number of editorials in the observer that were critical of other religions, and most controversial for his time, on the act of slavery.

On the evening of April 28th 1836 an angry and revengeful mob chained the escaped slave Francis L. McIntosh to a tree in Elijah's town of St. Louis, and burned him alive. The mob, which made up a Large portion of the town, Stood and watched as the flames rose far above Francis's head.

Earlier that day St. Louis's deputy sheriff George Hammond, Joined by the city's deputy constable, William Mull, arrested McIntosh because he had interfered with the arrest of two unruly Sailors. With McIntosh's help, the Sailors were able to run off. Hammond and Mull secured a warrant for Francis's incarceration and marched him off to the city jail, Located west of the courthouse.

When the group reached the corner of the Courthouse Square McIntosh drew a knife. He first struck at Mull, who dodged the blade. Swinging, McIntosh struck Hammond on the Lower chin and drove his knife into his neck. While trying to aid Hammond, Mull was stabbed in his abdomen. As Hammond Lay dying, Francis ran off, with Mull shouting out an alarm and chasing after him before passing out from massive blood Loss.

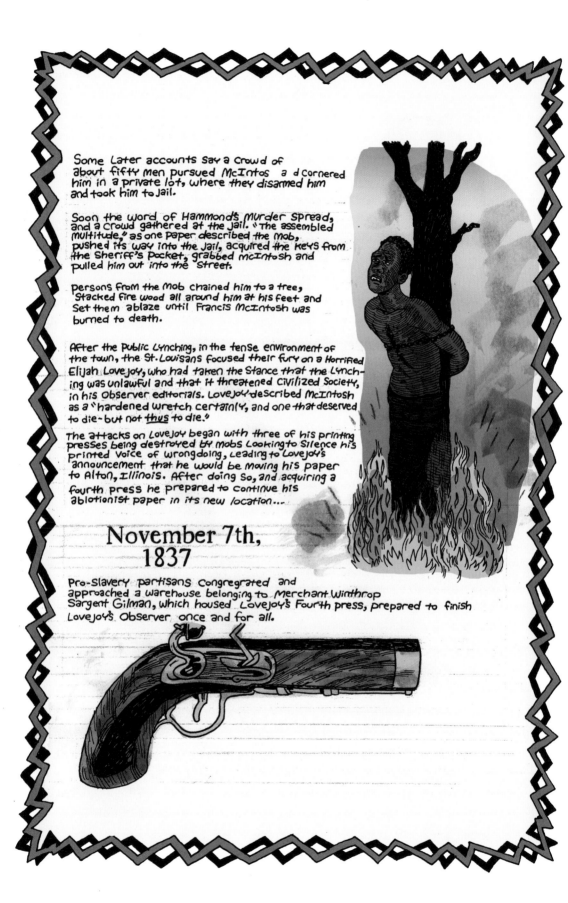

Some Later accounts say a crowd of about fifty men pursued McIntos a d cornered him in a private lot, where they disarmed him and took him to jail.

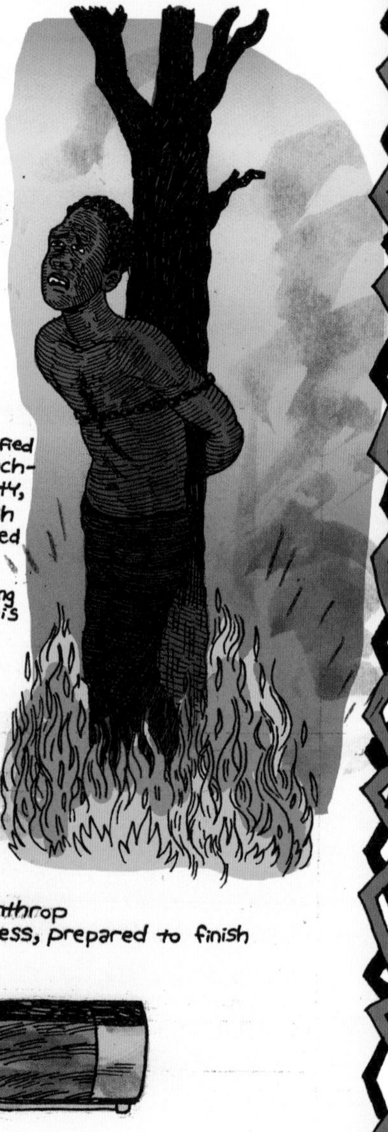

Soon the word of Hammond's murder spread, and a crowd gathered at the jail. "The assembled multitude," as one paper described the mob, pushed its way into the jail, acquired the keys from the sheriff's pocket, grabbed McIntosh and pulled him out into the street.

persons from the mob chained him to a tree, stacked fire wood all around him at his feet and set them ablaze until Francis McIntosh was burned to death.

After the public Lynching, in the tense environment of the town, the St. Louisans focused their fury on a Horrified Elijah Lovejoy, who had taken the stance that the Lynching was unlawful and that it threatened civilized society, in his Observer editorials. Lovejoy described McIntosh as a "hardened wretch certainly, and one that deserved to die-but not <u>thus</u> to die."

The attacks on Lovejoy began with three of his printing presses being destroyed by mobs Looking to Silence his printed voice of wrongdoing, Leading to Lovejoy's announcement that he would be moving his paper to Alton, Illinois. After doing so, and acquiring a fourth press he prepared to continue his ablotionist paper in its new location...

November 7th, 1837

Pro-Slavery partisans congregrated and approached a warehouse belonging to Merchant Winthrop Sargent Gilman, which housed Lovejoy's Fourth press, prepared to finish Lovejoy's Observer once and for all.

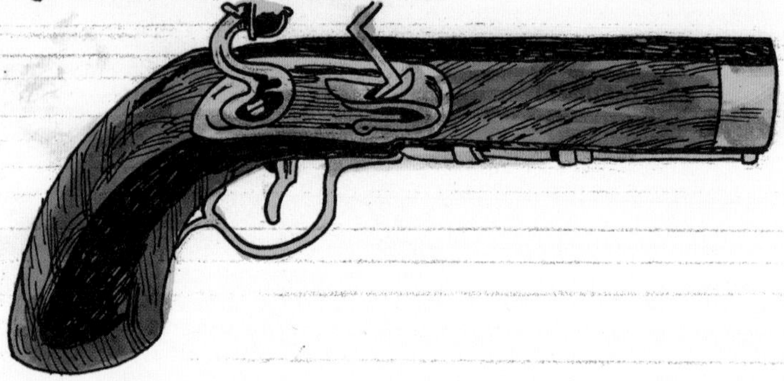

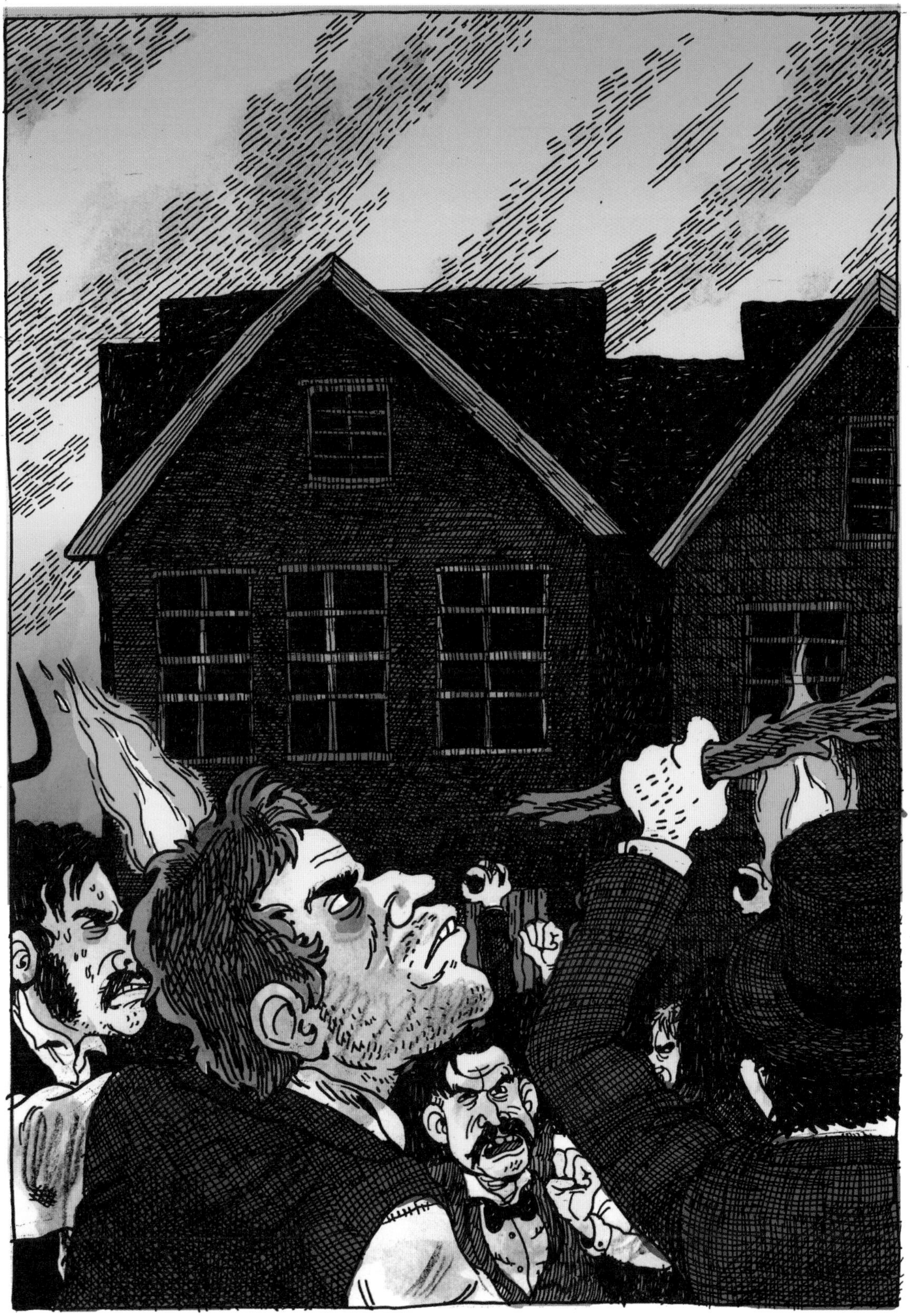

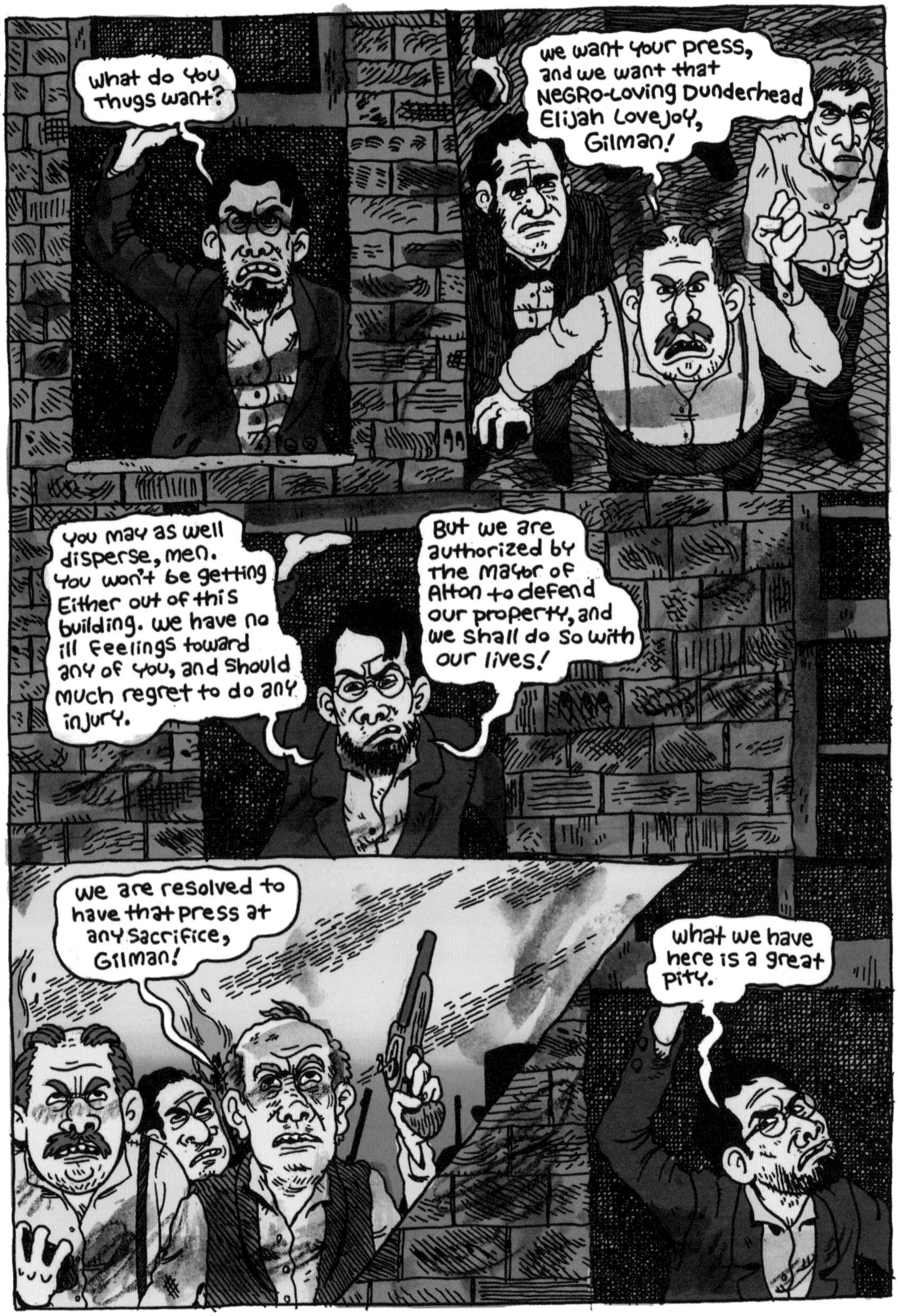
What do you Thugs want?
We want your press, and we want that NEGRO-LOVING Dunderhead Elijah Lovejoy, Gilman!
You may as well disperse, men. You won't be getting Either out of this building. We have no ill Feelings toward any of you, and should much regret to do any injury.
But we are authorized by the Mayor of Alton to defend our property, and we shall do so with our lives!
We are resolved to have that press at any sacrifice, Gilman!
What we have here is a great pity.

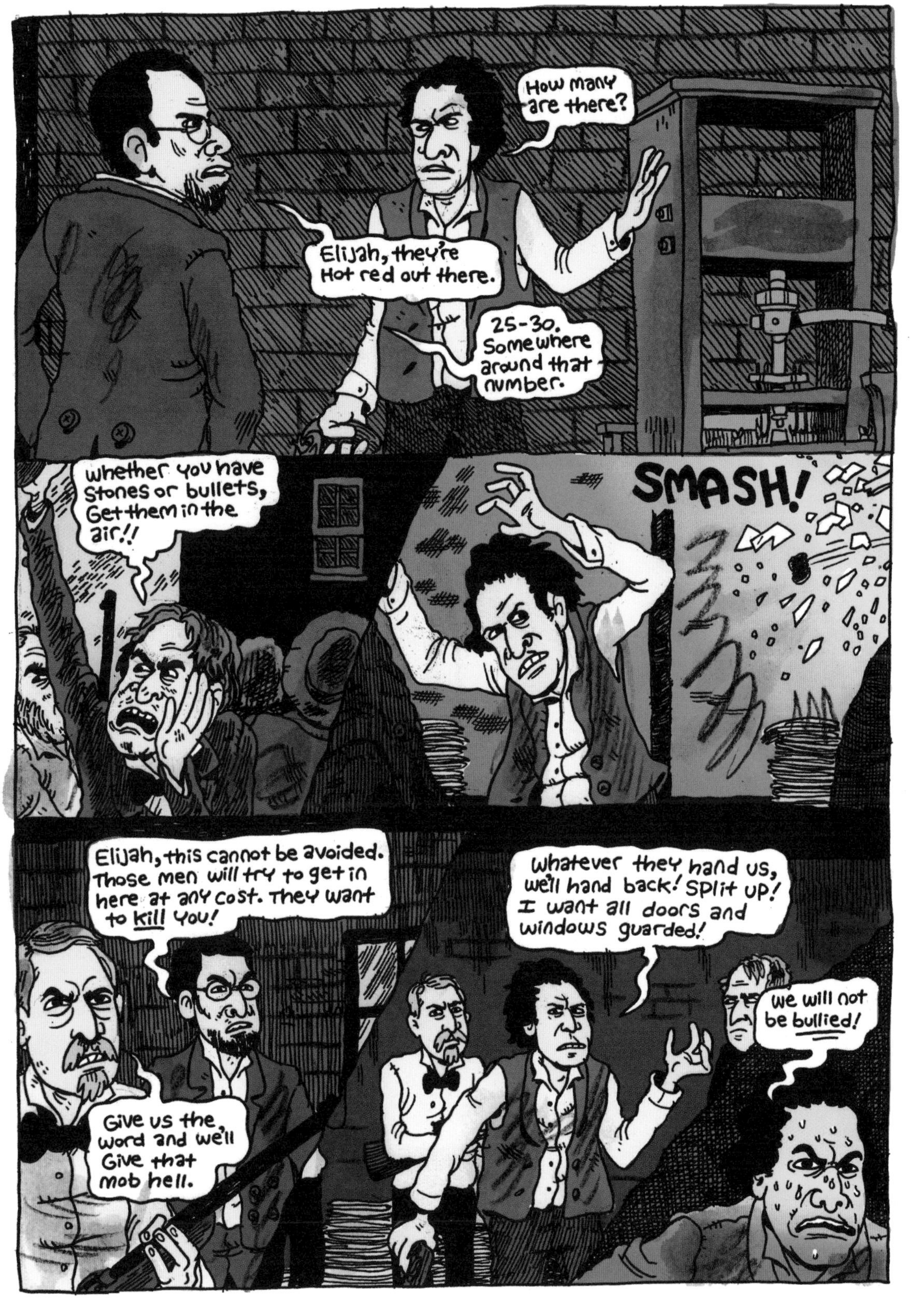
How many are there?
Elijah, they're Hot red out there.
25-30. Somewhere around that number.
whether you have Stones or bullets, Get them in the air!!
SMASH!
Elijah, this cannot be avoided. Those men will try to get in here at any cost. They want to kill you!
Give us the word and we'll Give that mob hell.
whatever they hand us, we'll hand back! Split up! I want all doors and windows guarded!
we will not be bullied!

a cut-away view

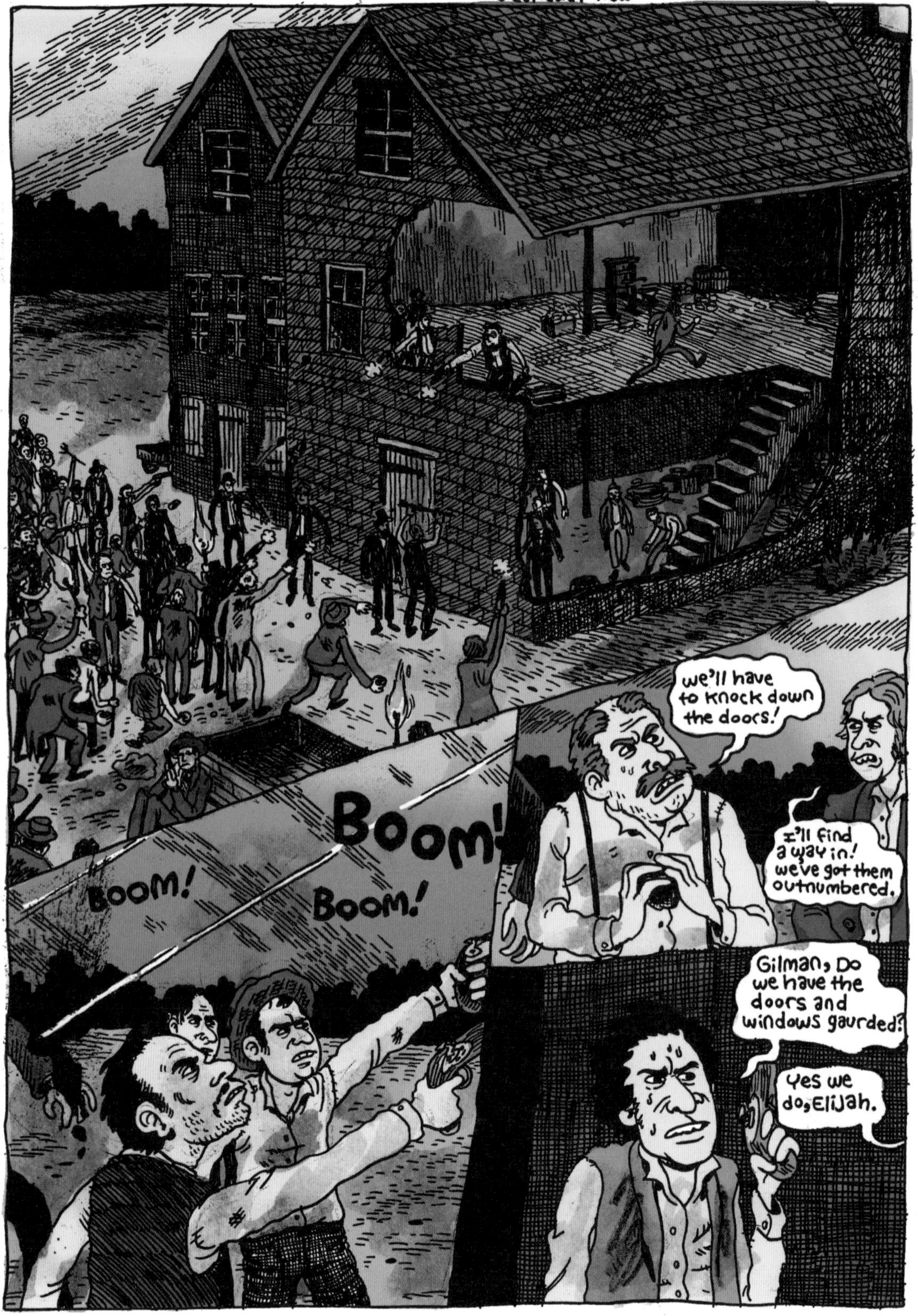

Boom!
Boom!
Boom!
we'll have to knock down the doors!
I'll find a way in! we've got them outnumbered.
Gilman, Do we have the doors and windows gaurded?
Yes we do, Elijah.

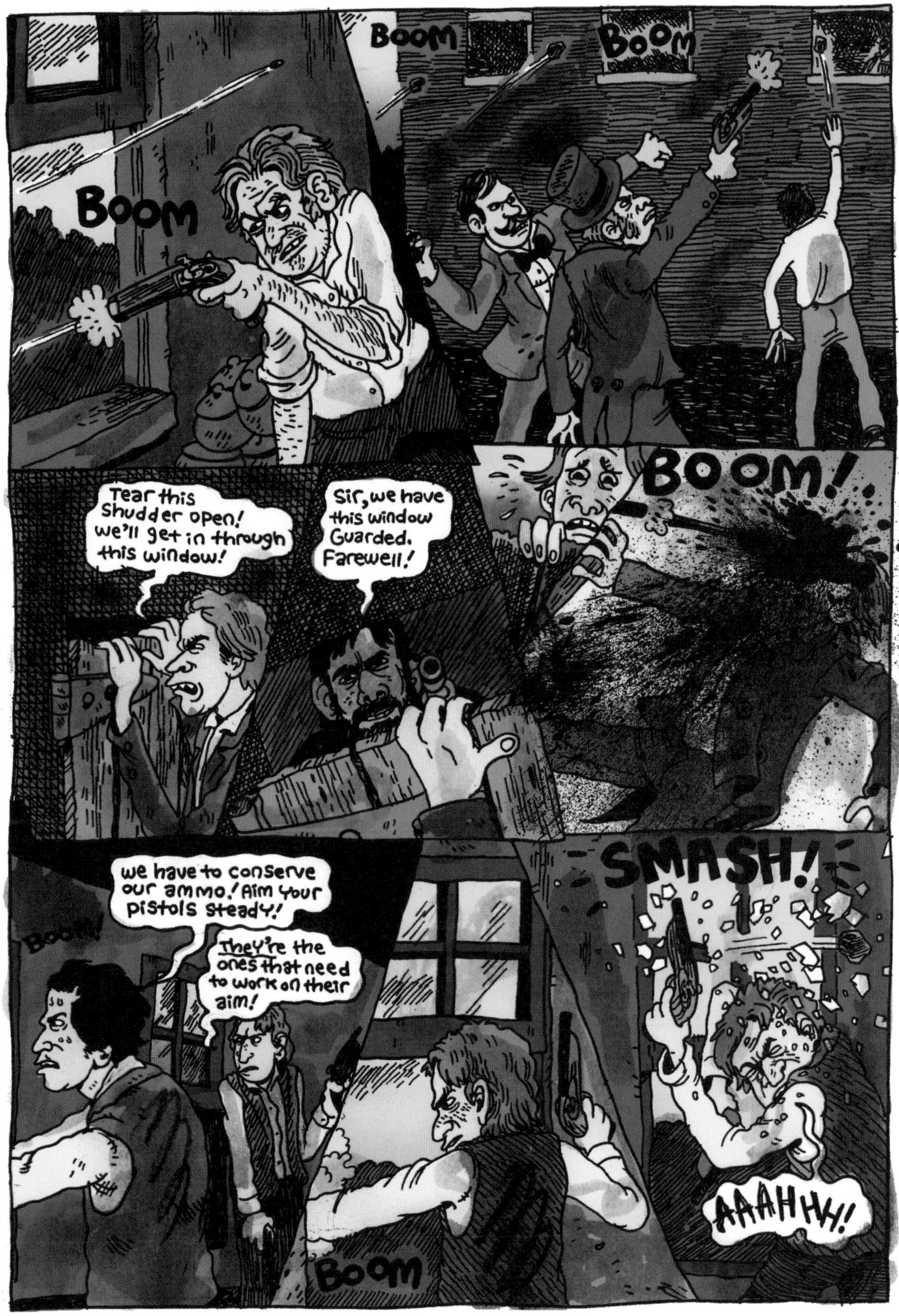
BOOM
BOOM
BOOM
Tear this Shudder open! we'll get in through this window!
Sir, we have this window Guarded. Farewell!
BOOM!
we have to conserve our ammo! Aim your pistols steady!
They're the ones that need to work on their aim!
SMASH!
AAAHHH!
BOOM

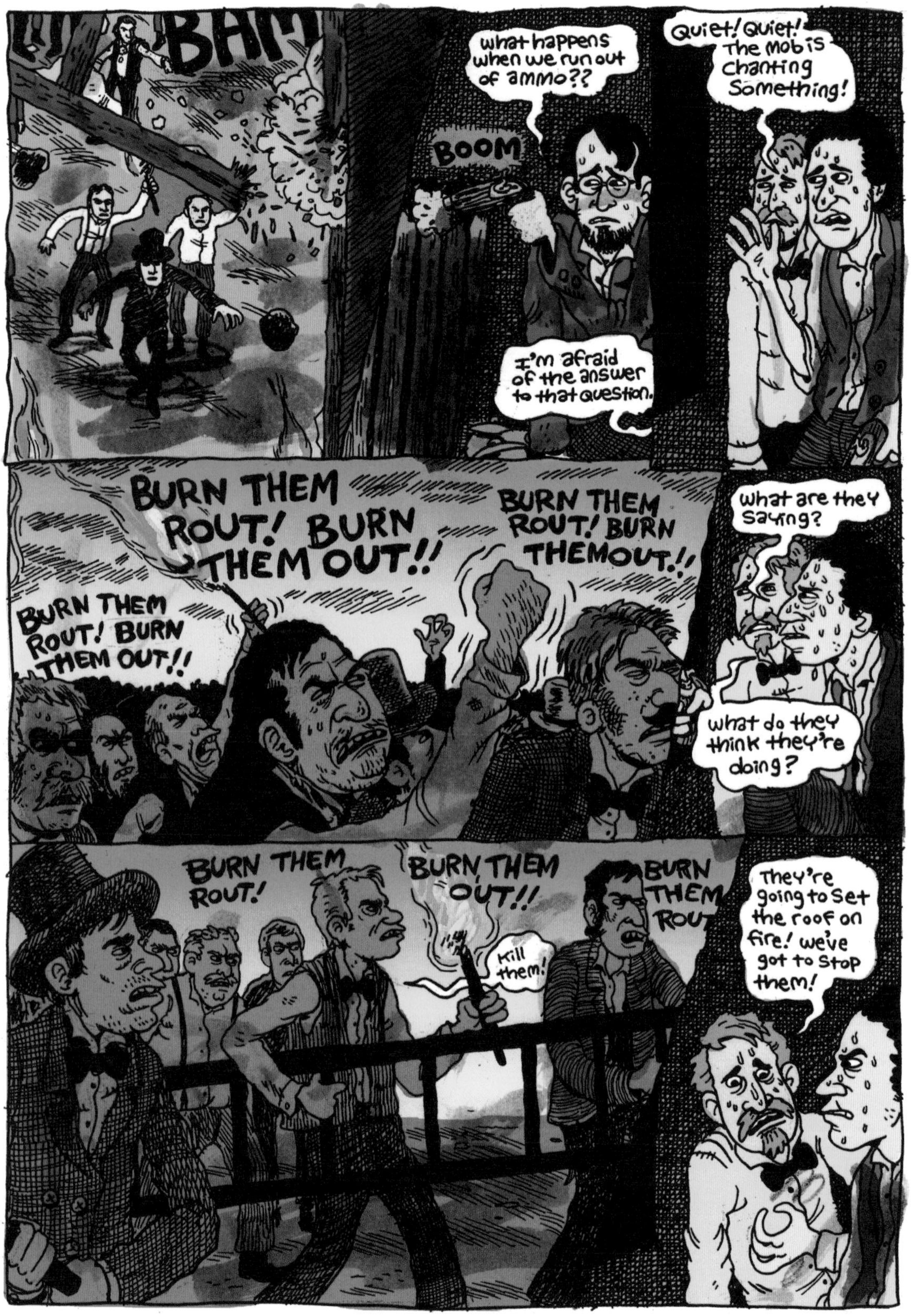
BAM
what happens when we run out of ammo??
BOOM
I'm afraid of the answer to that question.
Quiet! Quiet! The mob is chanting something!
BURN THEM ROUT! BURN THEM OUT!!
BURN THEM ROUT! BURN THEMOUT!!
BURN THEM ROUT! BURN THEM OUT!!
what are they saying?
what do they think they're doing?
BURN THEM ROUT!
BURN THEM OUT!!
Kill them!
BURN THEM ROUT
They're going to set the roof on fire! we've got to stop them!

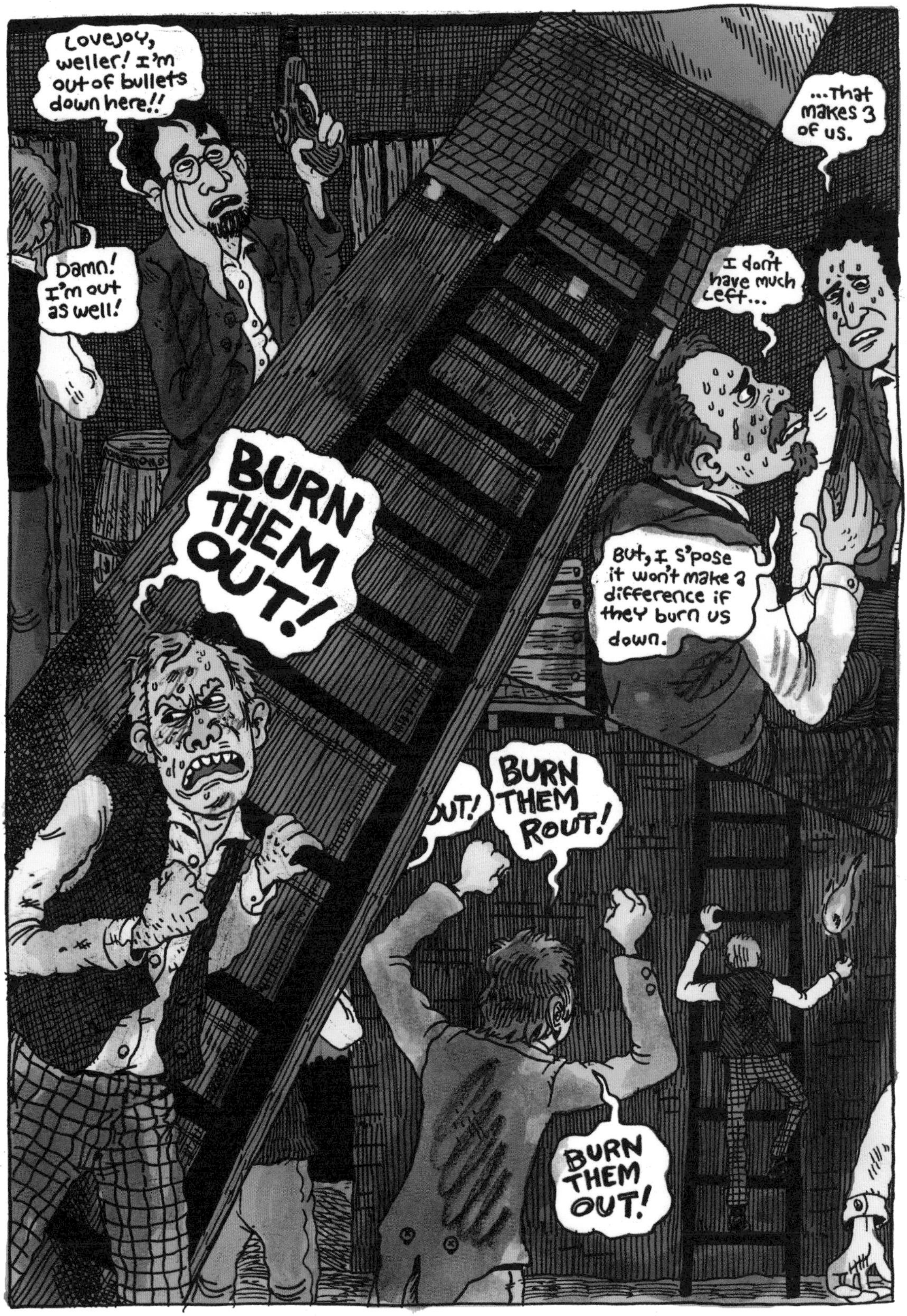
Lovejoy, weller! I'm out of bullets down here!!
Damn! I'm out as well!
...That makes 3 of us.
I don't have much left...
But, I s'pose it won't make a difference if they burn us down.
BURN THEM OUT!
OUT!
BURN THEM ROUT!
BURN THEM OUT!

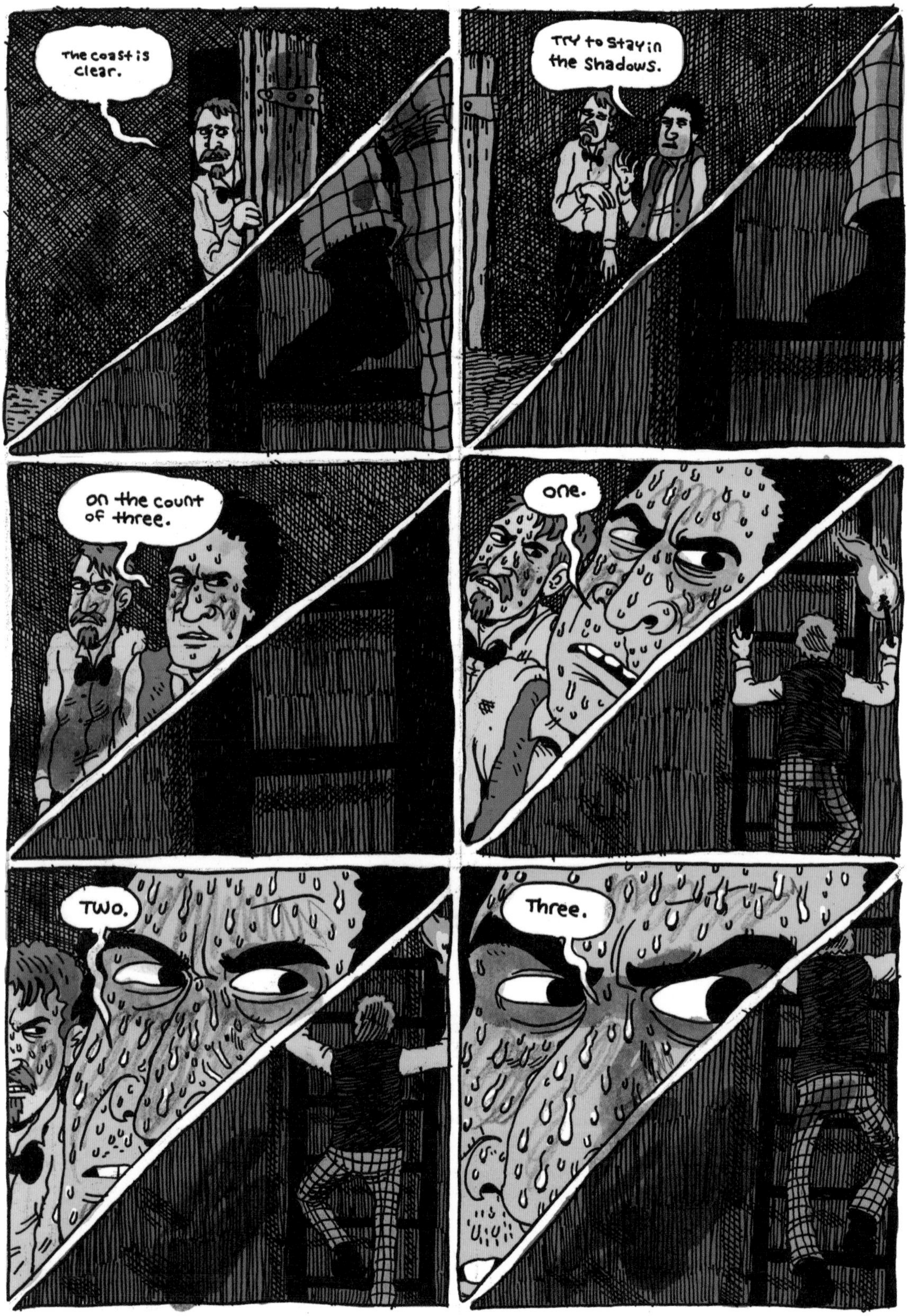
The coast is clear.
Try to stay in the shadows.
on the count of three.
one.
Two.
Three.

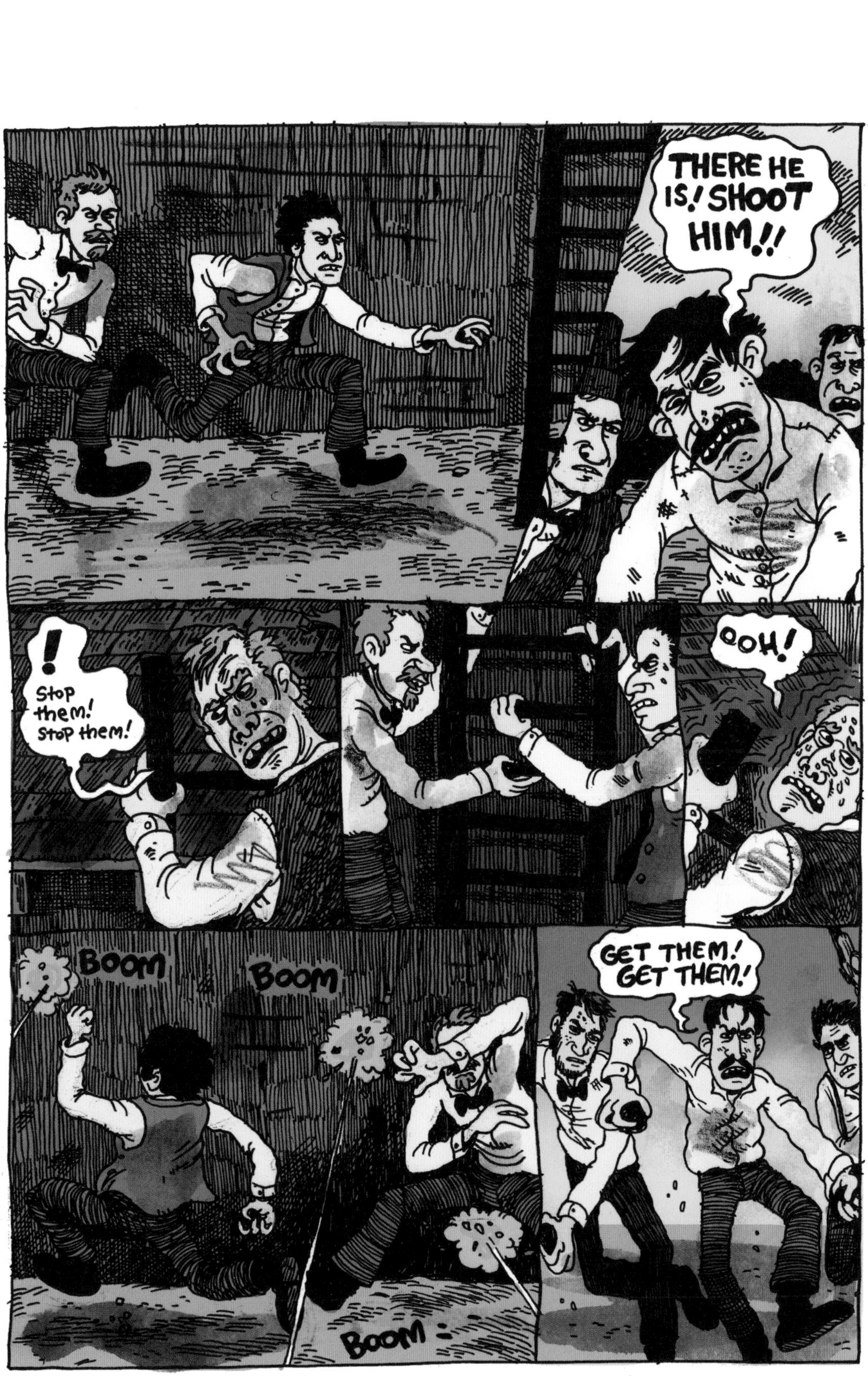
THERE HE IS! SHOOT HIM!!
!
Stop them! Stop them!
OOH!
Boom
Boom
Boom
GET THEM! GET THEM!

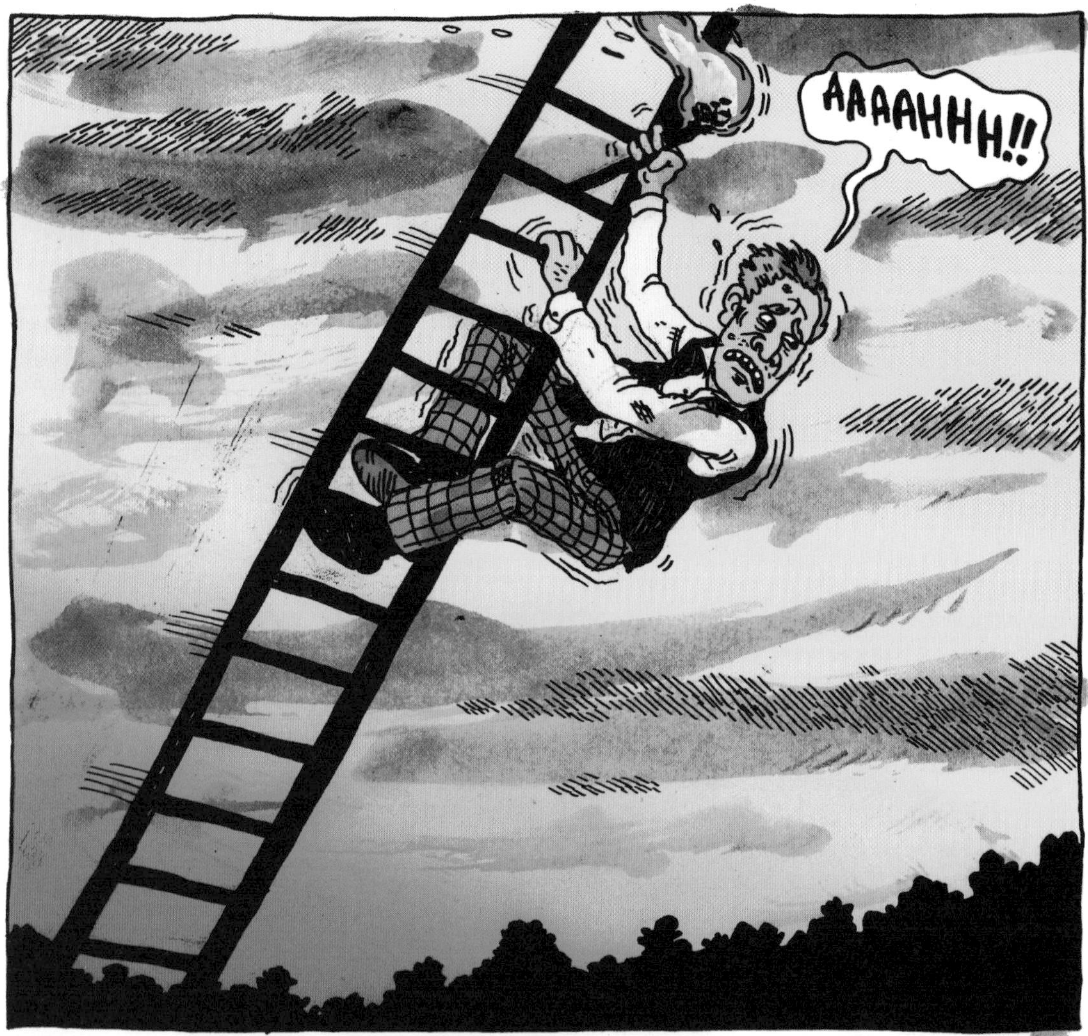
AAAAHHH!!

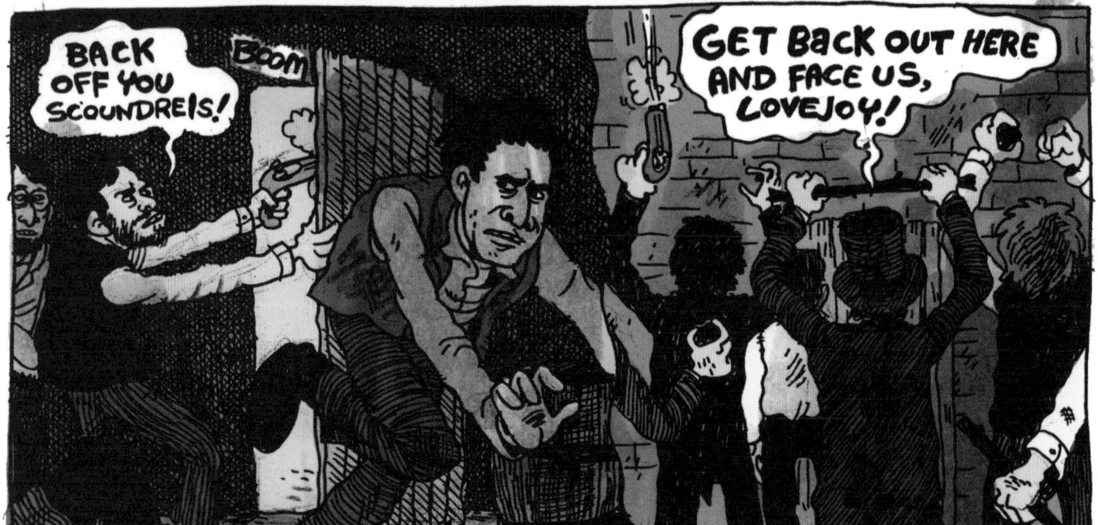
BACK OFF YOU SCOUNDRELS!
BOOM
GET BACK OUT HERE AND FACE US, LOVEJOY!

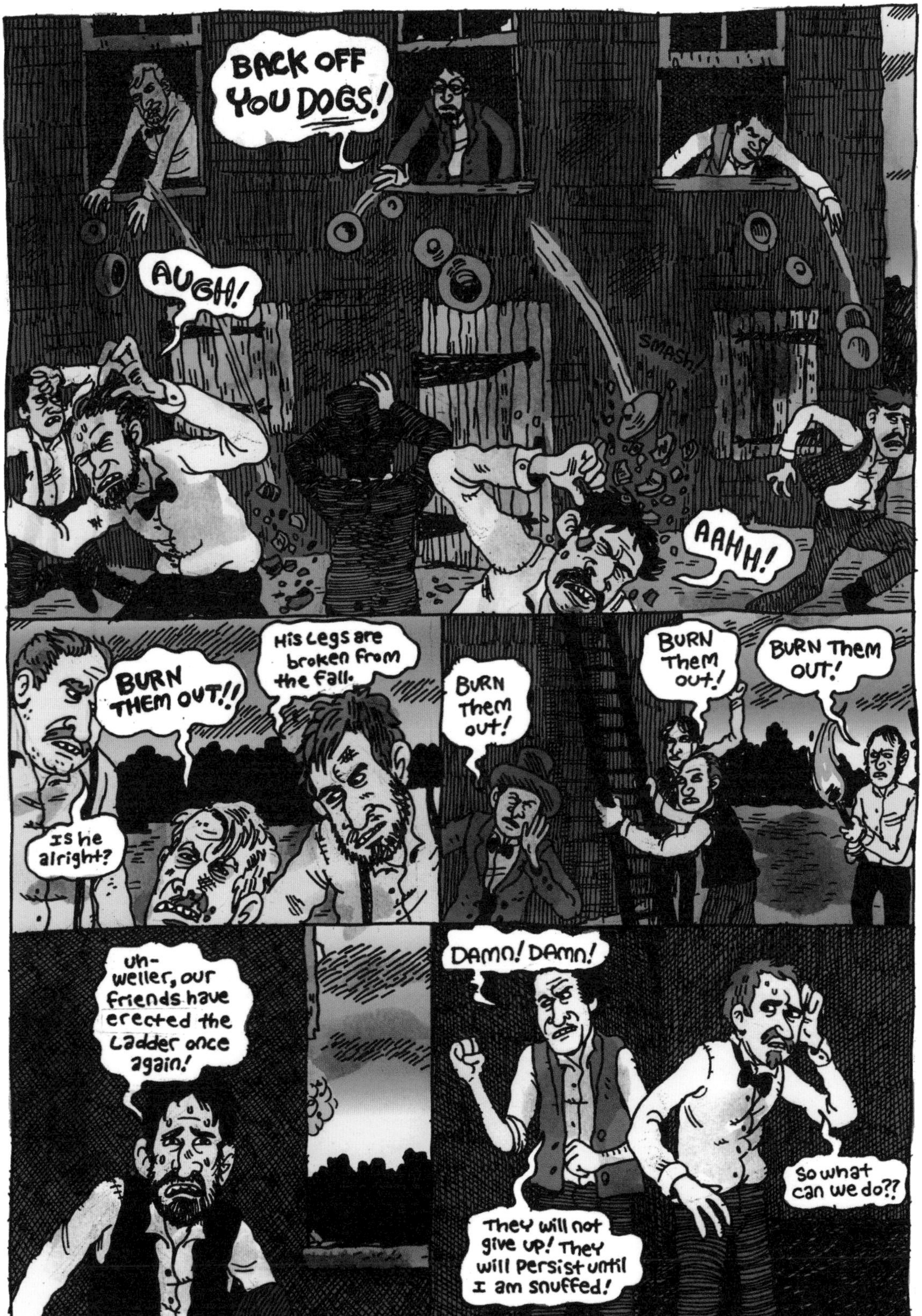
BACK OFF YOU DOGS!
AUGH!
SMASH!
AAHH!
BURN THEM OUT!!
Is he alright?
His Legs are broken from the fall.
BURN Them out!
BURN Them out!
BURN Them OUT!
uh-weller, our friends have erected the Ladder once again!
DAMN! DAMN!
They will not give up! They will persist until I am snuffed!
So what can we do??

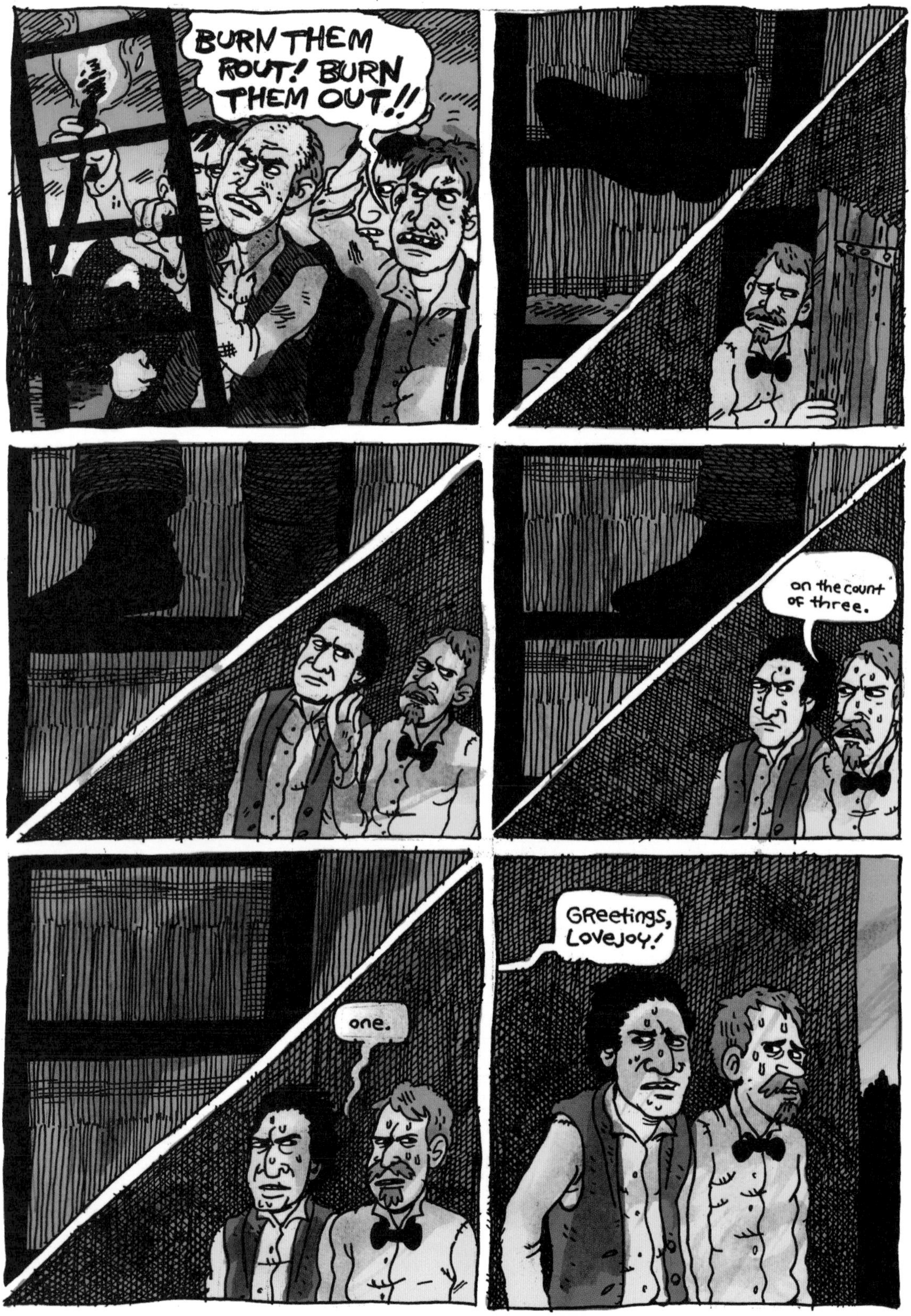
BURN THEM ROUT! BURN THEM OUT!!
on the count of three.
one.
GReetings, LoveJoy!

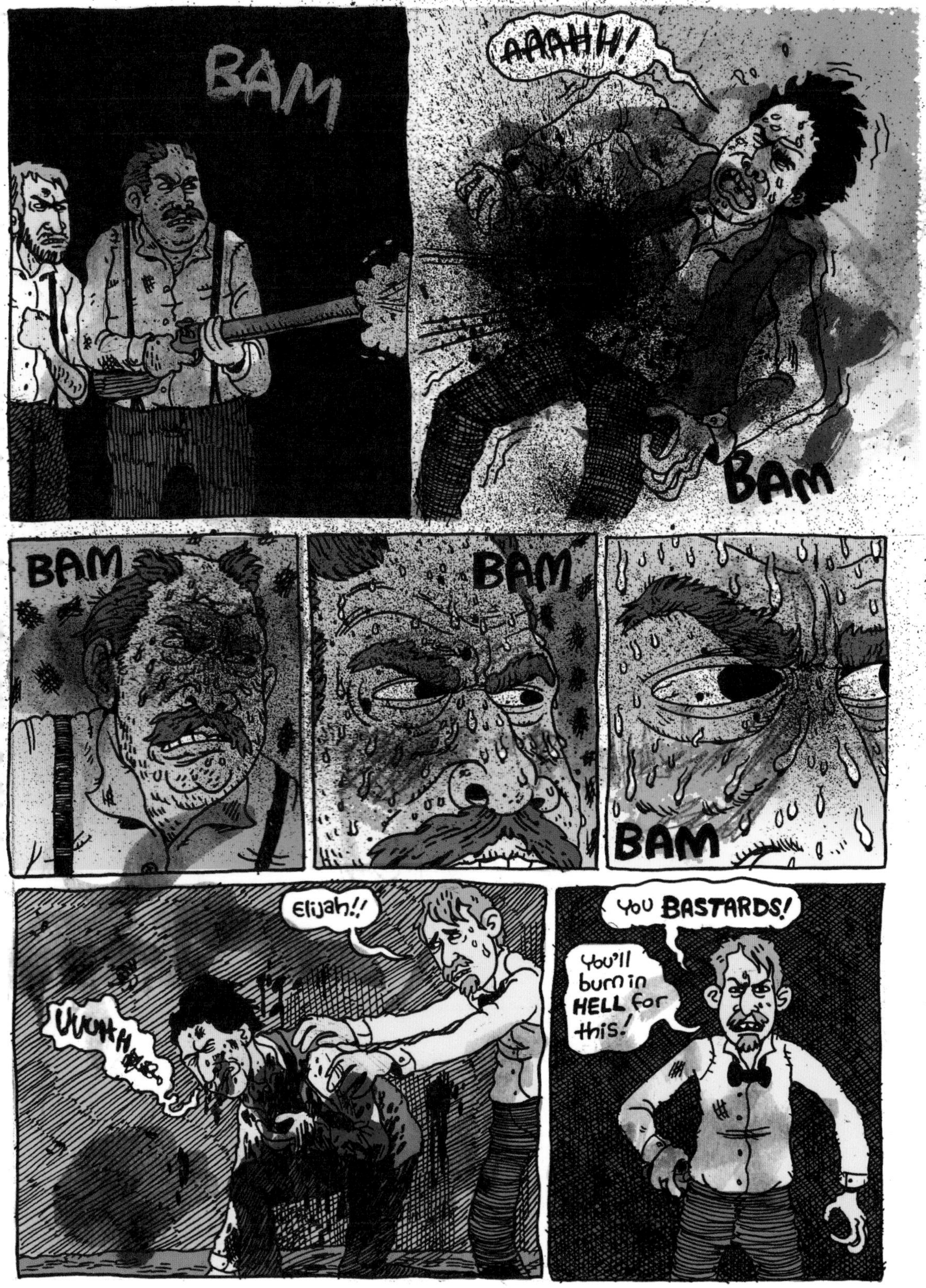
BAM
AAAHH!
BAM
BAM
BAM
BAM
Elijah!!
UUUH
You BASTARDS!
You'll burn in HELL for this!

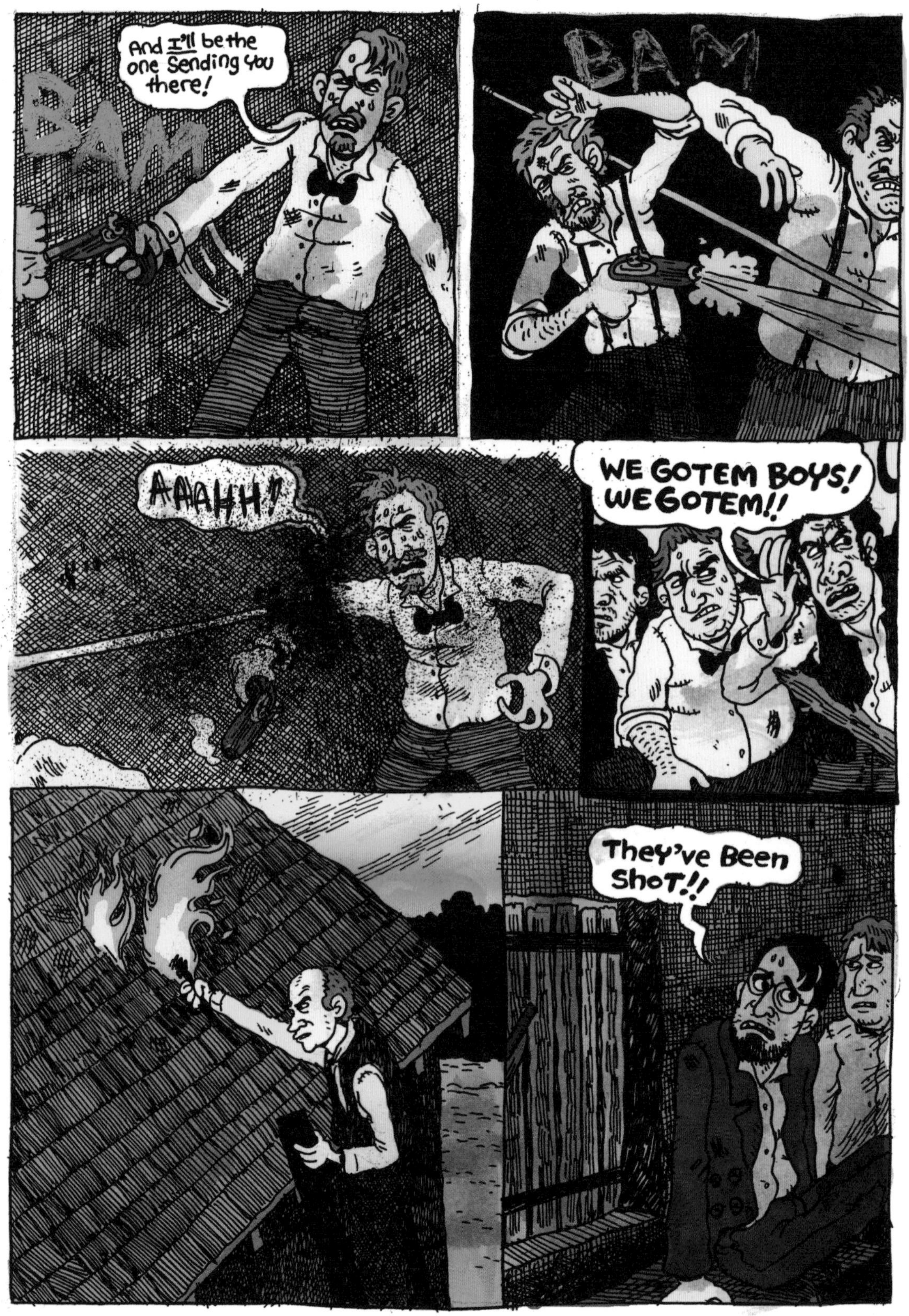
And I'll be the one sending you there!
BAM
BAM
AAAHH!!
WE GOTEM BOYS! WE GOTEM!!
They've Been ShoT!!

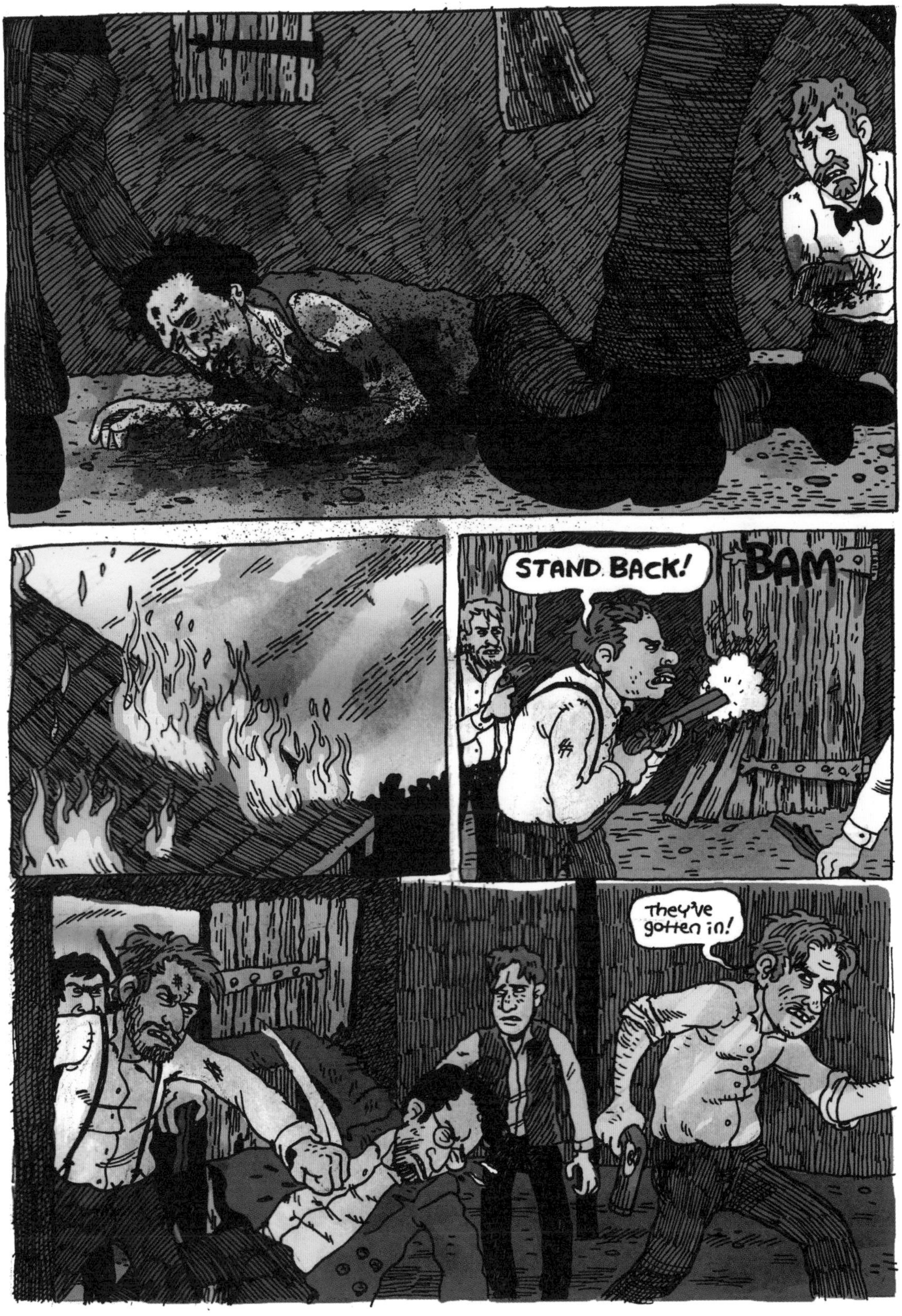
STAND BACK!
BAM
They've gotten in!

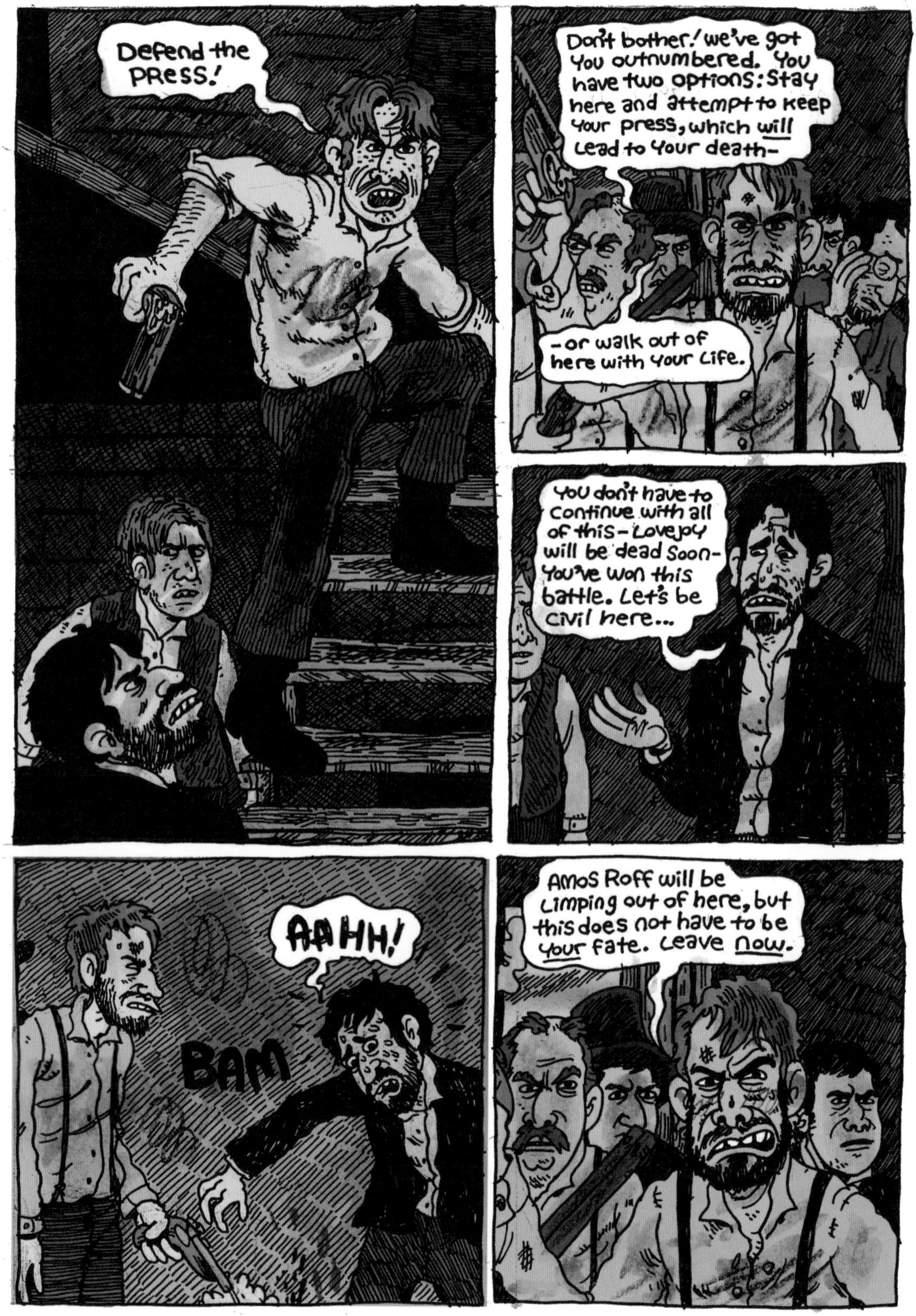
Defend the PRESS!
Don't bother! we've got you outnumbered. You have two options: Stay here and attempt to keep your press, which will lead to your death-
-or walk out of here with your life.
You don't have to continue with all of this-Lovejoy will be dead soon-You've won this battle. Let's be civil here...
AAHH!
BAM
Amos Roff will be limping out of here, but this does not have to be your fate. Leave now.

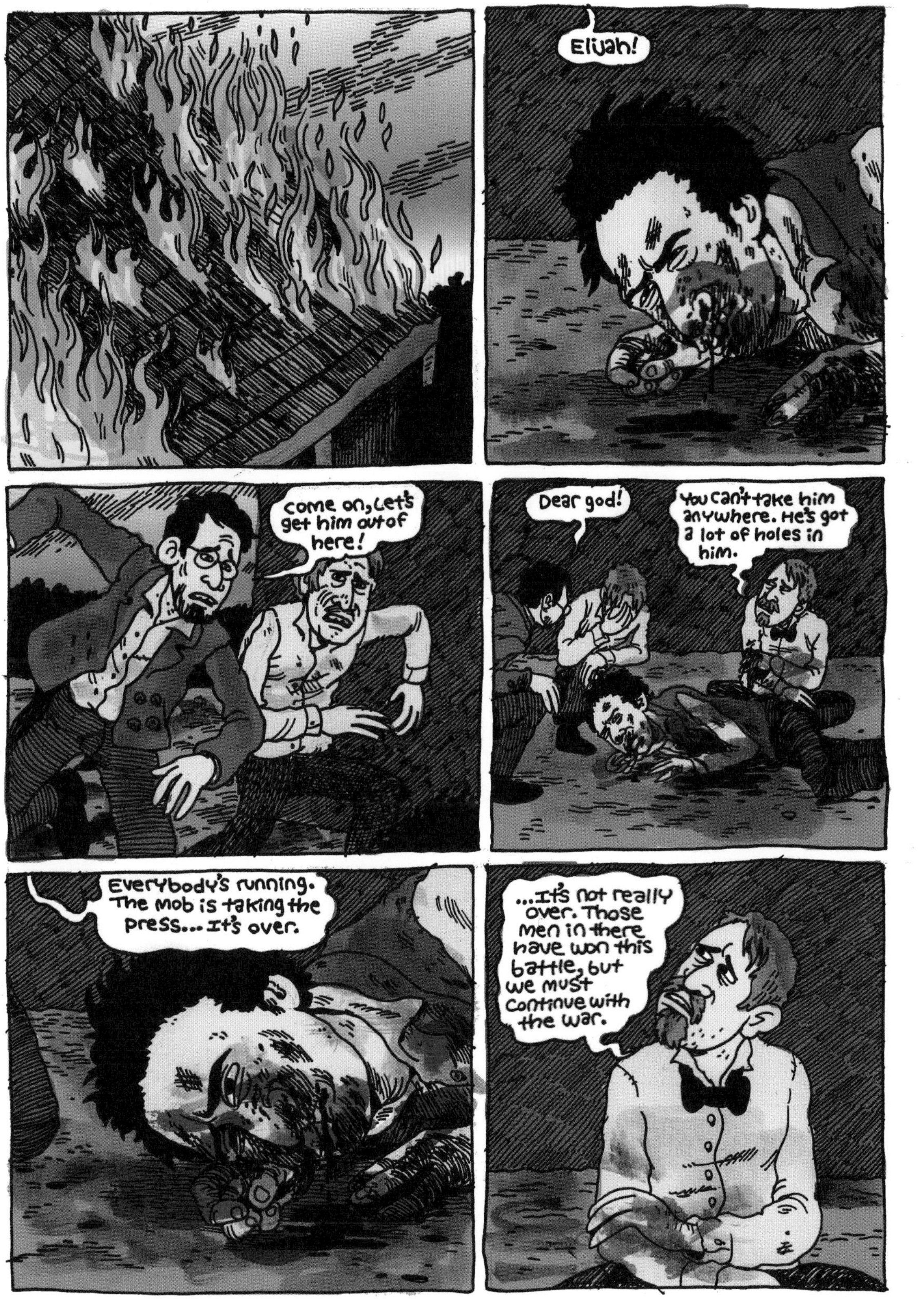
Elijah!
Come on, Let's get him out of here!
Dear god!
You can't take him anywhere. He's got a lot of holes in him.
Everybody's running. The mob is taking the press... It's over.
...It's not really over. Those men in there have won this battle, but we must continue with the war.

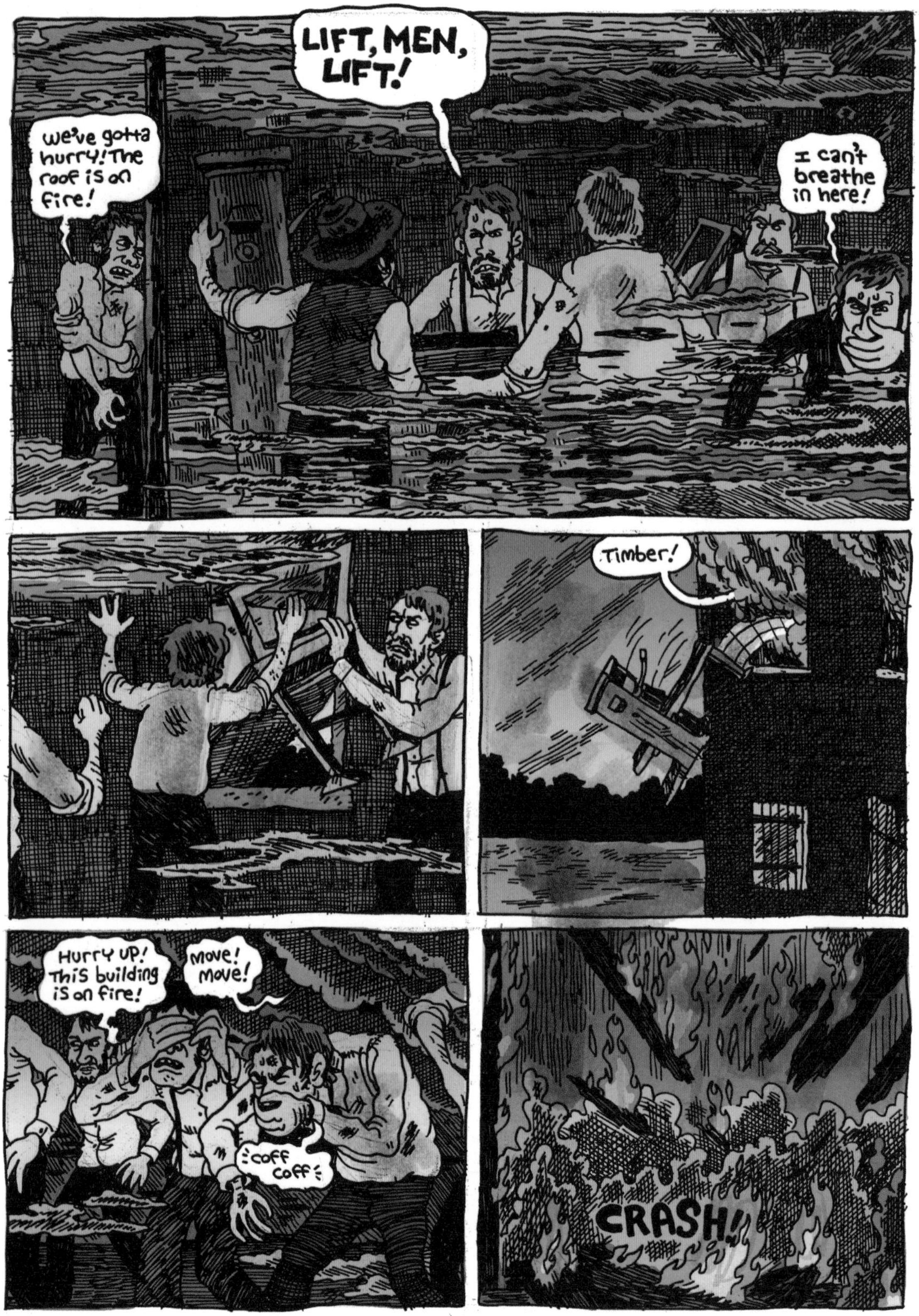
We've gotta hurry! The roof is on fire!
LIFT, MEN, LIFT!
I can't breathe in here!
Timber!
Hurry up! This building is on fire!
Move! Move!
coff coff
CRASH!

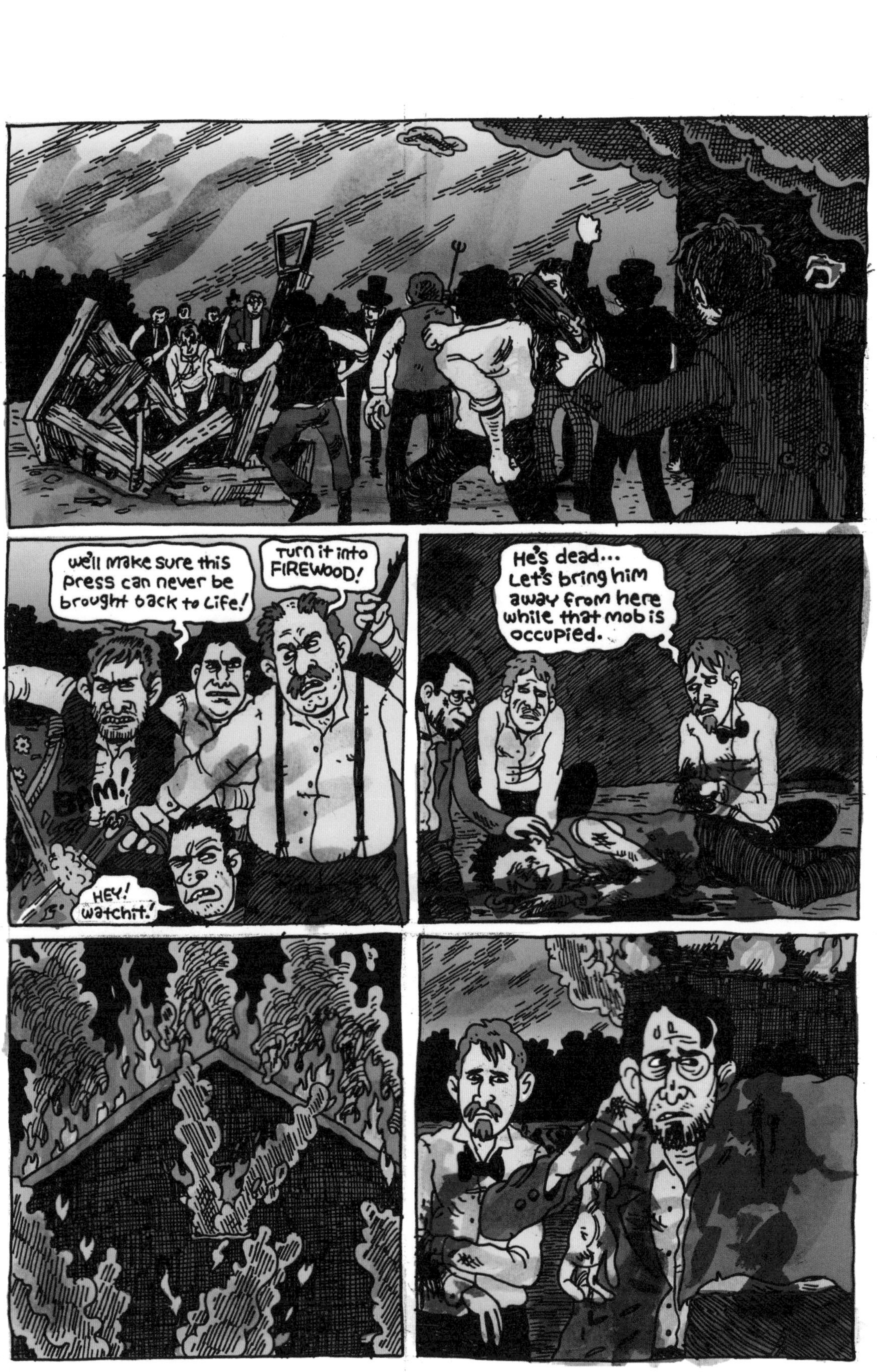
We'll make sure this press can never be brought back to life!
Turn it into FIREWOOD!
BAM!
HEY! Watchit!
He's dead... Let's bring him away from here while that mob is occupied.

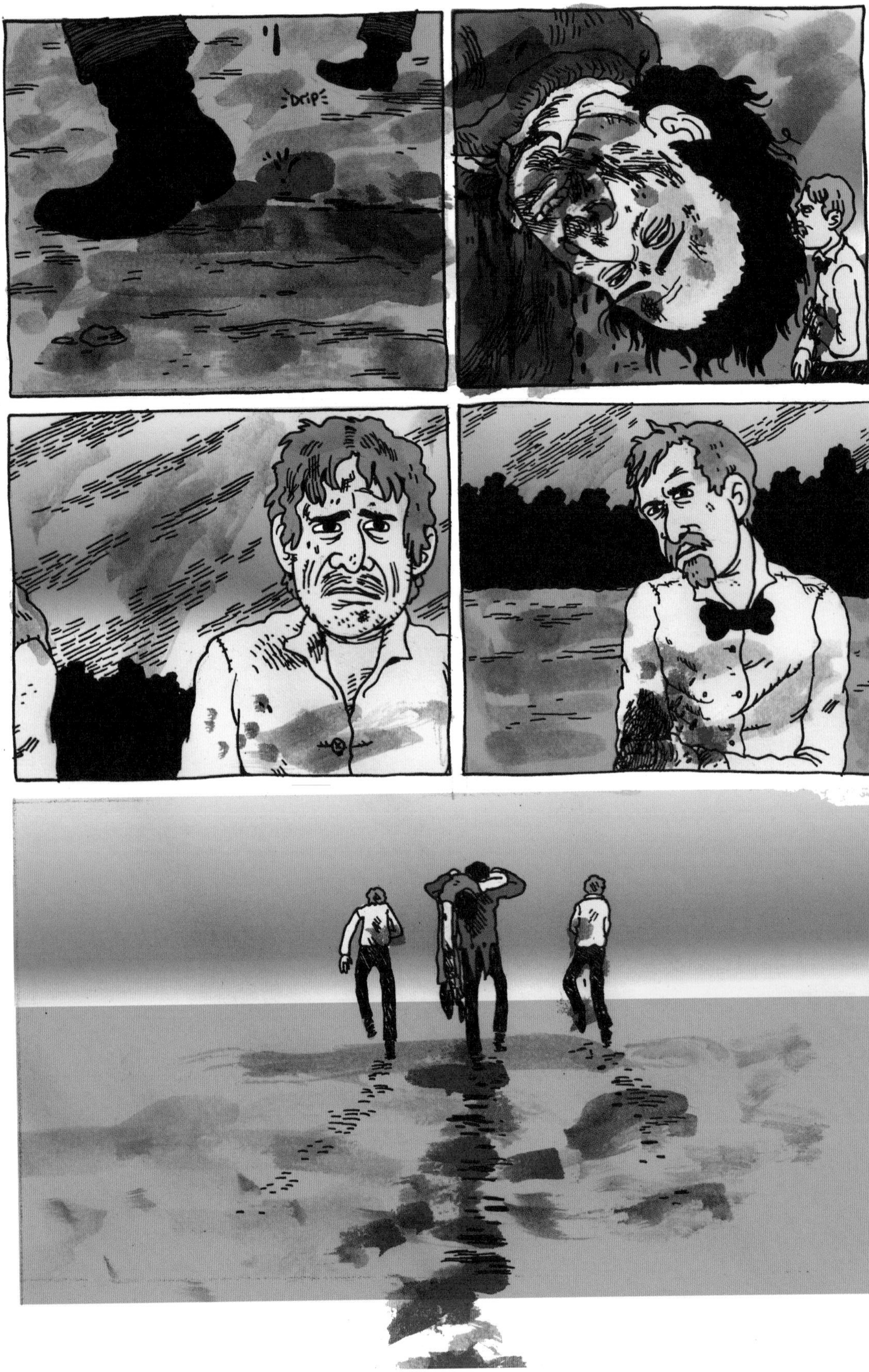
DRIP

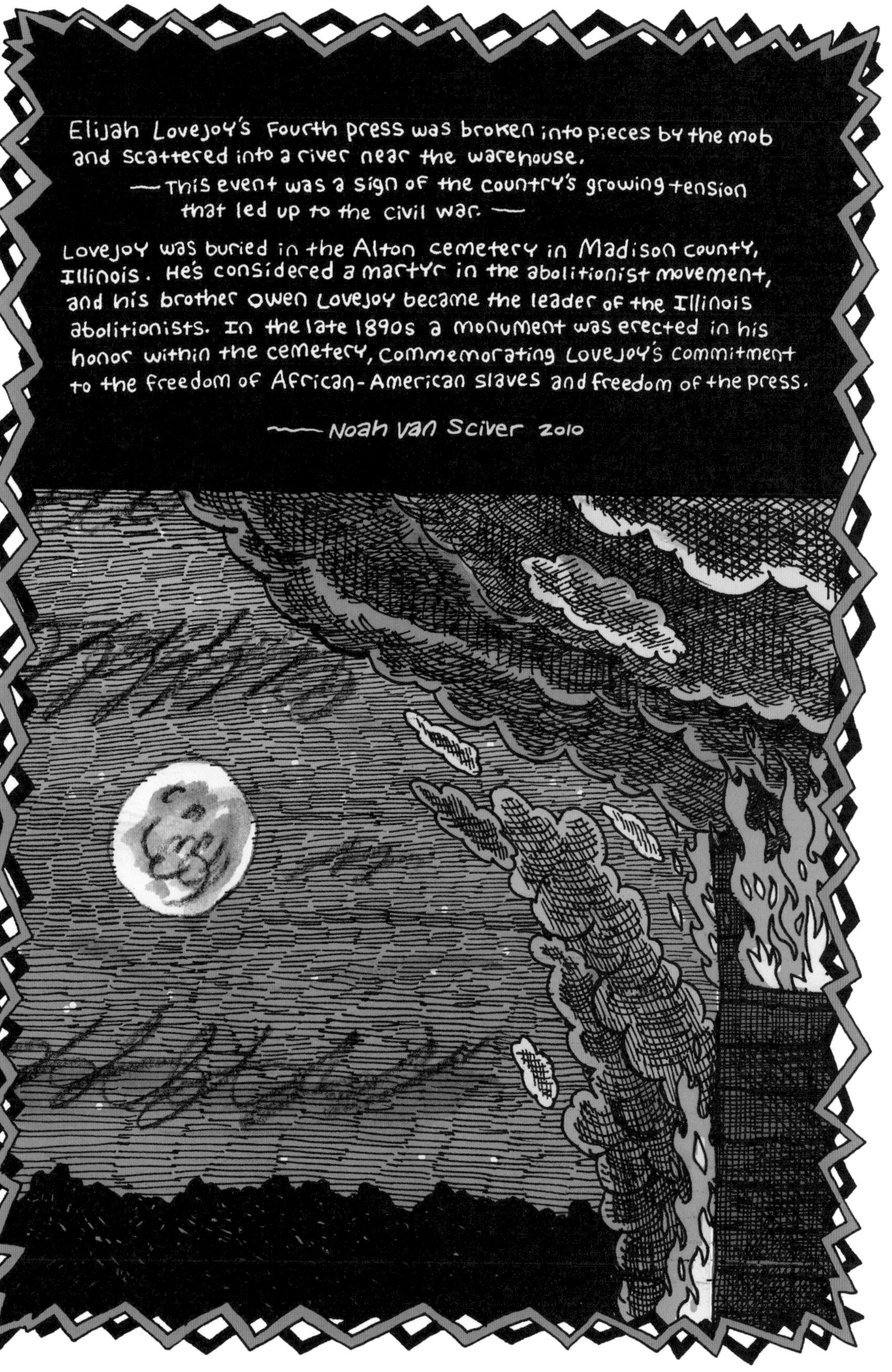
Elijah Lovejoy's Fourth press was broken into pieces by the mob and scattered into a river near the warehouse.
—This event was a sign of the country's growing tension that led up to the civil war.—
Lovejoy was buried in the Alton cemetery in Madison county, Illinois. He's considered a martyr in the abolitionist movement, and his brother Owen Lovejoy became the leader of the Illinois abolitionists. In the late 1890s a monument was erected in his honor within the cemetery, commemorating Lovejoy's commitment to the freedom of African-American slaves and freedom of the press.
—— Noah Van Sciver 2010

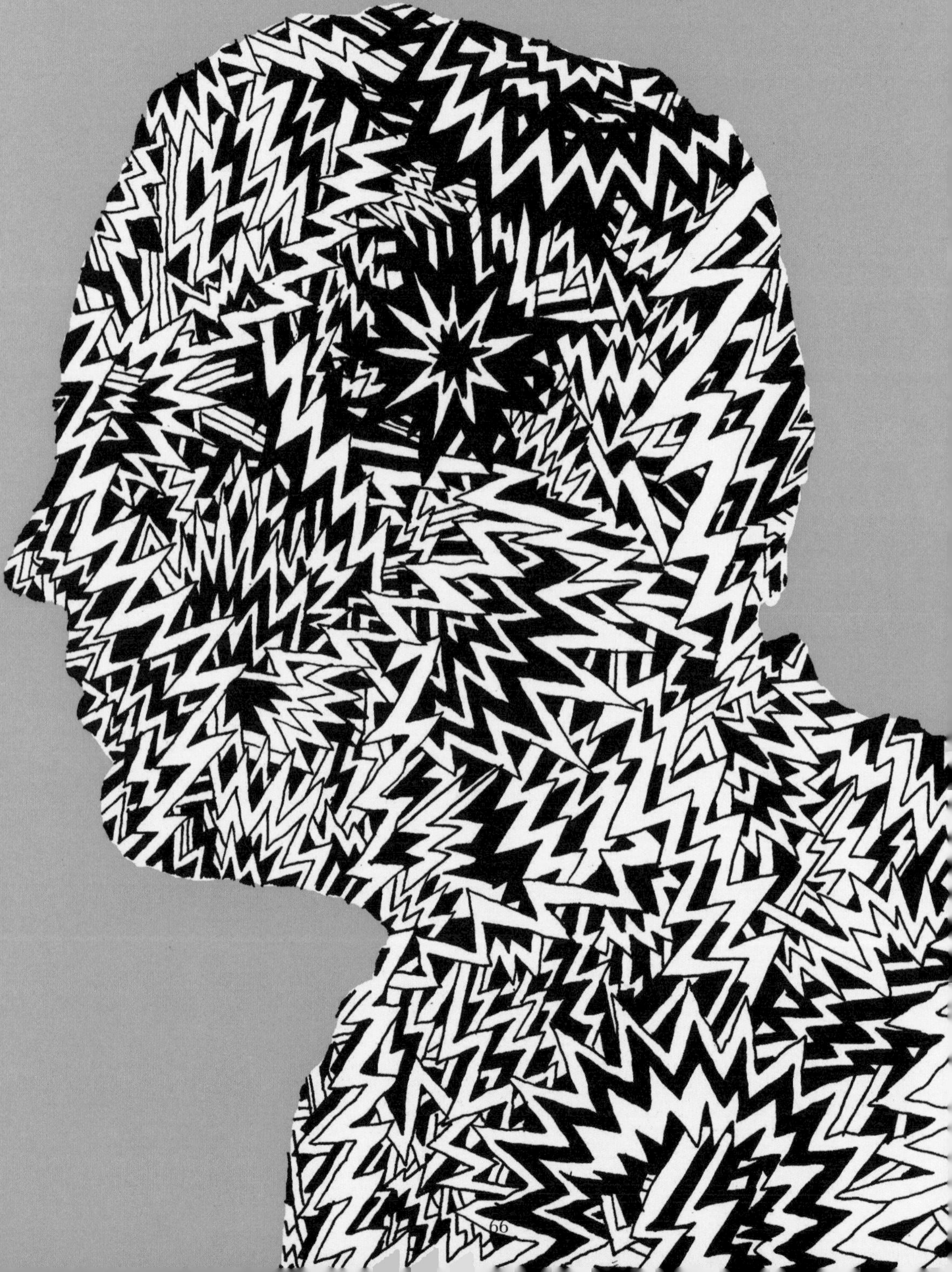

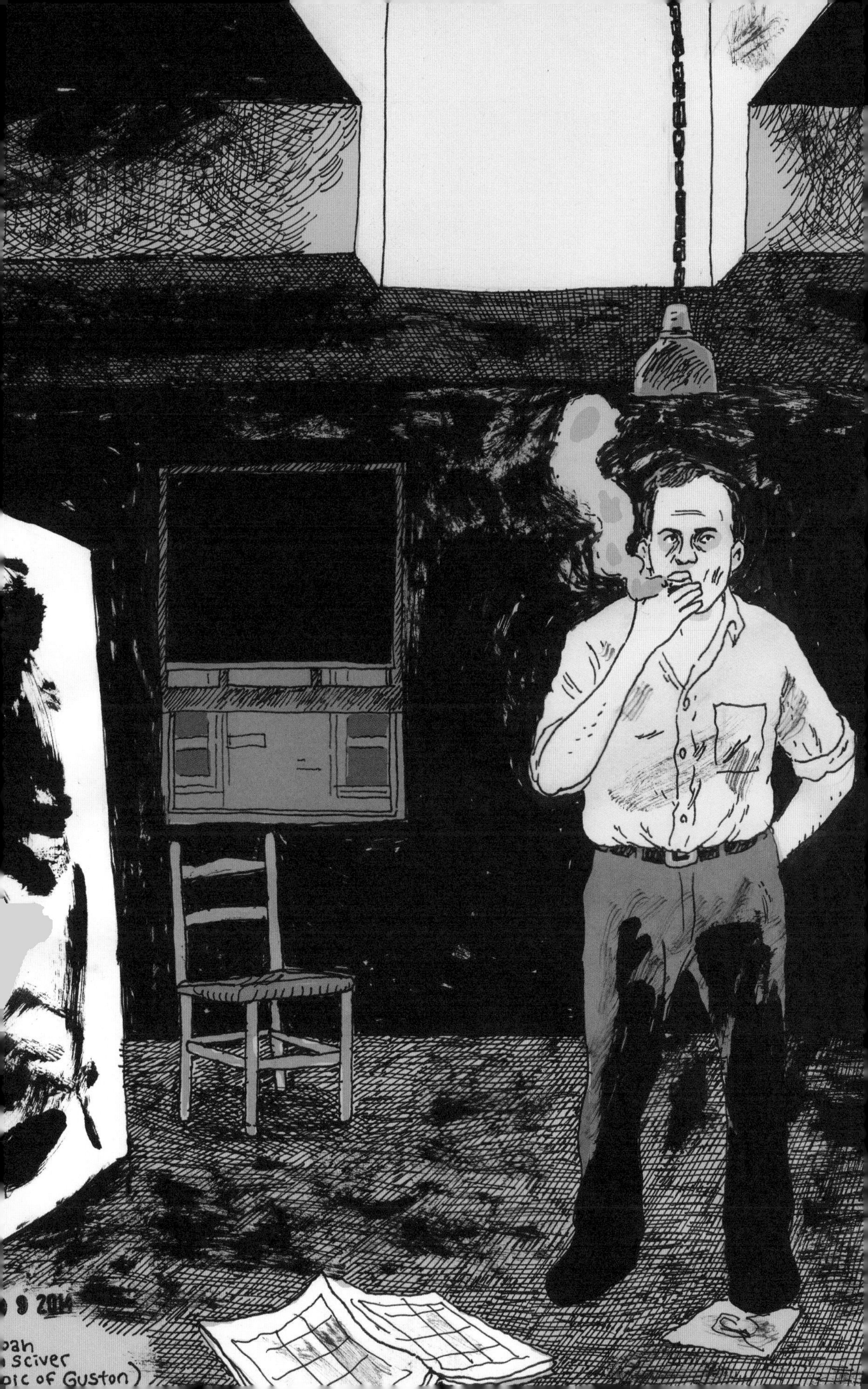
9 2014
oah
Sciver
pic of Guston)

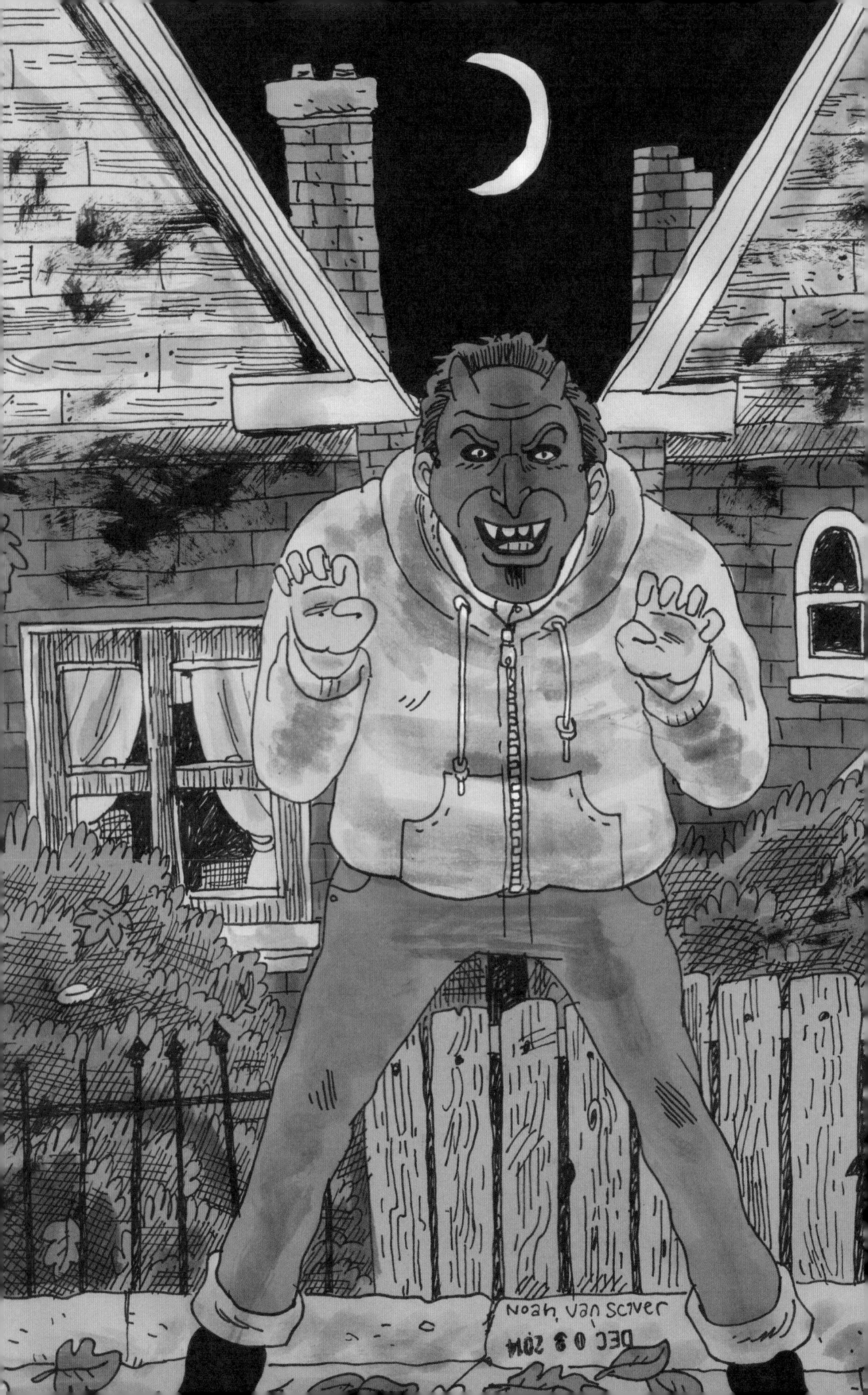
Noah Van Sciver
DEC 0 8 2014

NOAH VAN SCIVER
THE COW'S HEAD

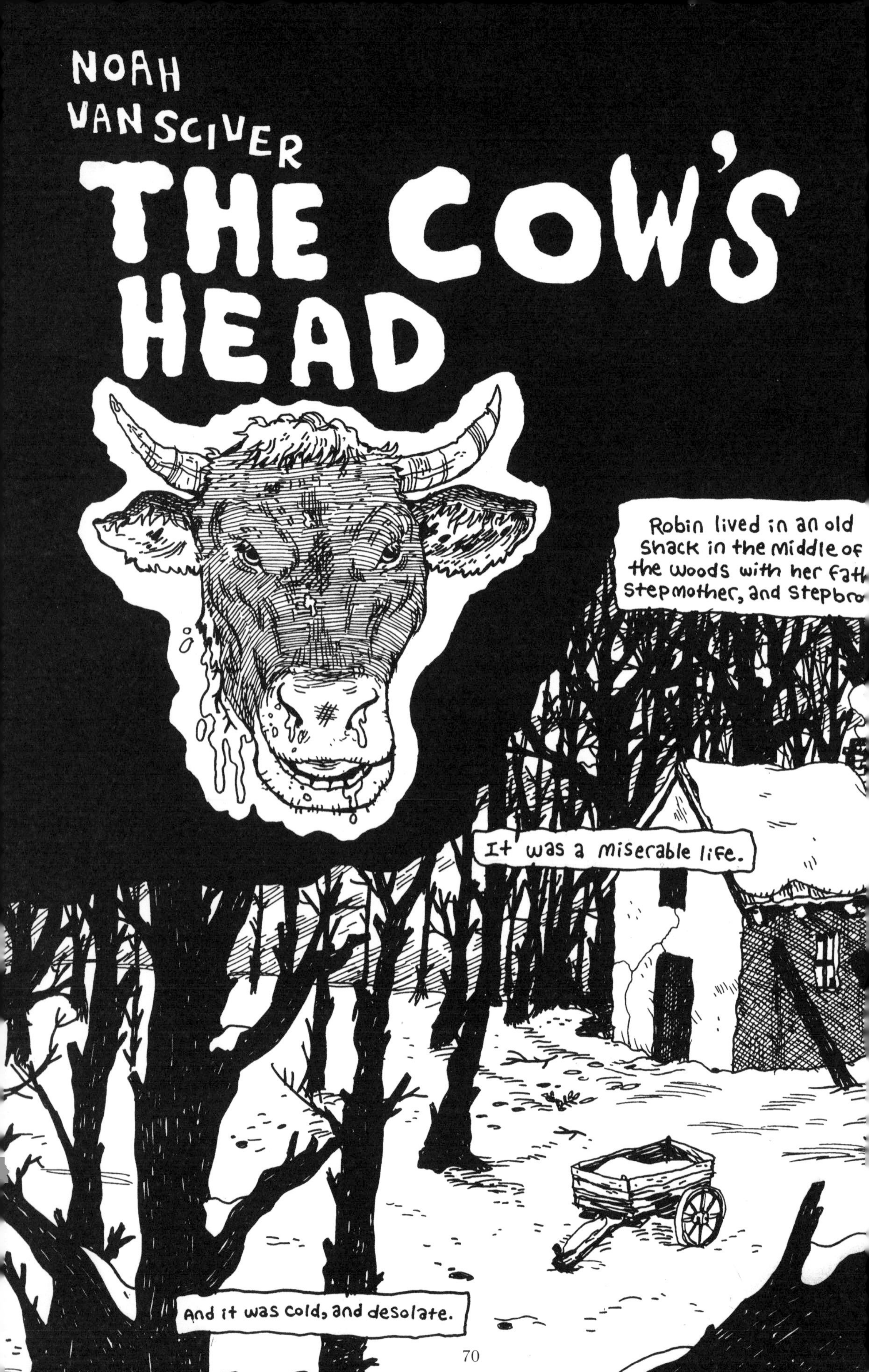
NOAH
VAN SCIVER
THE COW'S HEAD
Robin lived in an old
shack in the middle of
the woods with her fath
stepmother, and stepbro
It was a miserable life.
And it was cold, and desolate.

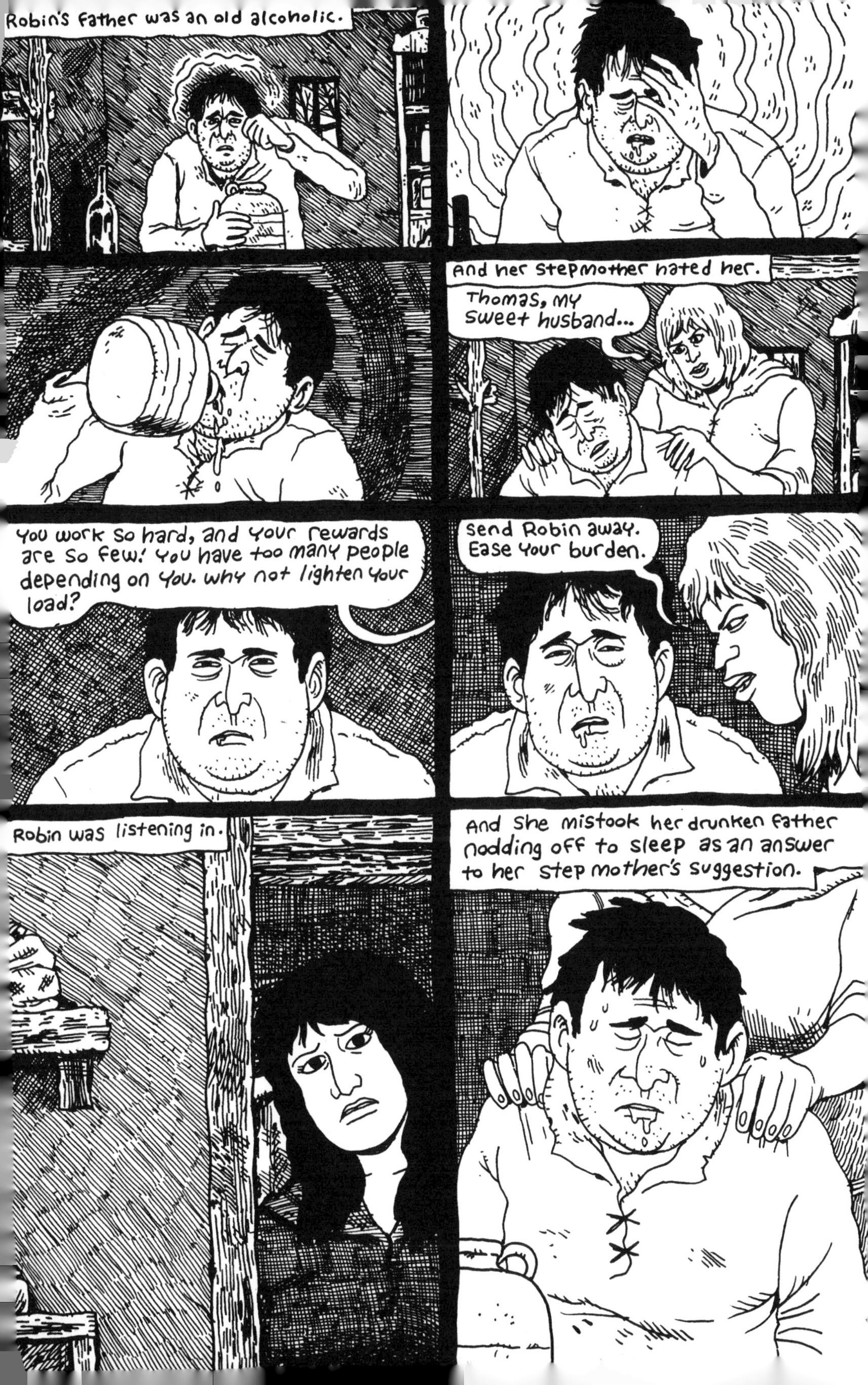
Robin's father was an old alcoholic.
And her stepmother hated her.
Thomas, my sweet husband...
You work so hard, and your rewards are so few! You have too many people depending on you. Why not lighten your load?
Send Robin away. Ease your burden.
Robin was listening in.
And she mistook her drunken father nodding off to sleep as an answer to her step mother's suggestion.

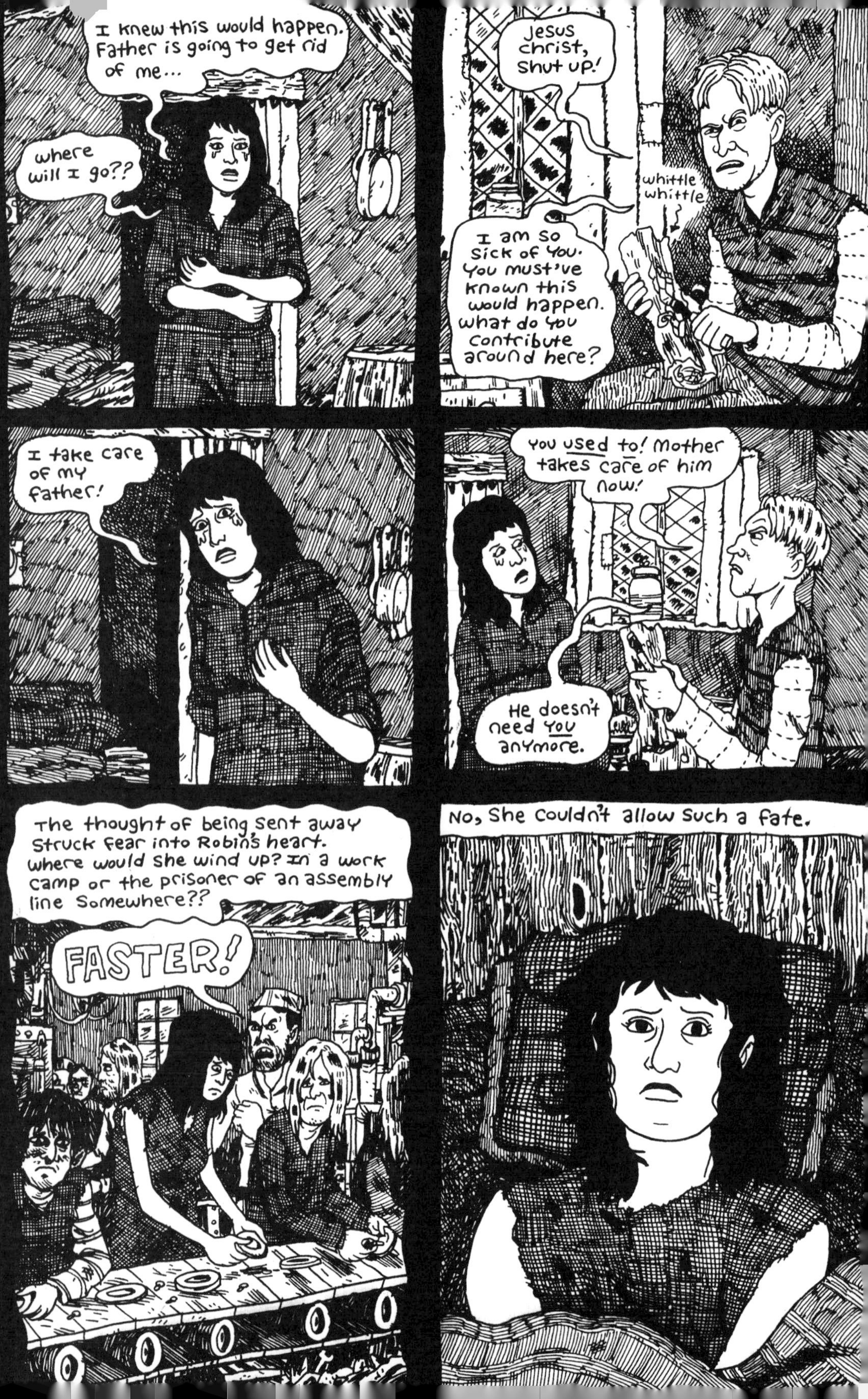
I knew this would happen. Father is going to get rid of me...
where will I go??
Jesus christ, shut up!
whittle whittle
I am so sick of you. You must've known this would happen. what do you contribute around here?
I take care of my father!
You used to! Mother takes care of him now!
He doesn't need you anymore.
The thought of being sent away struck fear into Robin's heart. where would she wind up? In a work camp or the prisoner of an assembly line somewhere??
FASTER!
No, she couldn't allow such a fate.

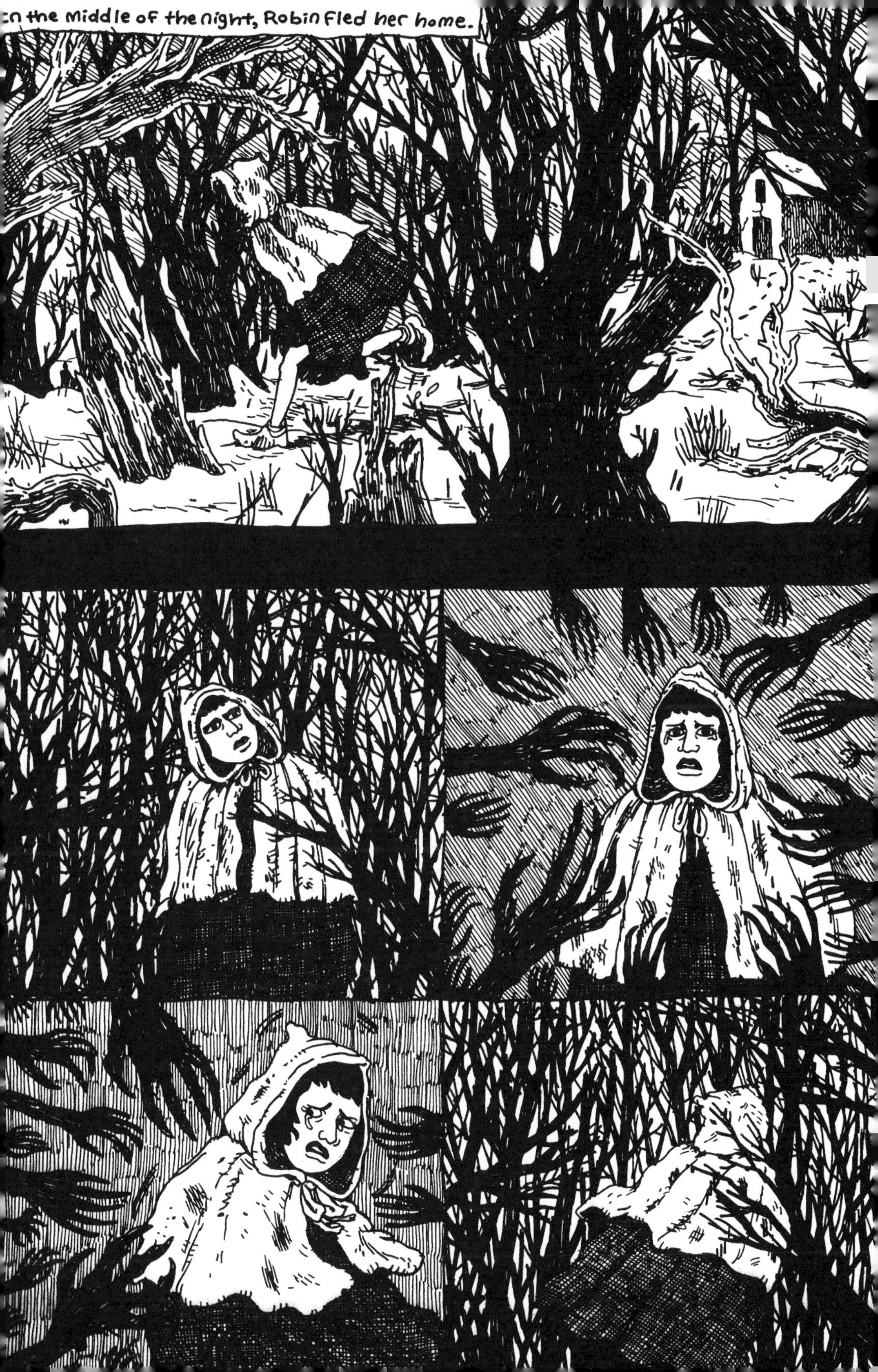
In the middle of the night, Robin fled her home.

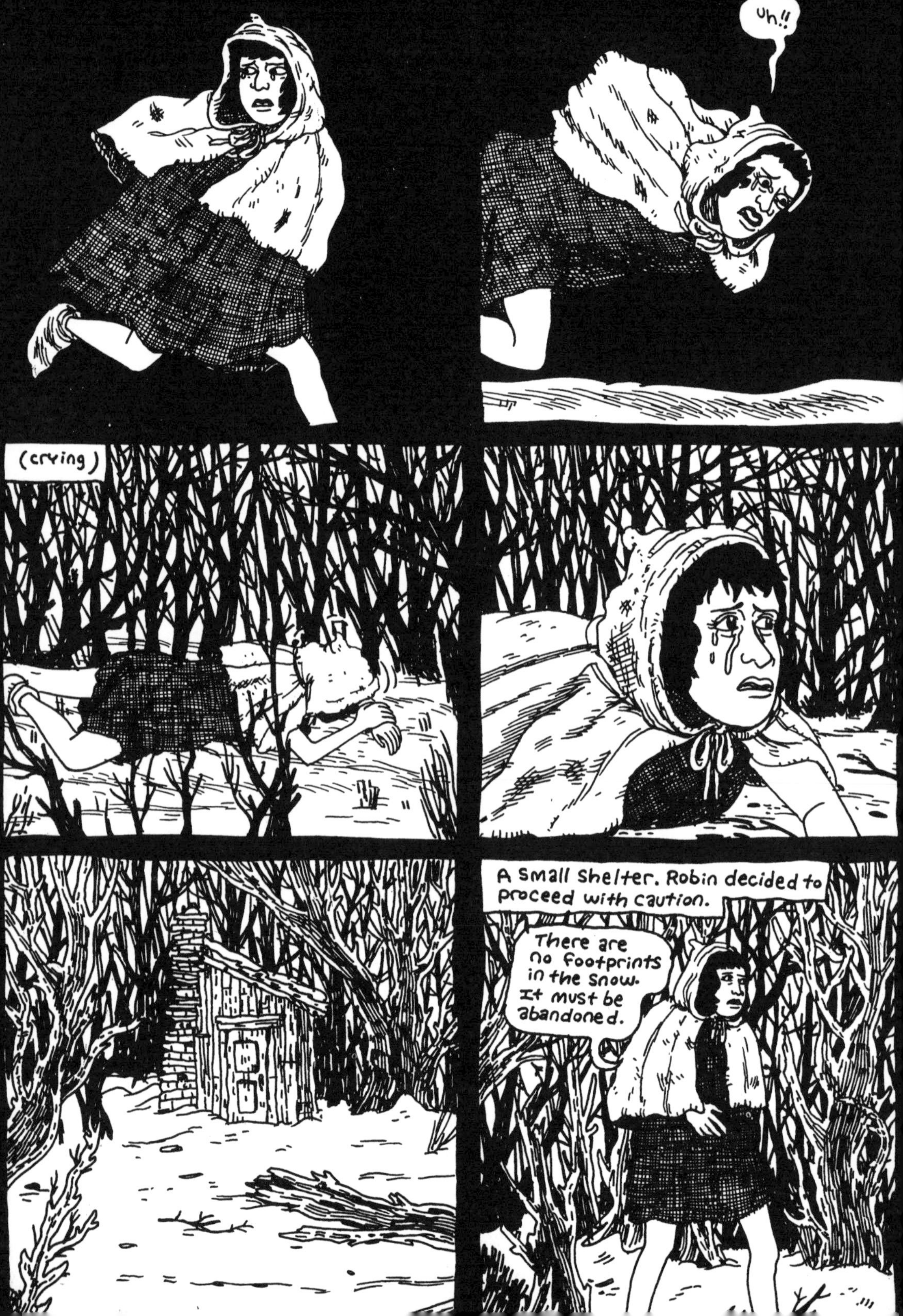
uh!!
(crying)
A small shelter. Robin decided to proceed with caution.
There are no footprints in the snow. It must be abandoned.

She knocked and waited...

KNOCK
KNOCK
KNOCK

Hello?
IS anybody
home?

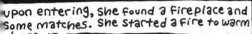
upon entering, she found a fireplace and some matches. she started a fire to warm herself.

In a small box she found some bread, cheese, and garlic. Robin melted some snow for water and used the food and water to cook a stew over the fire.

The smell of the stew twisted through the gnarled trees of the lonely woods...

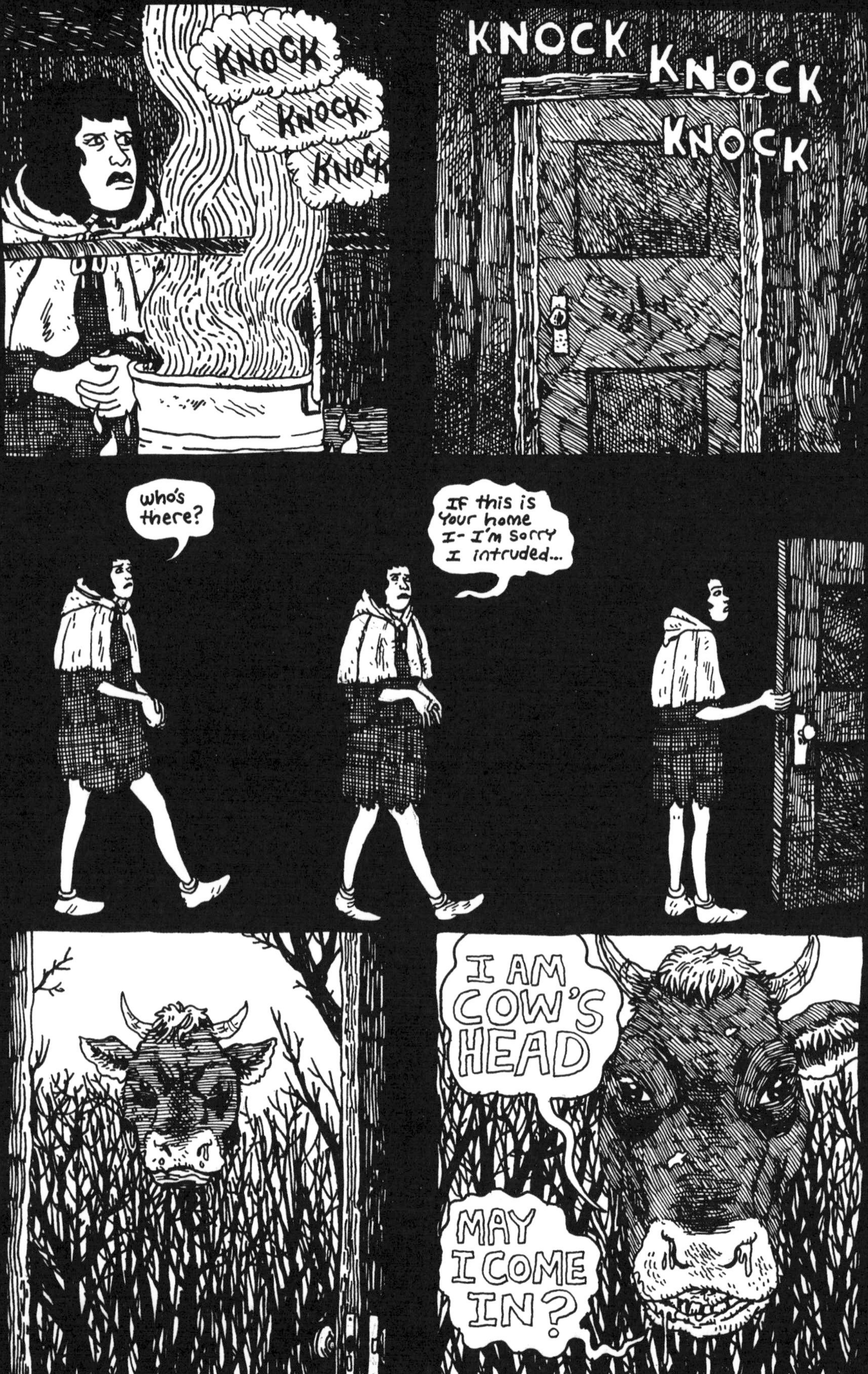
KNOCK
KNOCK
KNOCK
KNOCK
KNOCK
KNOCK
who's there?
If this is your home I- I'm sorry I intruded...
I AM COW'S HEAD
MAY I COME IN?

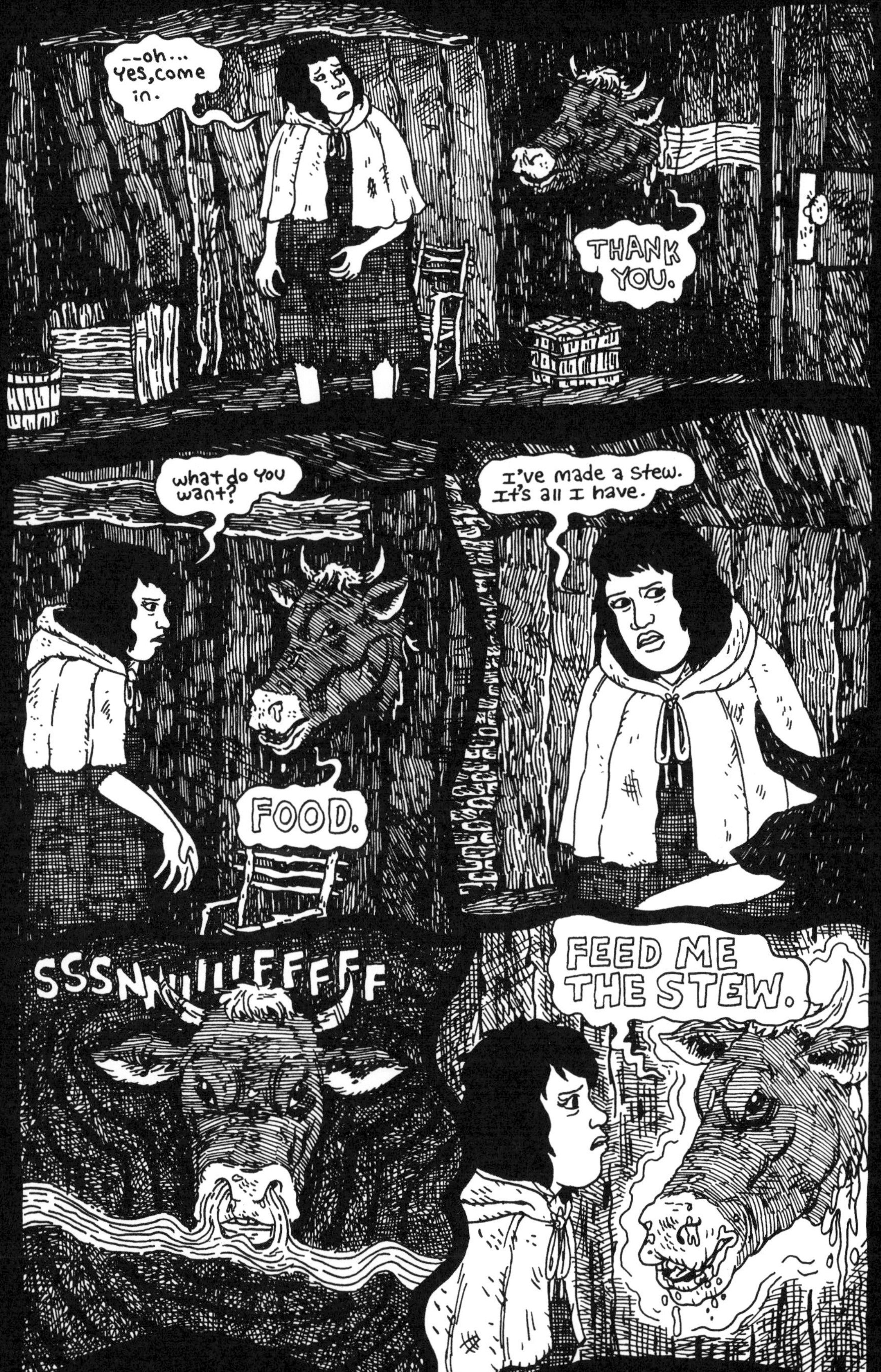
--oh...
Yes, come in.
THANK YOU.
what do you want?
FOOD.
I've made a stew.
It's all I have.
SSSNNIIIIFFFFFF
FEED ME THE STEW.

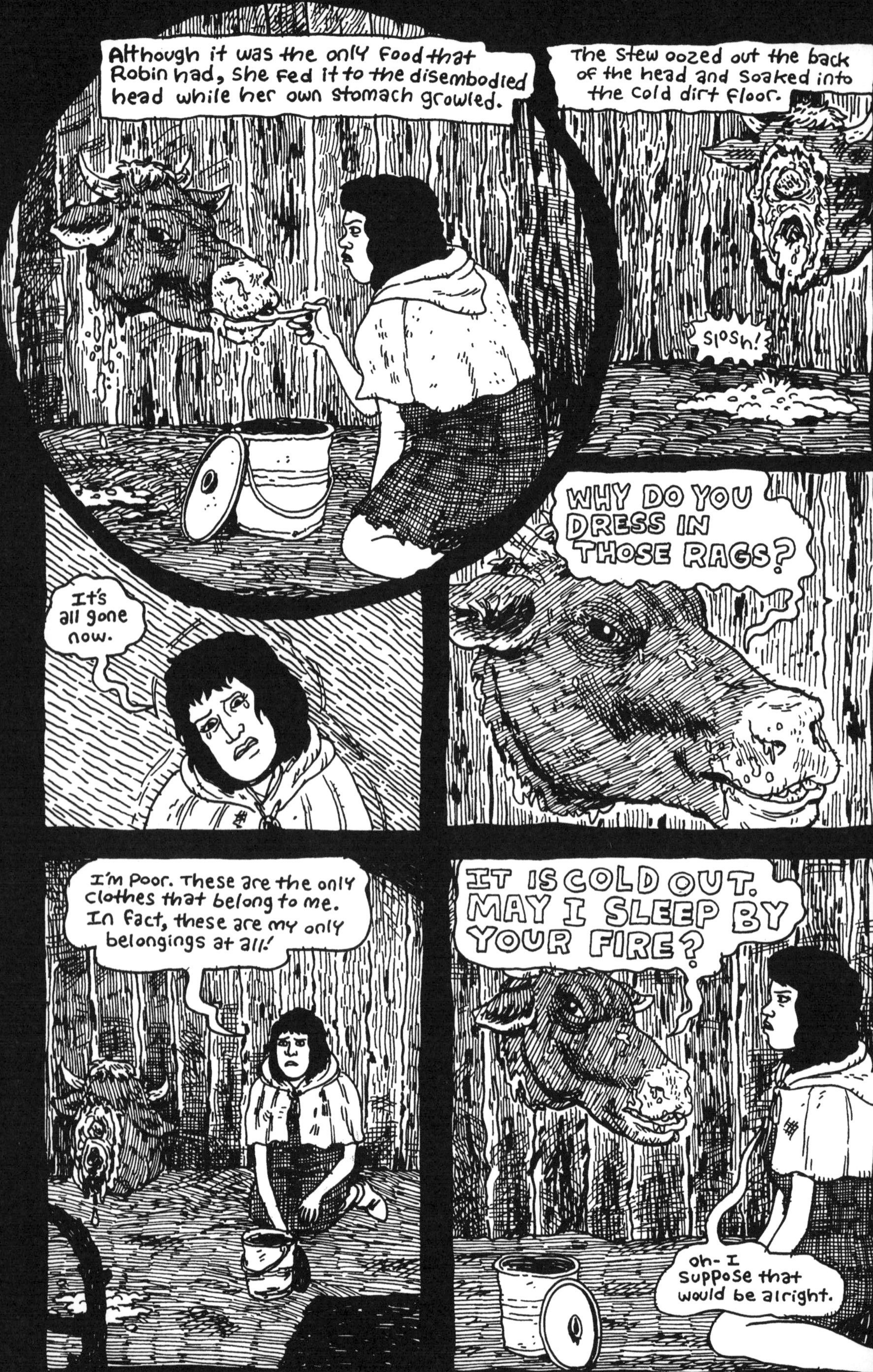
Although it was the only food that Robin had, she fed it to the disembodied head while her own stomach growled.
The stew oozed out the back of the head and soaked into the cold dirt floor.
SLOSH!
It's all gone now.
WHY DO YOU DRESS IN THOSE RAGS?
I'm poor. These are the only clothes that belong to me. In fact, these are my only belongings at all!
IT IS COLD OUT. MAY I SLEEP BY YOUR FIRE?
Oh- I suppose that would be alright.

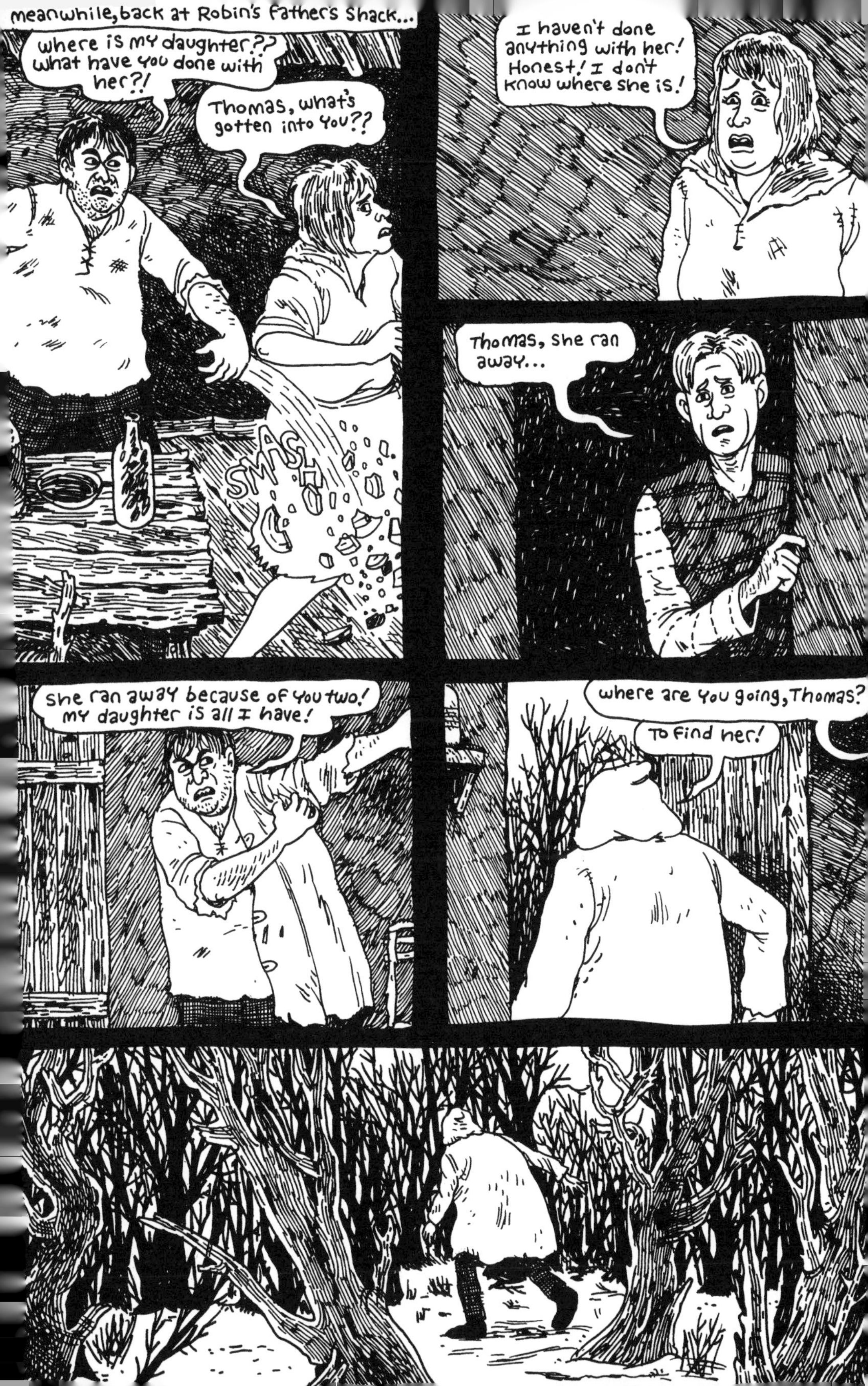
Meanwhile, back at Robin's Father's Shack...
Where is my daughter?? What have you done with her?!
Thomas, what's gotten into you??
SMASH
I haven't done anything with her! Honest! I don't know where she is!
Thomas, she ran away...
She ran away because of you two! My daughter is all I have!
Where are you going, Thomas?
To find her!

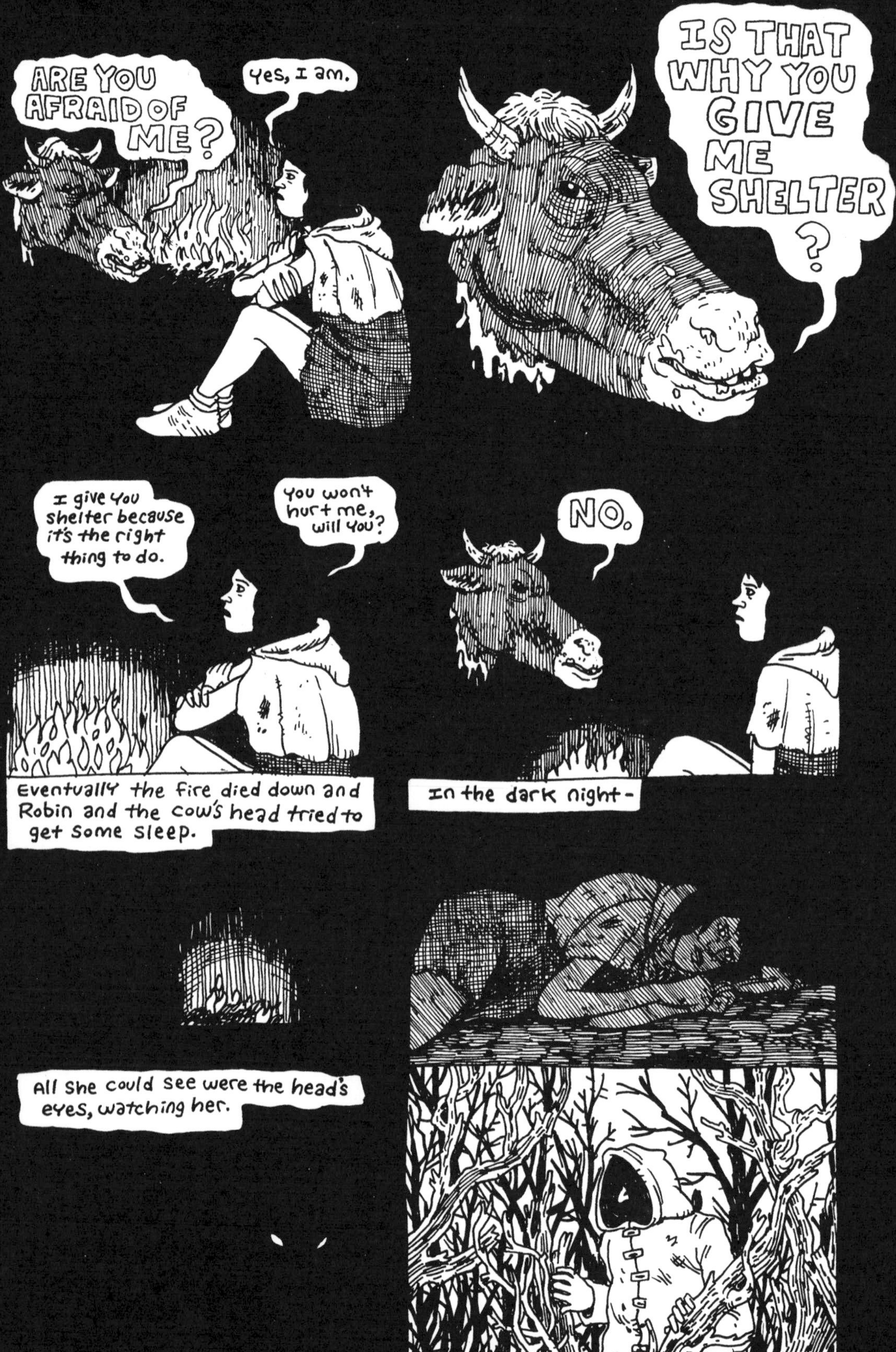
ARE YOU AFRAID OF ME?
Yes, I am.
IS THAT WHY YOU GIVE ME SHELTER?
I give you shelter because it's the right thing to do.
You won't hurt me, will you?
Eventually the fire died down and Robin and the cow's head tried to get some sleep.
NO.
In the dark night-
All she could see were the head's eyes, watching her.

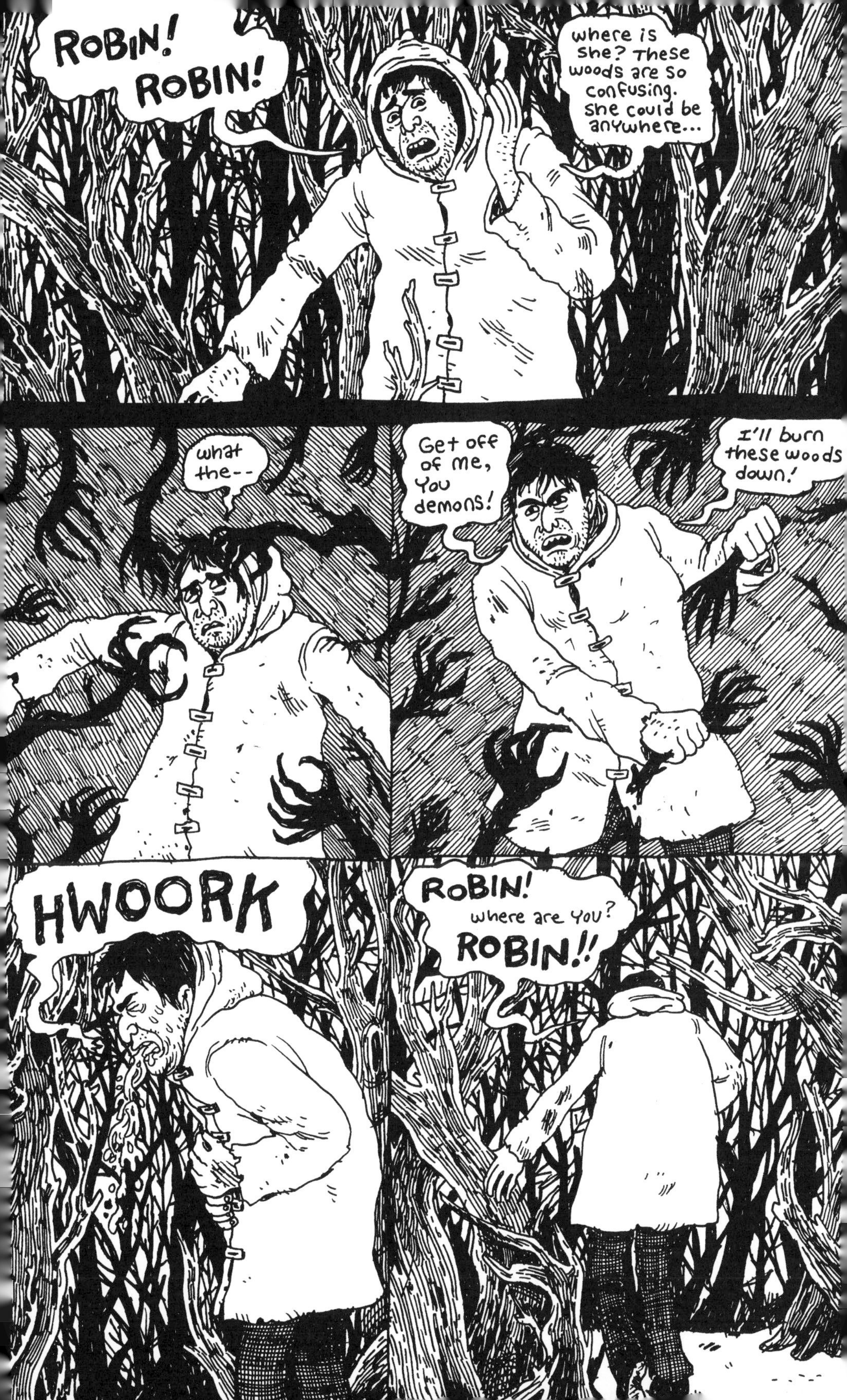
ROBIN! ROBIN!
where is she? These woods are so confusing. she could be anywhere...
what the--
Get off of me, You demons!
I'll burn these woods down!
HWOORK
ROBIN! where are you? ROBIN!!

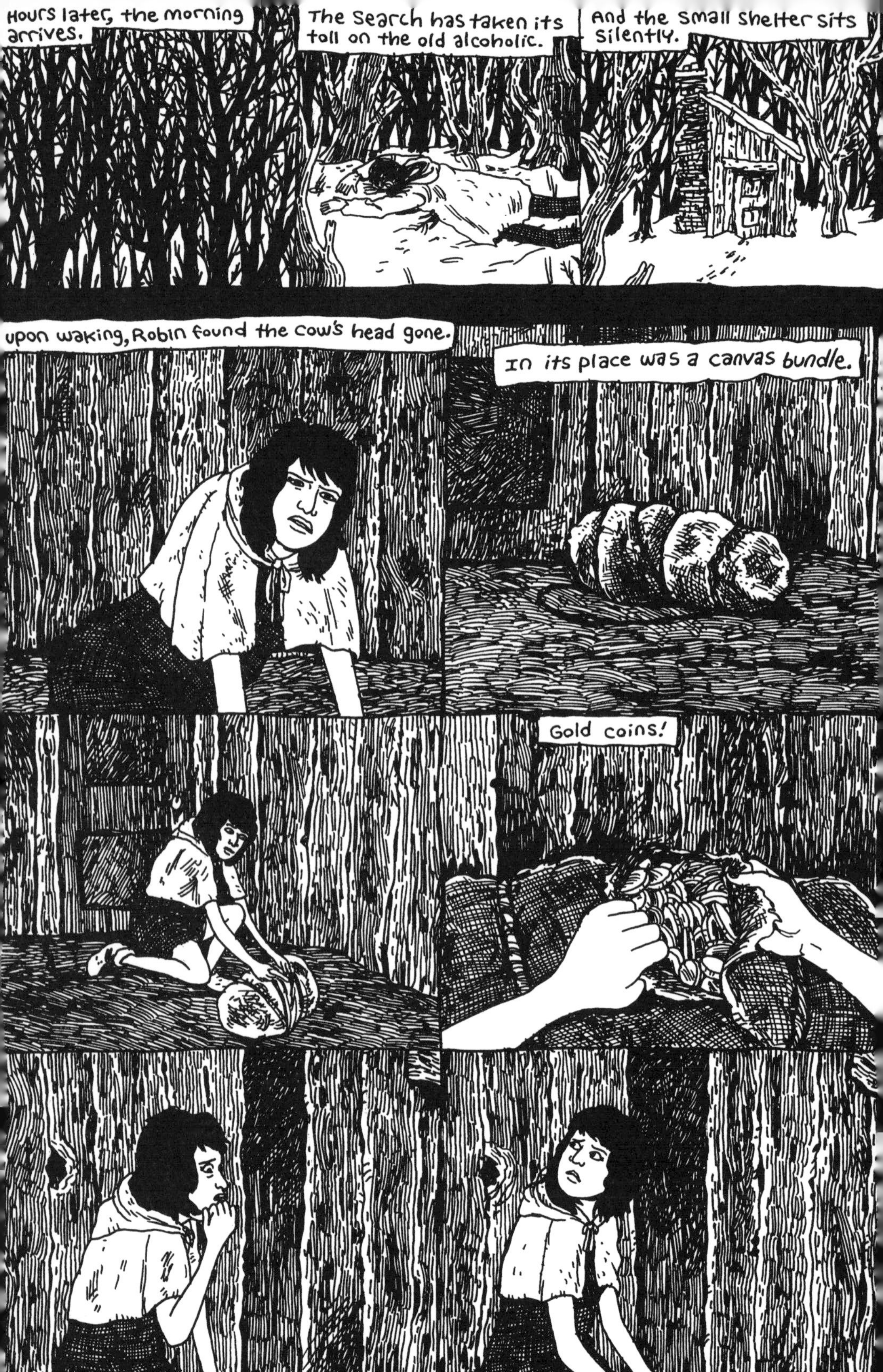
Hours later, the morning arrives.
The search has taken its toll on the old alcoholic.
And the small shelter sits silently.
upon waking, Robin found the cow's head gone.
In its place was a canvas bundle.
Gold coins!

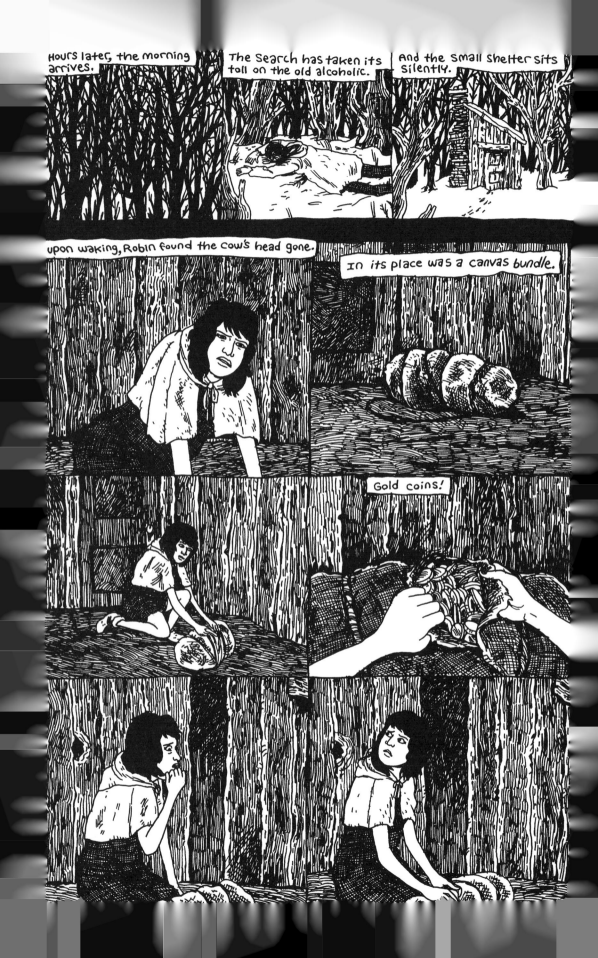

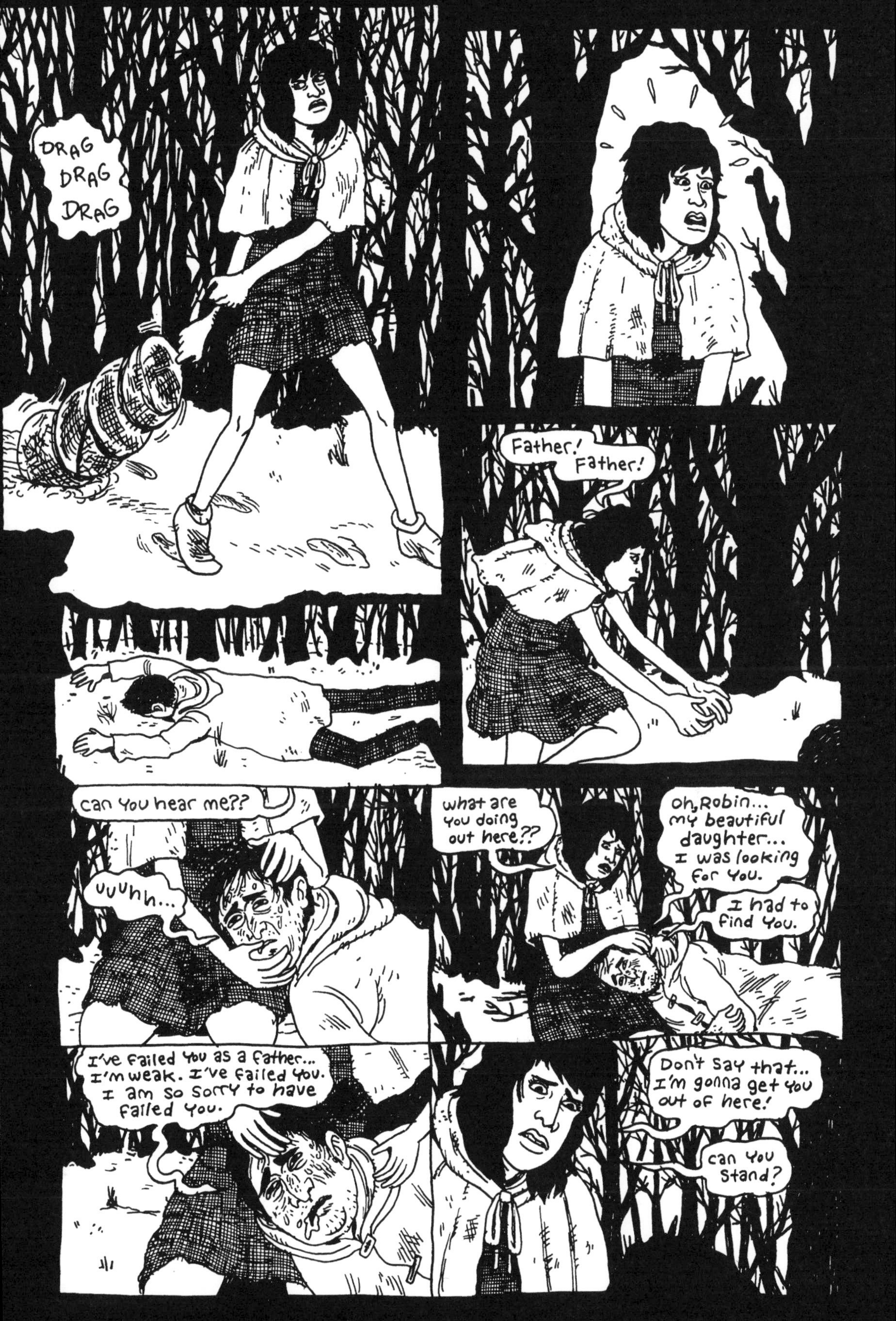
DRAG DRAG DRAG
Father! Father!
can you hear me??
uuuhh...
what are you doing out here??
Oh, Robin... my beautiful daughter... I was looking for you.
I had to find you.
I've failed you as a father... I'm weak. I've failed you. I am so sorry to have failed you.
Don't say that... I'm gonna get you out of here!
can you stand?

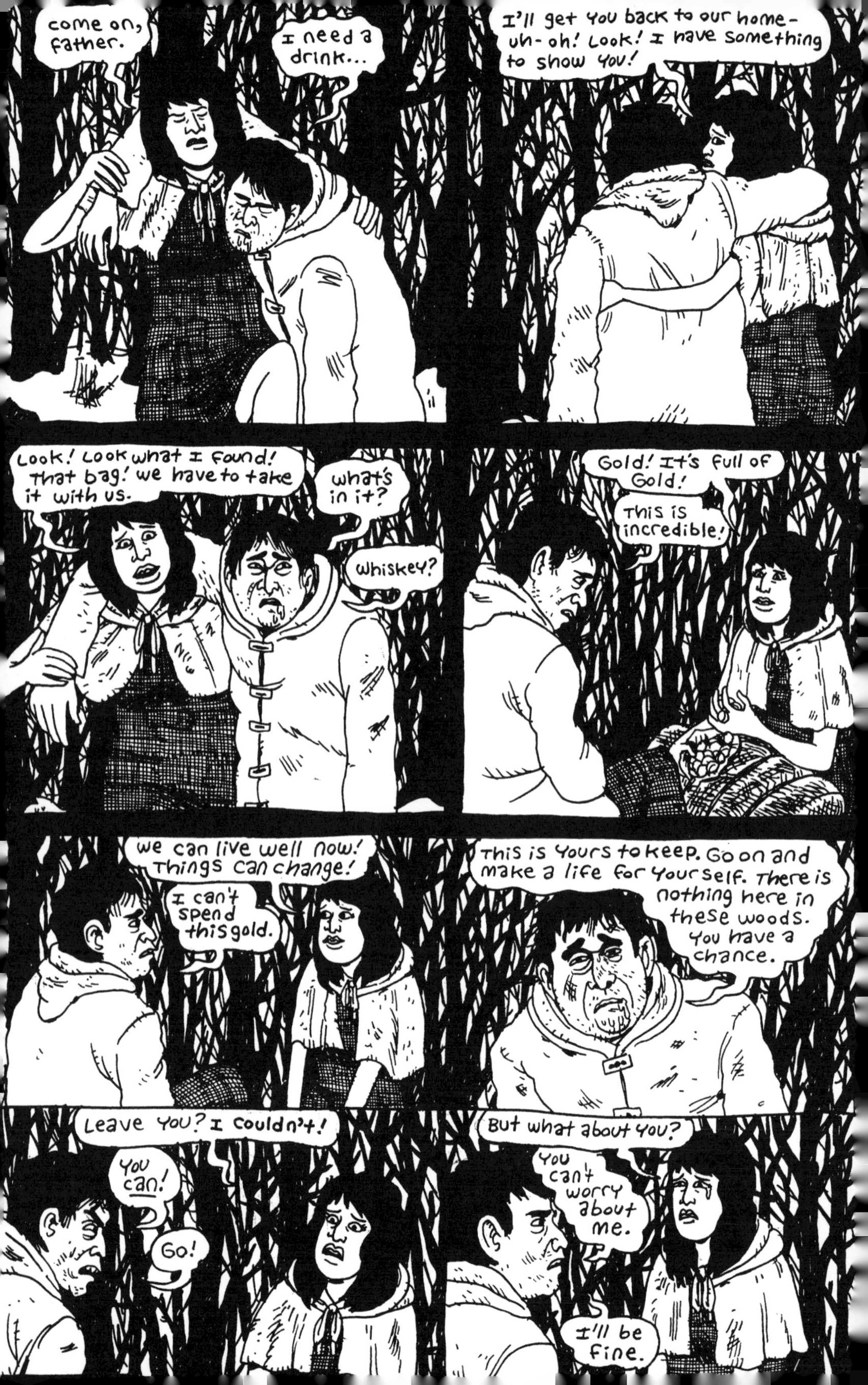
come on, father.
I need a drink...
I'll get you back to our home- uh-oh! Look! I have something to show you!
Look! Look what I found! That bag! we have to take it with us.
what's in it?
Whiskey?
Gold! It's full of Gold!
This is incredible!
we can live well now! Things can change!
I can't spend this gold.
This is yours to keep. Go on and make a life for yourself. There is nothing here in these woods. You have a chance.
Leave you? I couldn't!
You can!
Go!
But what about you?
You can't worry about me.
I'll be fine.

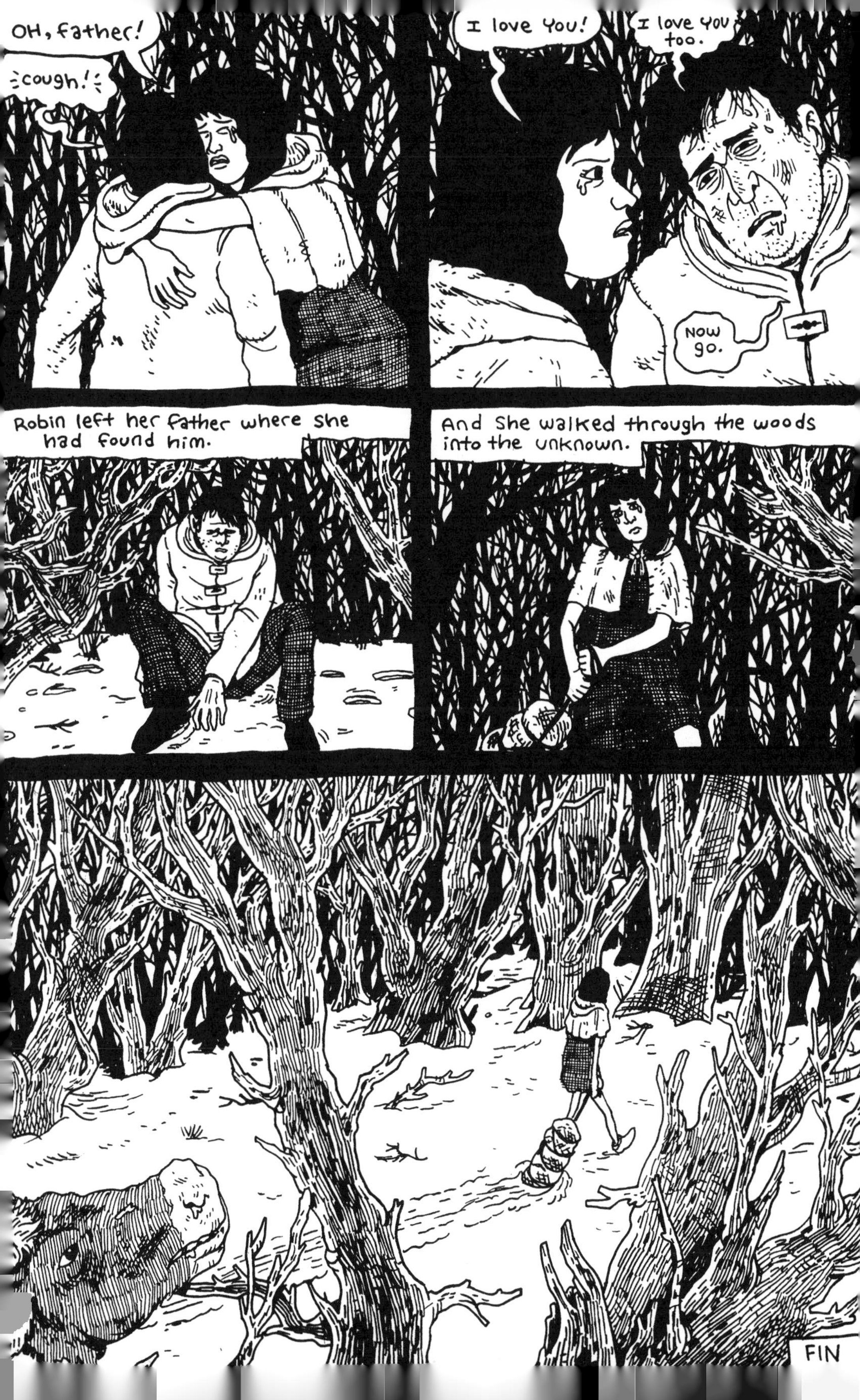
OH, father!
cough!
I love You!
I love You too.
Now go.
Robin left her father where she had found him.
And she walked through the woods into the unknown.
FIN

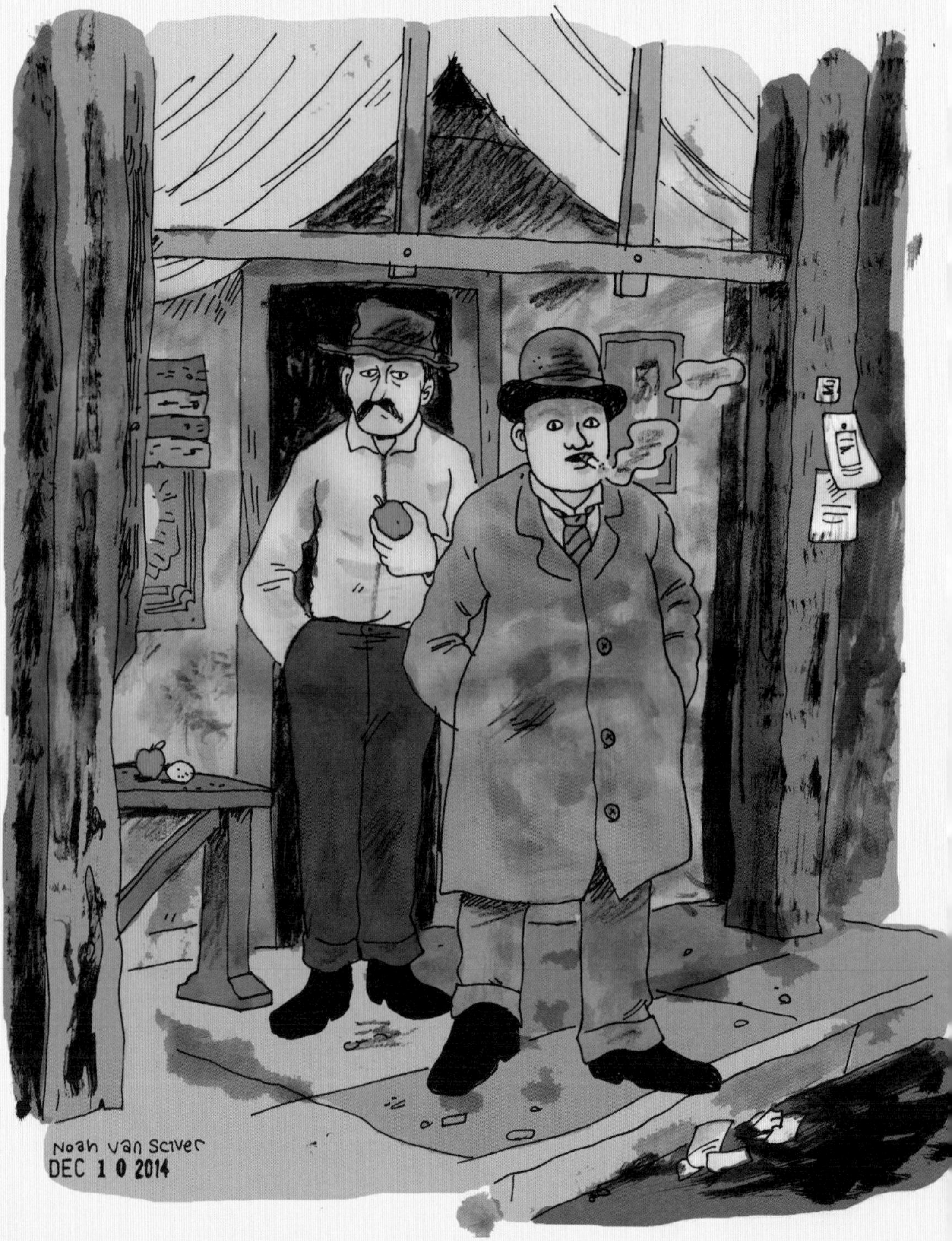
Noah van Sciver
DEC 1 0 2014

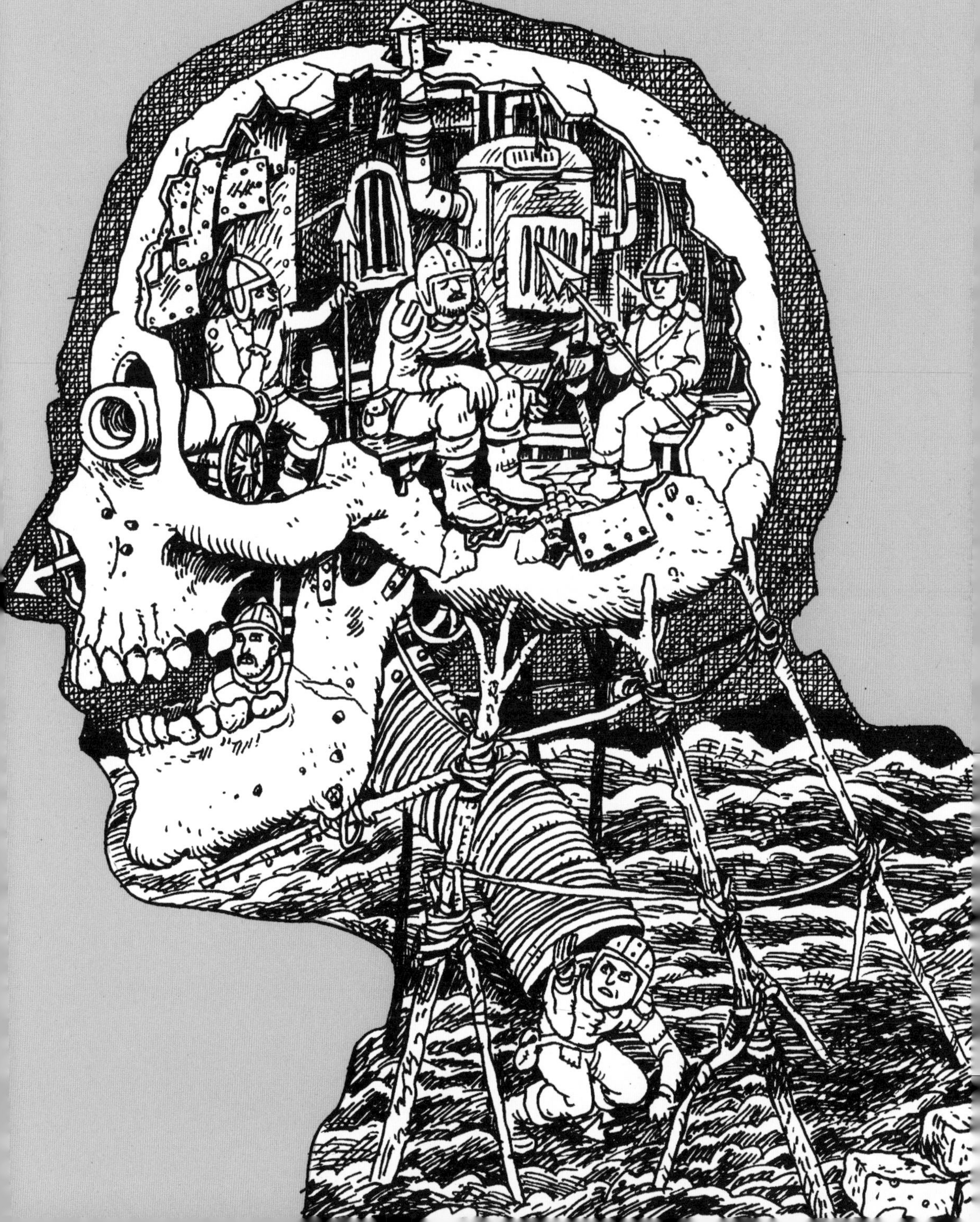

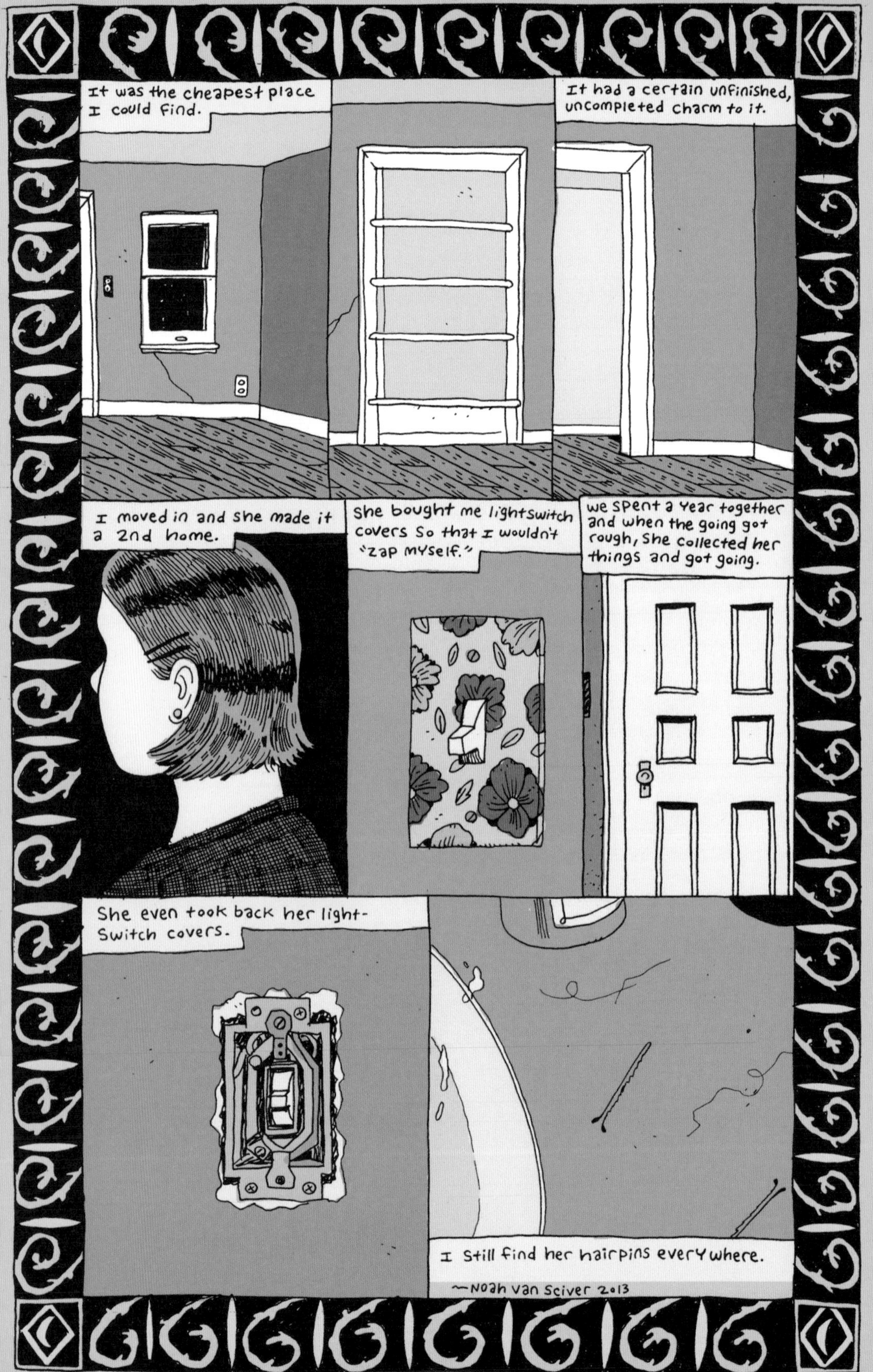
It was the cheapest place I could find.
It had a certain unfinished, uncompleted charm to it.
I moved in and she made it a 2nd home.
She bought me lightswitch covers so that I wouldn't "zap myself."
We spent a year together and when the going got rough, she collected her things and got going.
She even took back her light-switch covers.
I still find her hairpins everywhere.
~Noah Van Sciver 2013

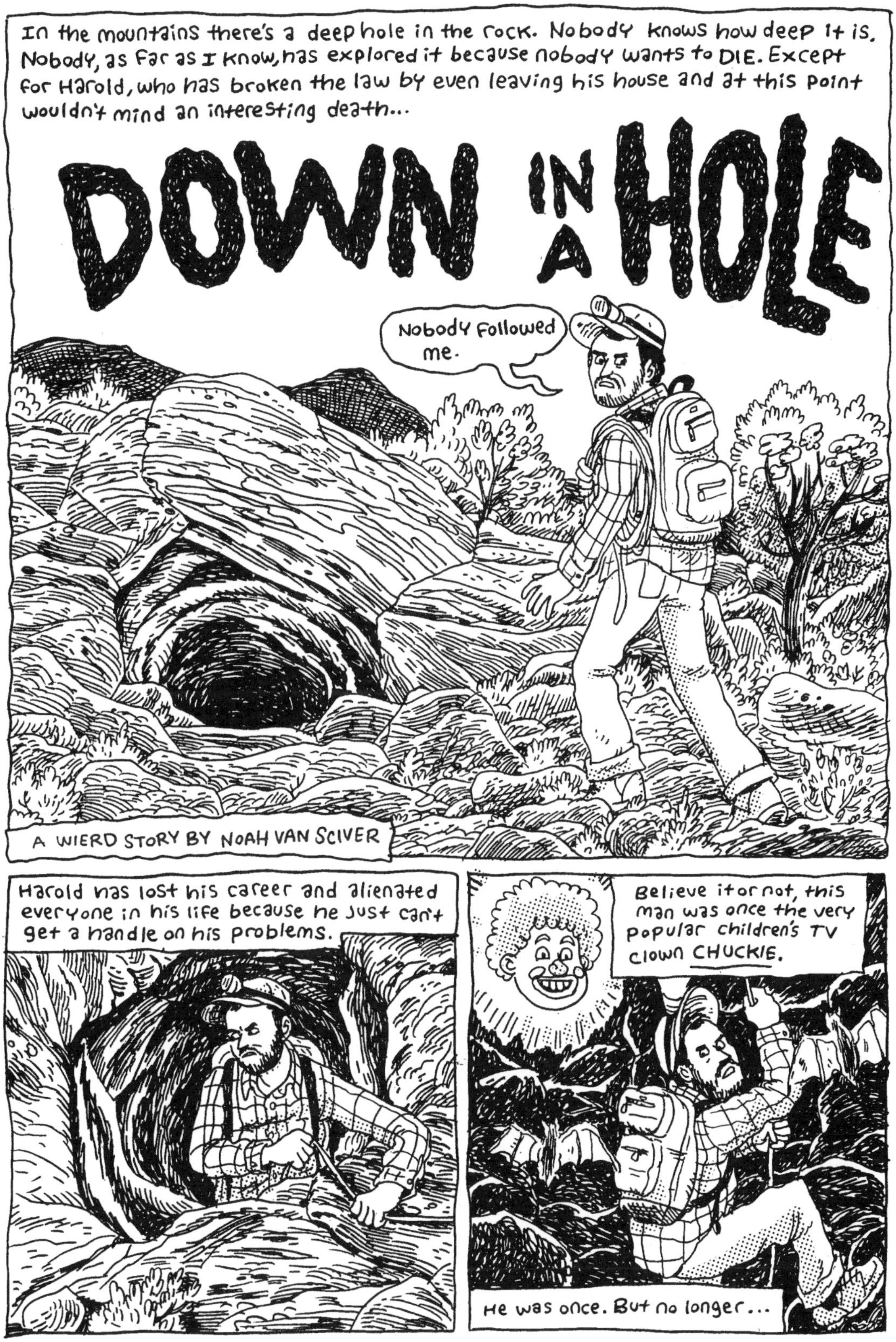

In the mountains there's a deep hole in the rock. Nobody knows how deep it is. Nobody, as far as I know, has explored it because nobody wants to DIE. Except for Harold, who has broken the law by even leaving his house and at this point wouldn't mind an interesting death...
DOWN IN A HOLE
Nobody followed me.
A WIERD STORY BY NOAH VAN SCIVER
Harold has lost his career and alienated everyone in his life because he just can't get a handle on his problems.
Believe it or not, this man was once the very popular children's TV clown CHUCKIE.
He was once. But no longer...

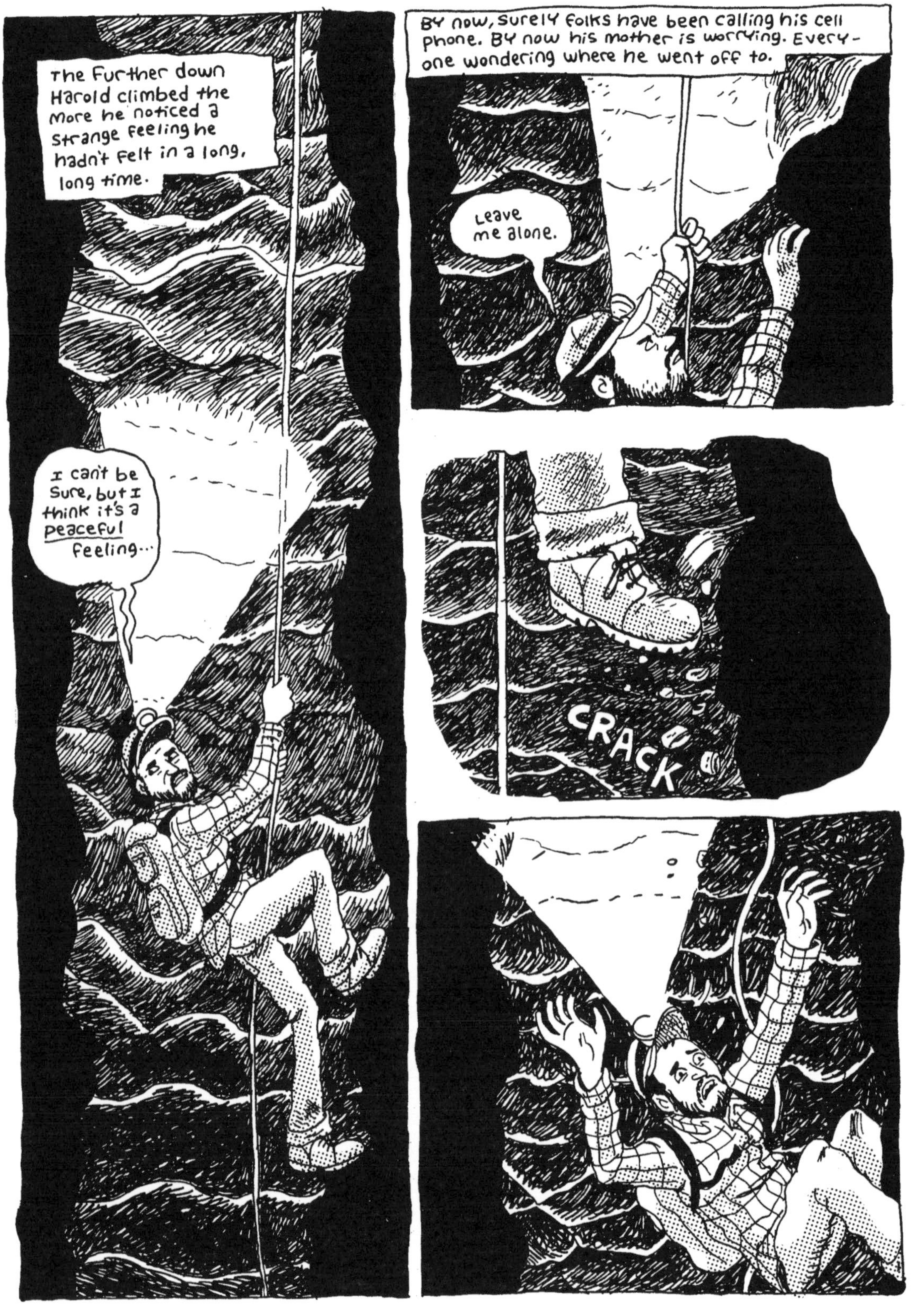
The Further down Harold climbed the more he noticed a strange feeling he hadn't felt in a long, long time.
I can't be sure, but I think it's a peaceful feeling...
By now, surely folks have been calling his cell phone. By now his mother is worrying. Every-one wondering where he went off to.
Leave me alone.
CRACK

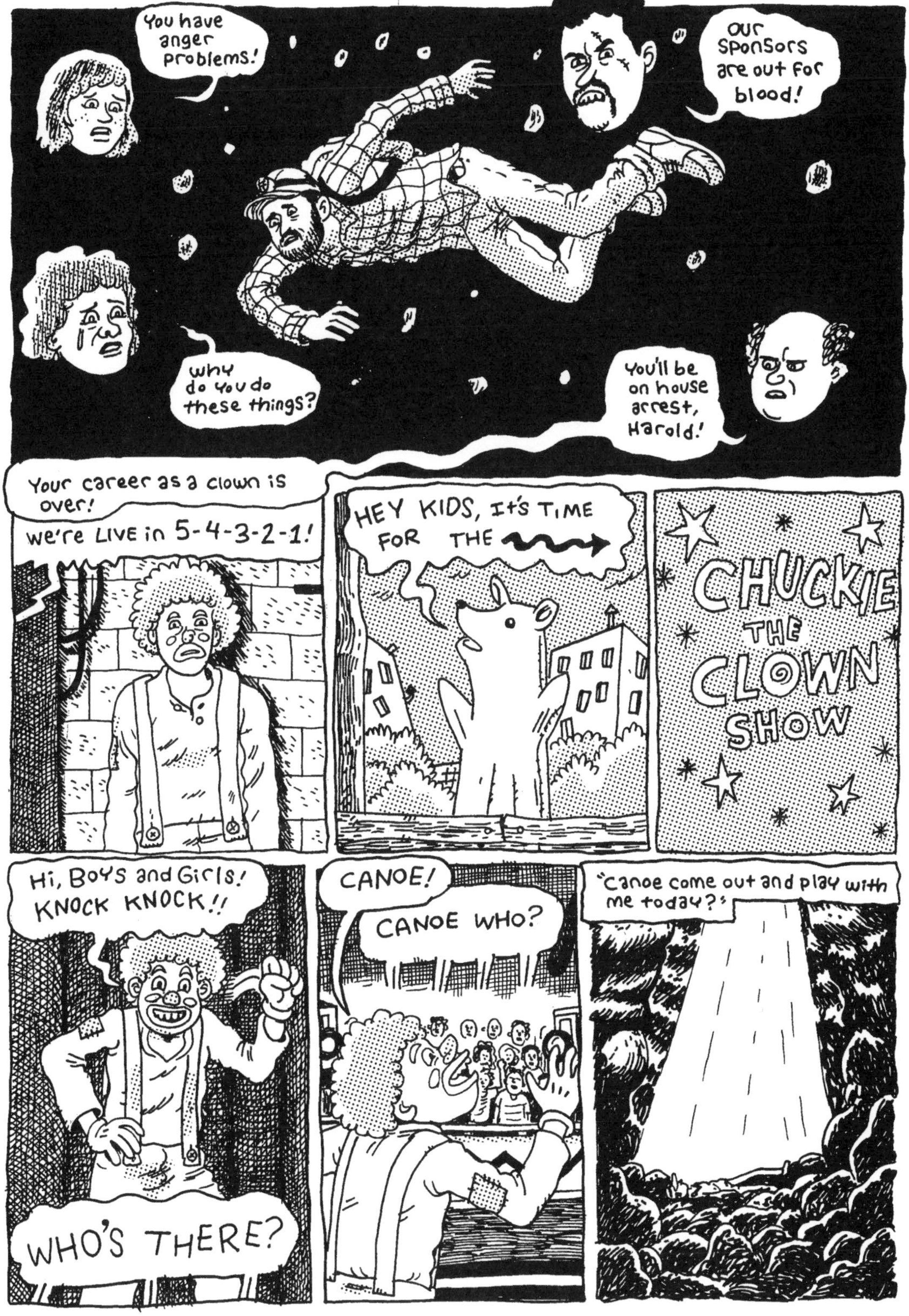
You have anger problems!
Our sponsors are out for blood!
why do you do these things?
You'll be on house arrest, Harold!
Your career as a clown is over!
we're LIVE in 5-4-3-2-1!
HEY KIDS, It's TIME FOR THE
CHUCKIE THE CLOWN SHOW
Hi, Boys and Girls! KNOCK KNOCK!!
WHO'S THERE?
CANOE!
CANOE WHO?
"Canoe come out and play with me today?"

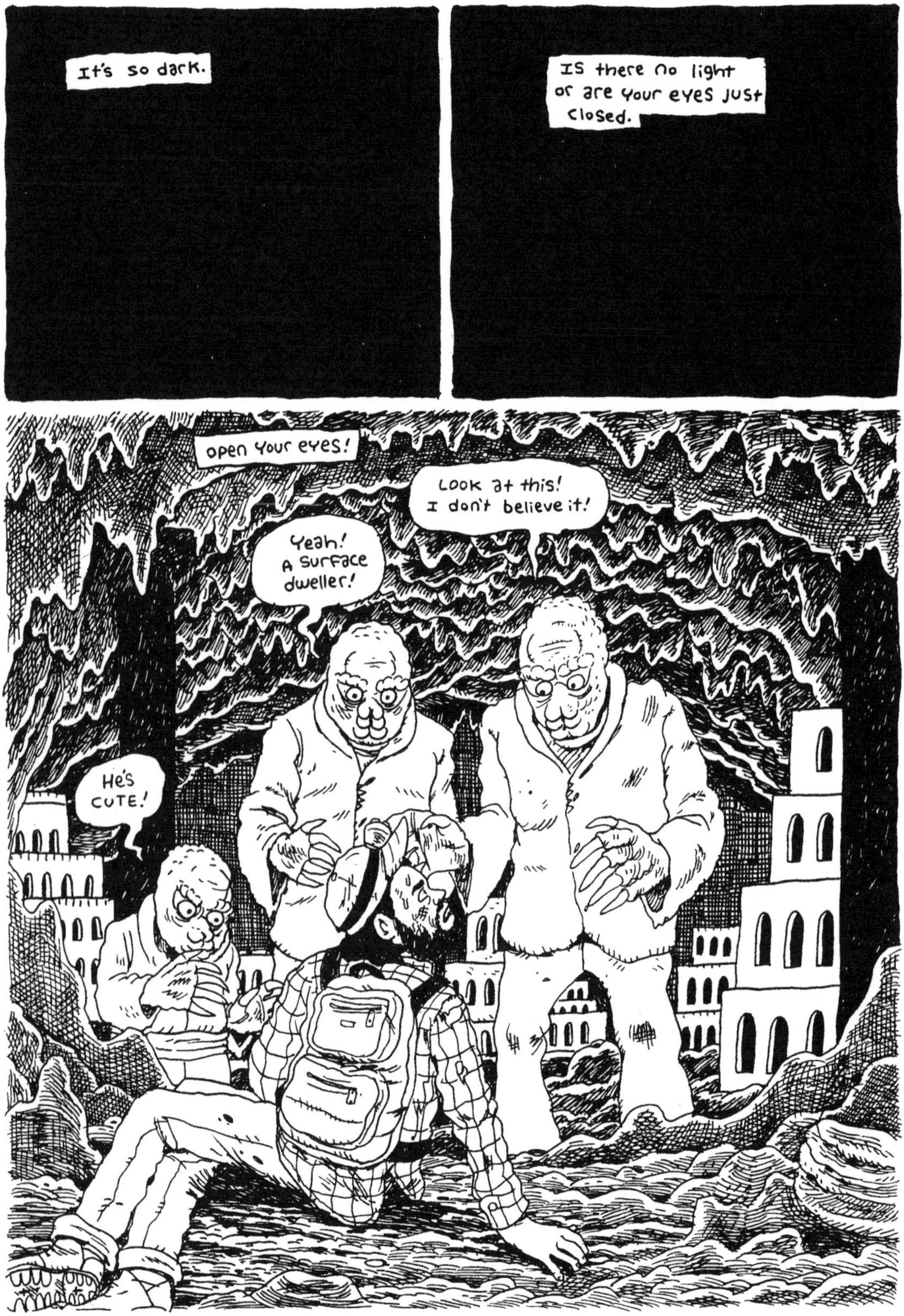
It's so dark.
IS there no light or are your eyes just closed.
open your eyes!
Look at this! I don't believe it!
Yeah! A surface dweller!
He's CUTE!

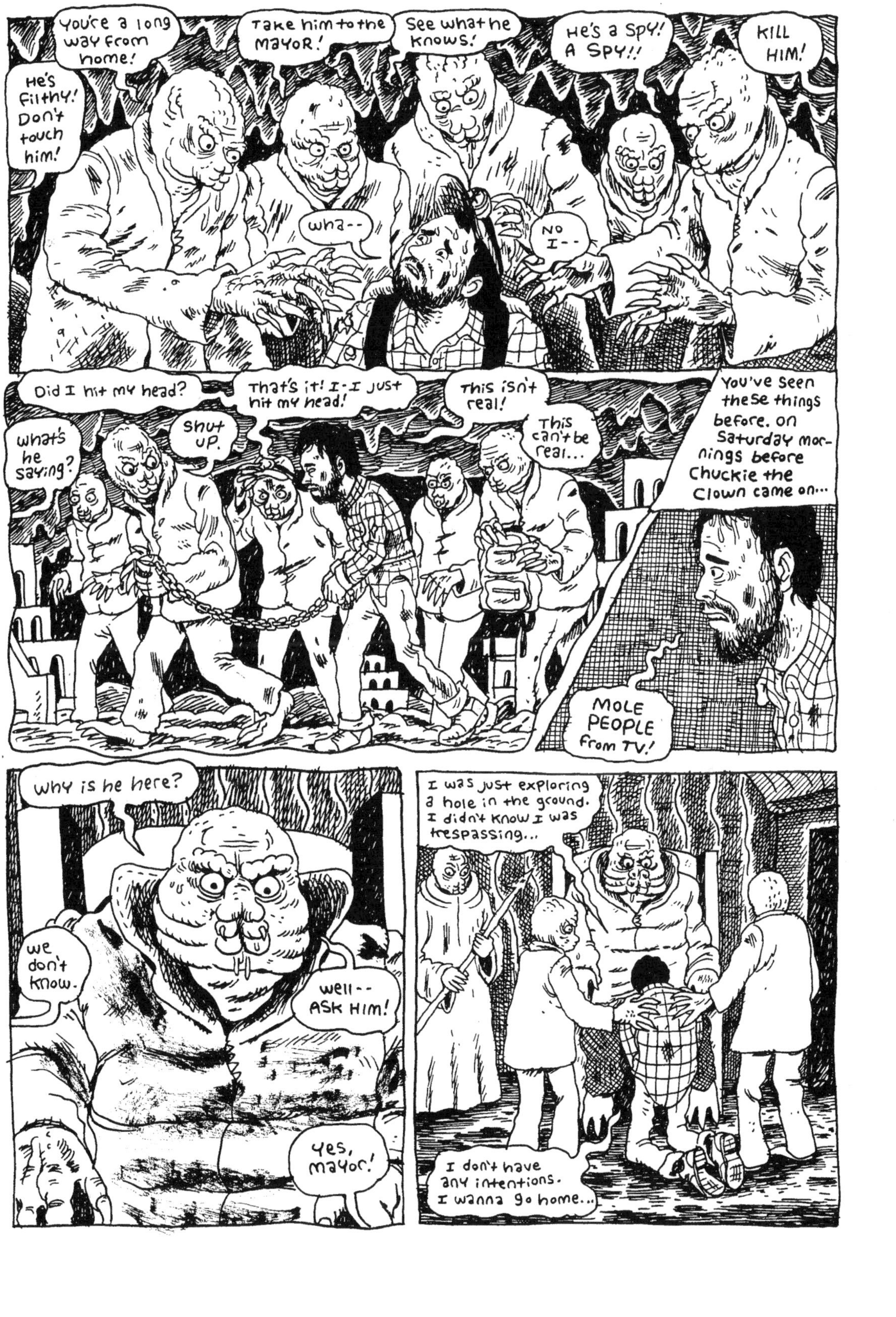
You're a long way from home!
He's filthy! Don't touch him!
Take him to the MAYOR!
See what he knows!
He's a SPY! A SPY!!
KILL HIM!
wha--
NO I--
Did I hit my head?
what's he saying?
Shut up.
That's it! I-I just hit my head!
This isn't real!
This can't be real...
You've seen these things before. on Saturday mornings before Chuckie the Clown came on...
MOLE PEOPLE from TV!
why is he here?
we don't know.
well-- ASK HIM!
yes, mayor!
I was just exploring a hole in the ground. I didn't know I was trespassing...
I don't have any intentions. I wanna go home...

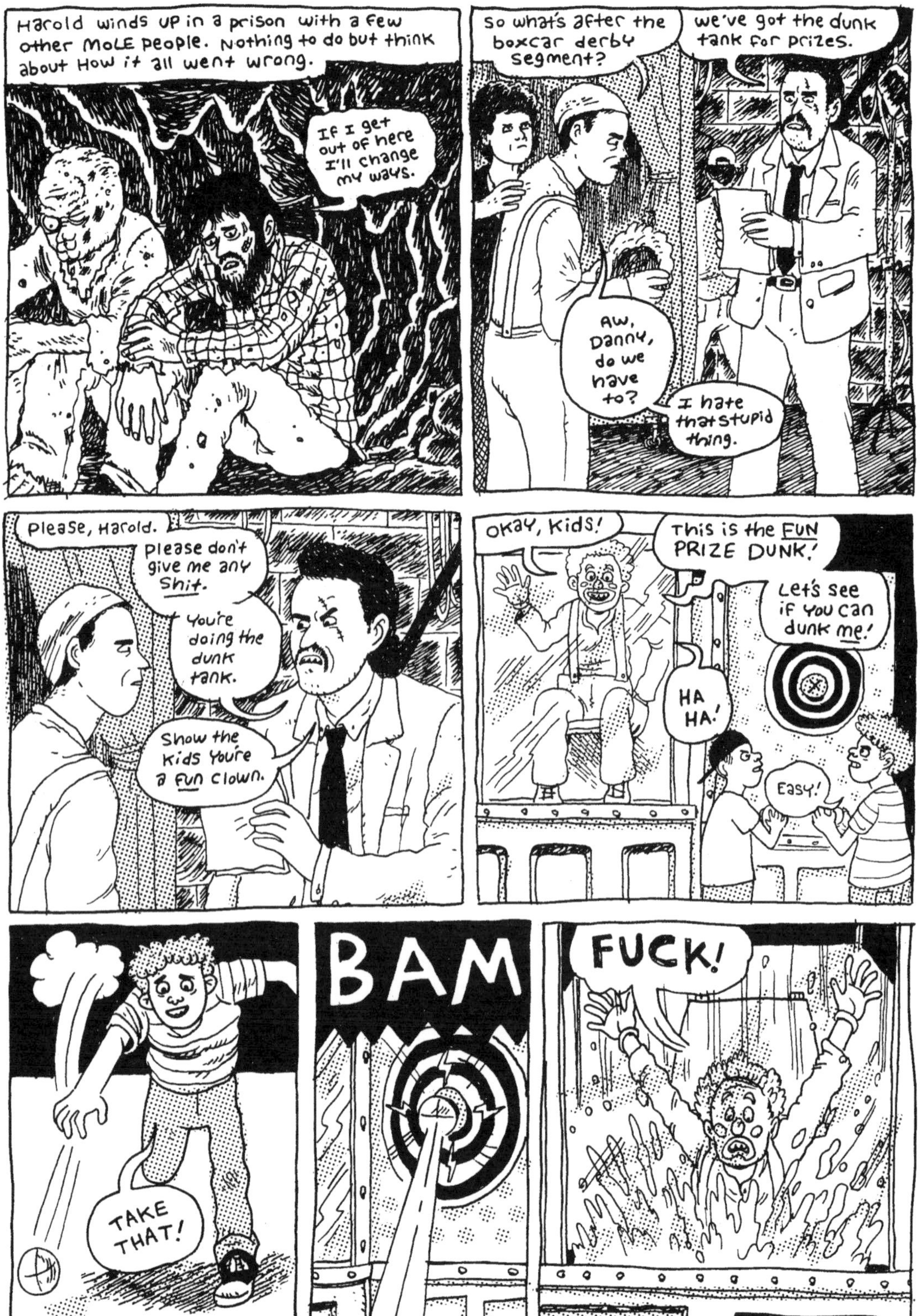
Harold winds up in a prison with a few other MOLE People. Nothing to do but think about How it all went wrong.
If I get out of here I'll change my ways.
So what's after the boxcar derby segment?
we've got the dunk tank for prizes.
Aw, Danny, do we have to?
I hate that stupid thing.
Please, Harold.
Please don't give me any Shit.
You're doing the dunk tank.
Show the kids You're a FUN clown.
OKAY, Kids!
This is the FUN PRIZE DUNK!
Let's see if you can dunk me!
HA HA!
Easy!
TAKE THAT!
BAM
FUCK!

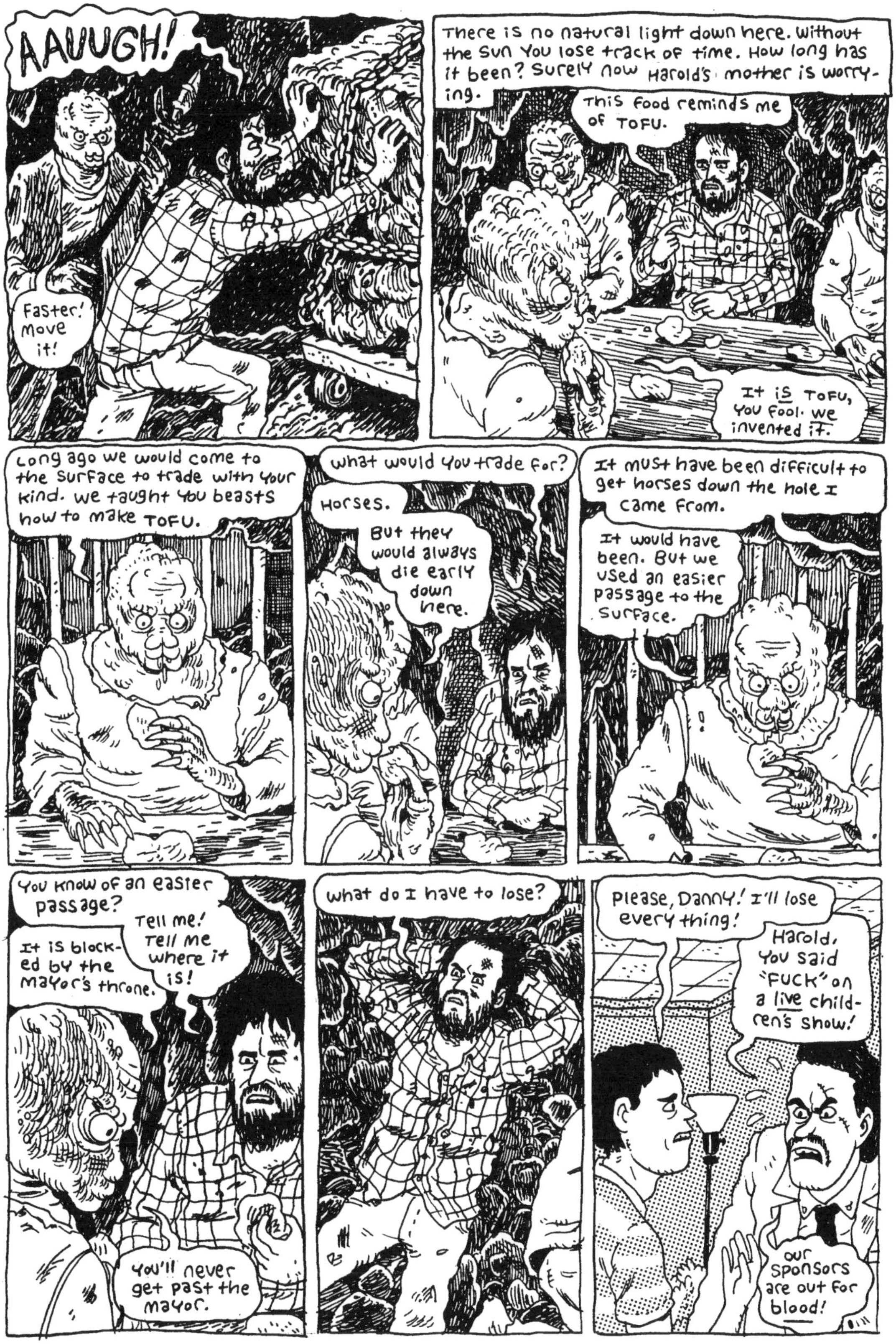
AAUUGH!
Faster! Move it!
There is no natural light down here. Without the sun you lose track of time. How long has it been? Surely now Harold's mother is worrying.
This food reminds me of TOFU.
It IS TOFU, you fool. We invented it.
Long ago we would come to the surface to trade with your kind. We taught you beasts how to make TOFU.
What would you trade for?
Horses.
But they would always die early down here.
It must have been difficult to get horses down the hole I came from.
It would have been. But we used an easier passage to the surface.
You know of an easier passage?
Tell me! Tell me where it is!
It is blocked by the mayor's throne.
You'll never get past the mayor.
What do I have to lose?
Please, Danny! I'll lose everything!
Harold, you said "FUCK" on a live children's show!
Our sponsors are out for blood!

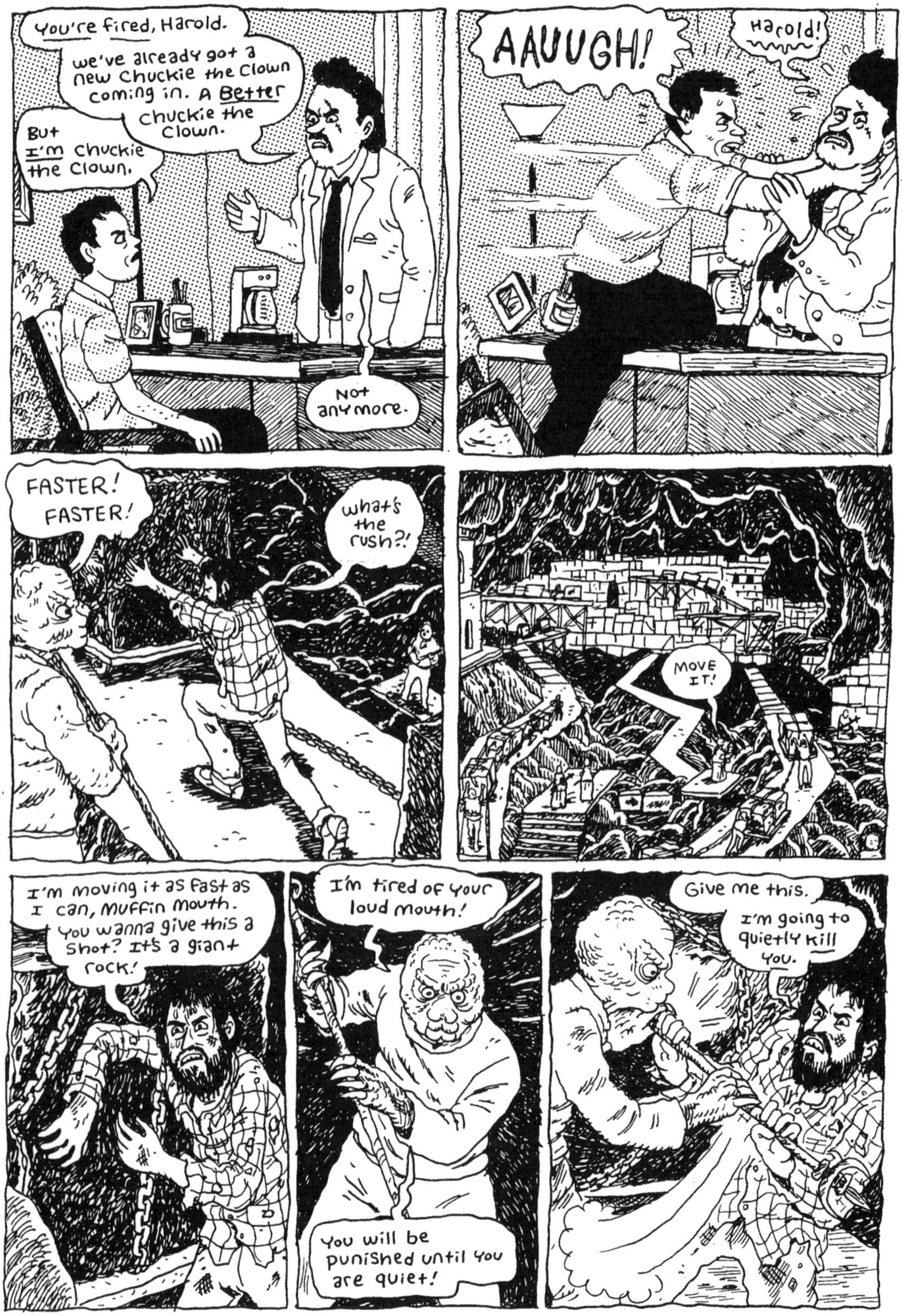
You're fired, Harold.
we've already got a new Chuckie the Clown coming in. A Better Chuckie the Clown.
But I'm Chuckie the Clown.
Not anymore.
AAUUGH!
Harold!
FASTER! FASTER!
what's the rush?!
MOVE IT!
I'm moving it as fast as I can, Muffin Mouth. You wanna give this a shot? It's a giant rock!
I'm tired of your loud mouth!
You will be punished until you are quiet!
Give me this.
I'm going to quietly kill you.

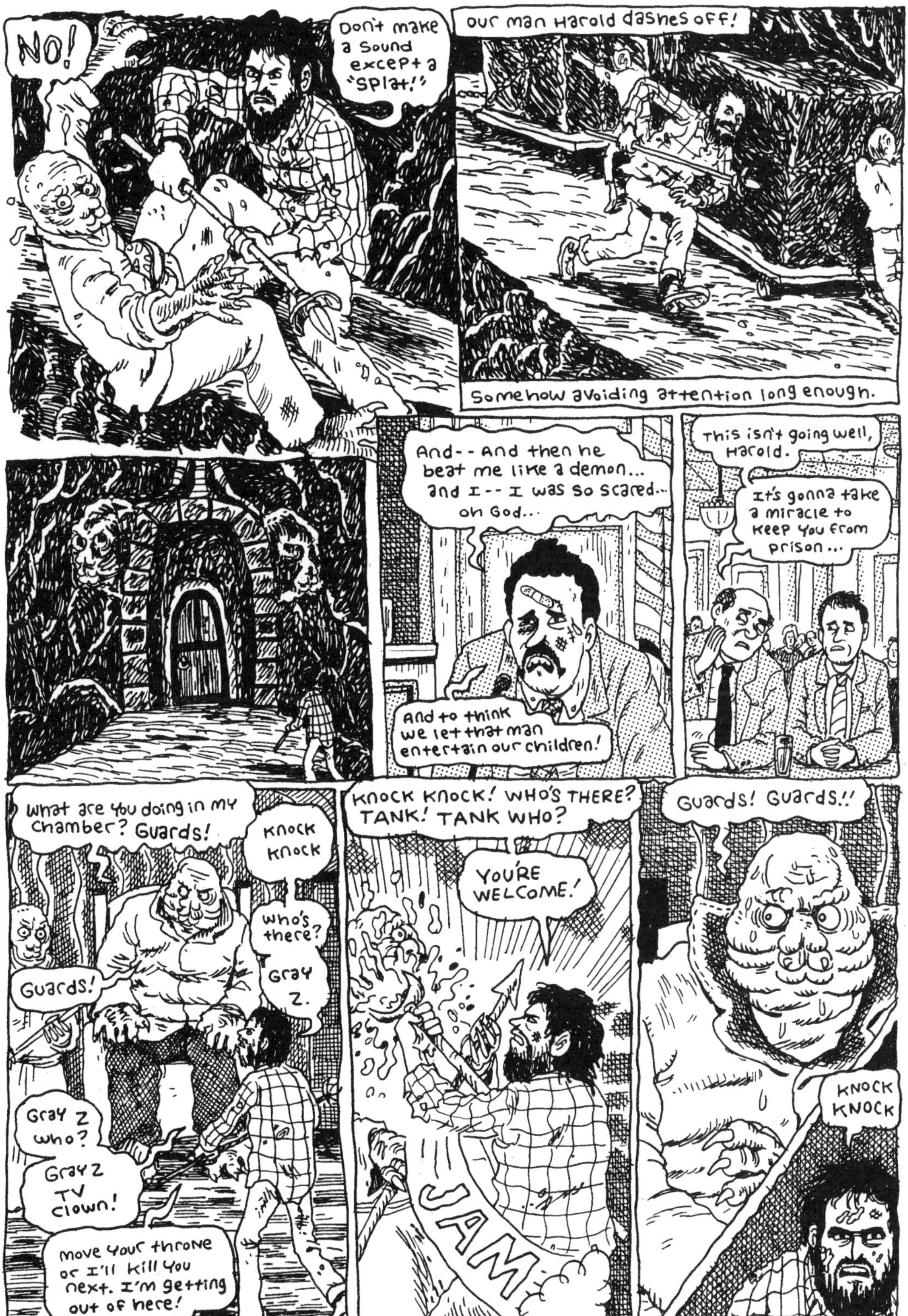
NO!
Don't make a Sound except a "splat!"
Our man Harold dashes off!
Somehow avoiding attention long enough.
And-- And then he beat me like a demon... and I-- I was so scared... oh God...
And to think we let that man entertain our children!
This isn't going well, Harold.
It's gonna take a miracle to keep you from prison...
What are you doing in my chamber? Guards!
Knock knock
Who's there?
Gray Z.
Guards!
Gray Z who?
Gray Z TV clown!
Move your throne or I'll kill you next. I'm getting out of here!
KNOCK KNOCK! WHO'S THERE? TANK! TANK WHO?
YOU'RE WELCOME!
JAM
Guards! Guards!!
KNOCK KNOCK

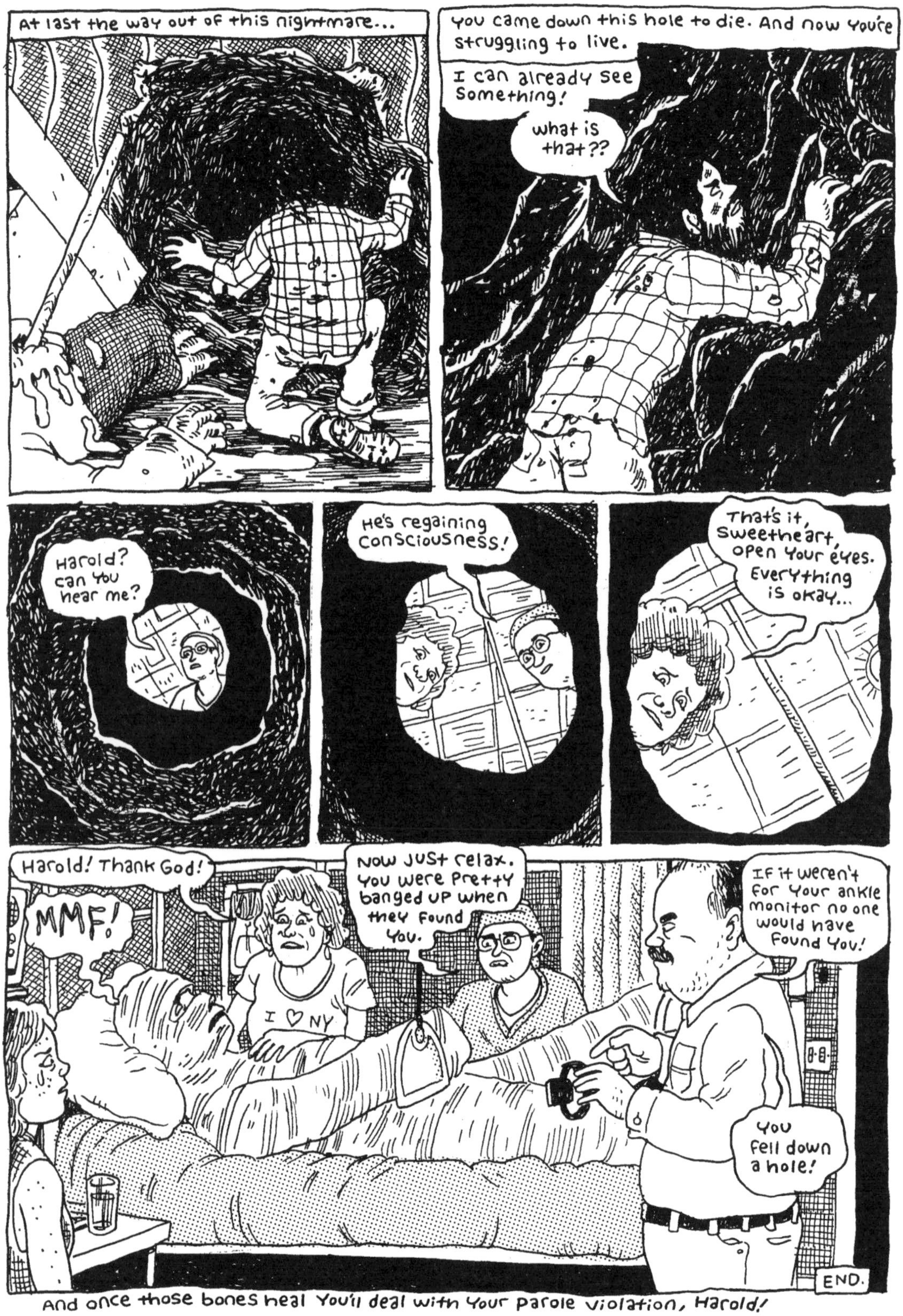
At last the way out of this nightmare...
You came down this hole to die. And now you're struggling to live.
I can already see something!
what is that??
Harold? can you hear me?
He's regaining consciousness!
That's it, sweetheart, open your eyes. Everything is okay...
Harold! Thank God!
MMF!
Now just relax. You were pretty banged up when they found you.
If it weren't for your ankle monitor no one would have found you!
You fell down a hole!
END.
And once those bones heal you'll deal with your parole violation, Harold!

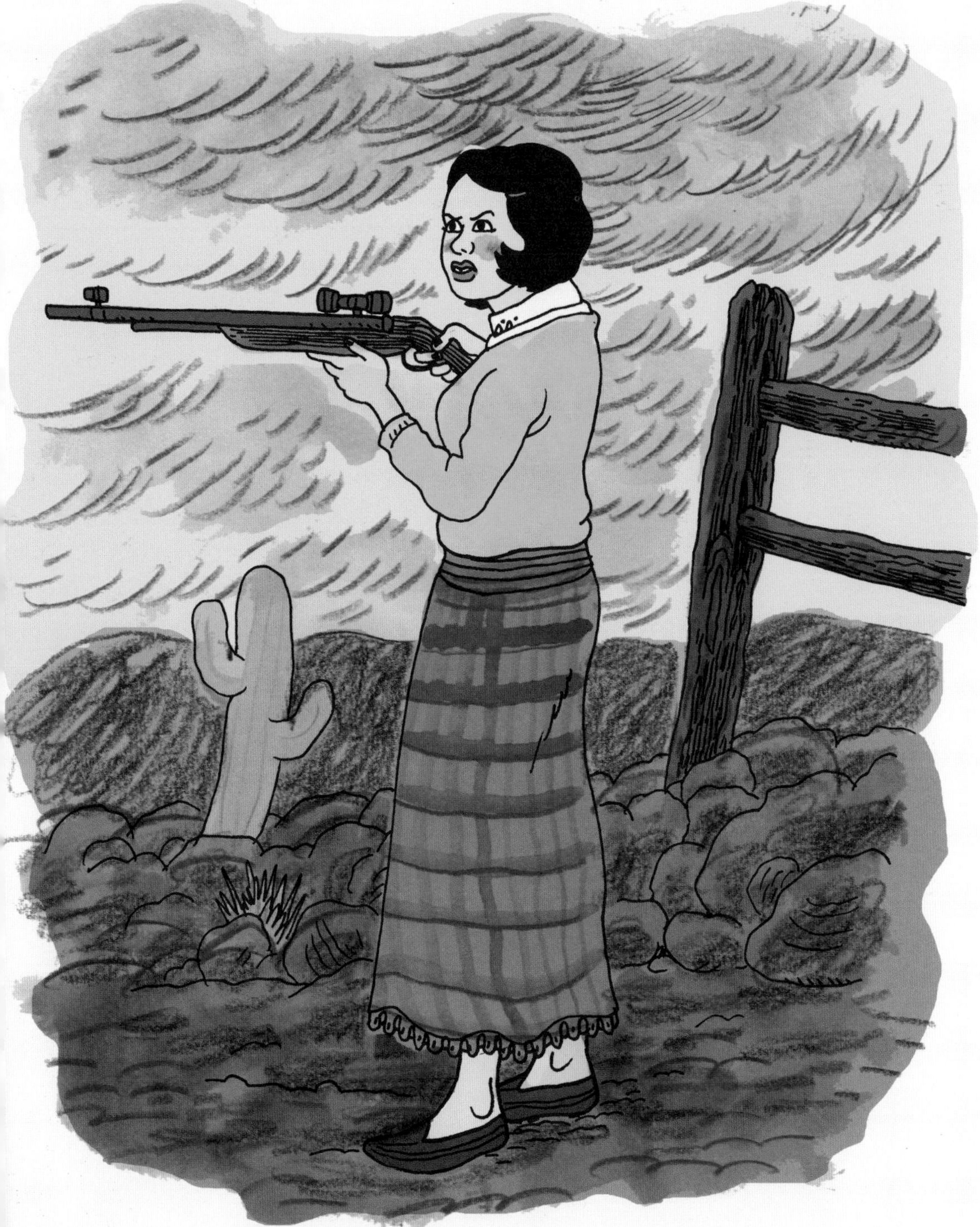

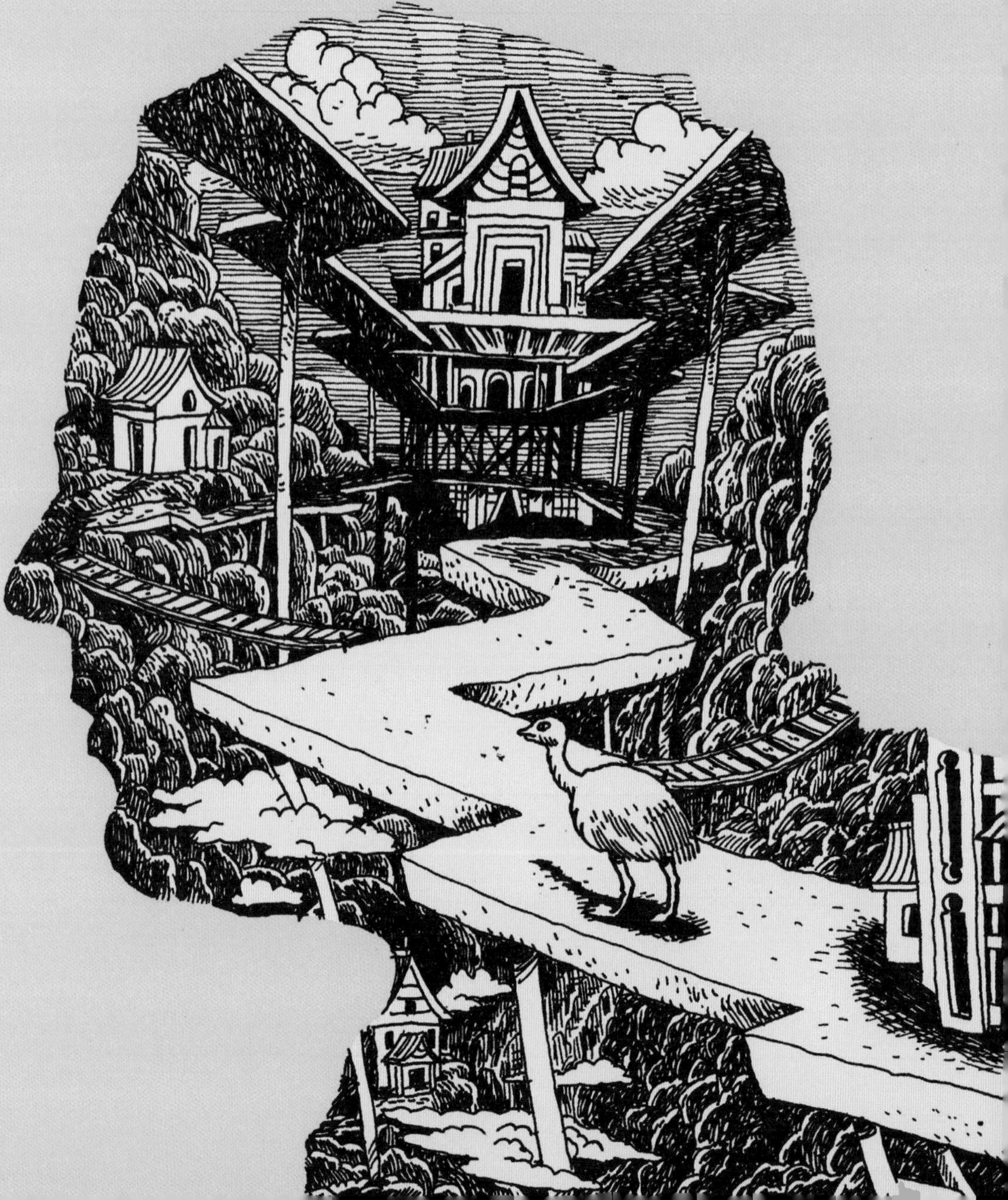

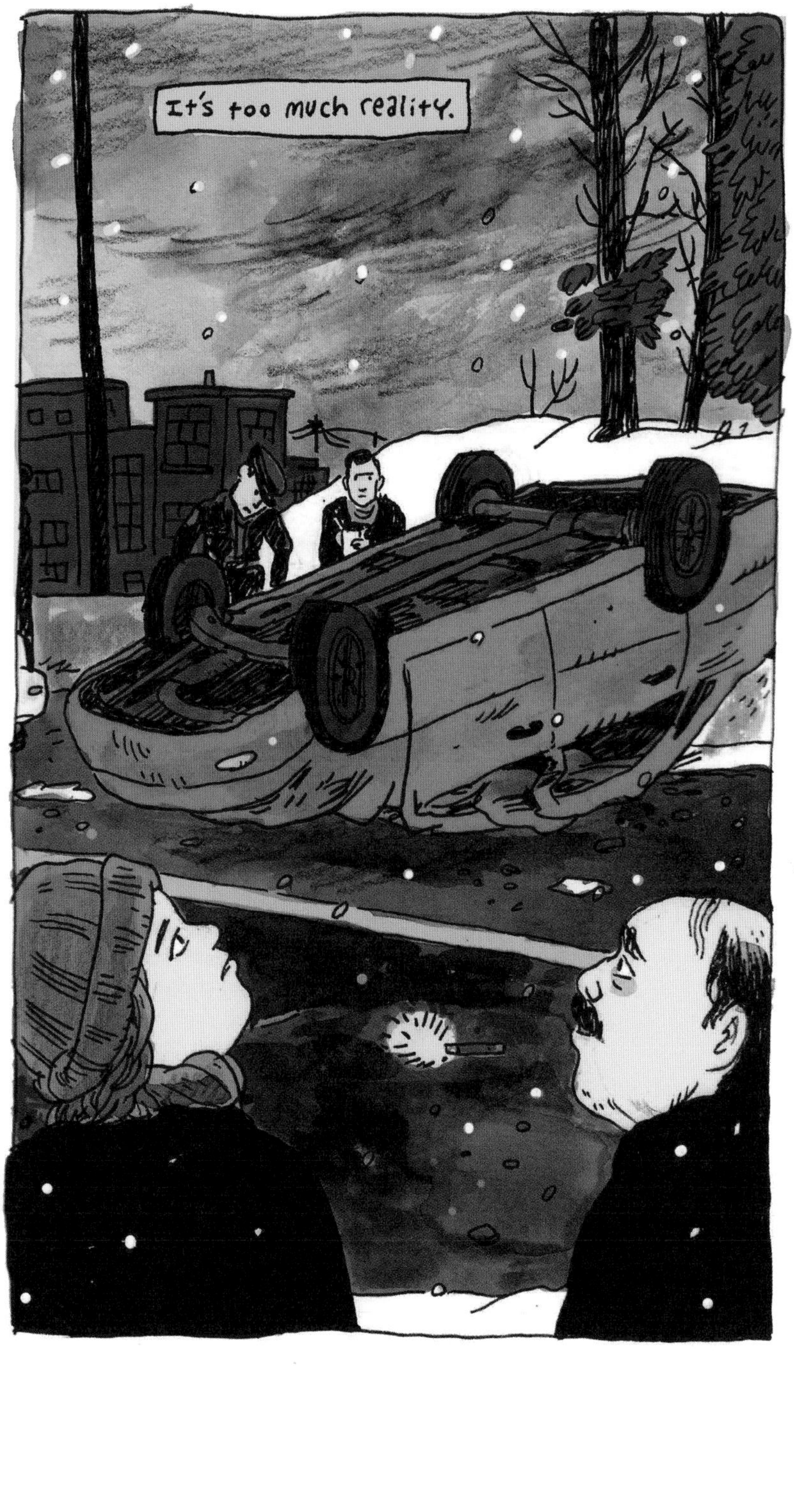
It's too much reality.

on Christmas Eve I rode my bike to a church in my neighborhood for midnight mass. I I hadn't been inside a church in I don't know how long. Since I was really little.

It was an old building. Built in the 1800s, and I wondered how many midnight masses had happened there. And I wondered where all of the people who had attended the first midnight mass are buried.

where are they now?

with the lord in heaven, my dear.

I'm 30. I can't even fake feeling any kind of magic or holiness. I'm too cynical. There's no Lord's presence here. I'm not getting what I wanted to out of this.

It's so nice to see a new face!

I'm Tim.

I'm Sarah. This is such a beautiful church!

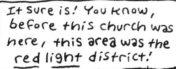

It sure is! You know, before this church was here, this area was the red light district!

Wild stuff, don't you think?

Is this flirtation?

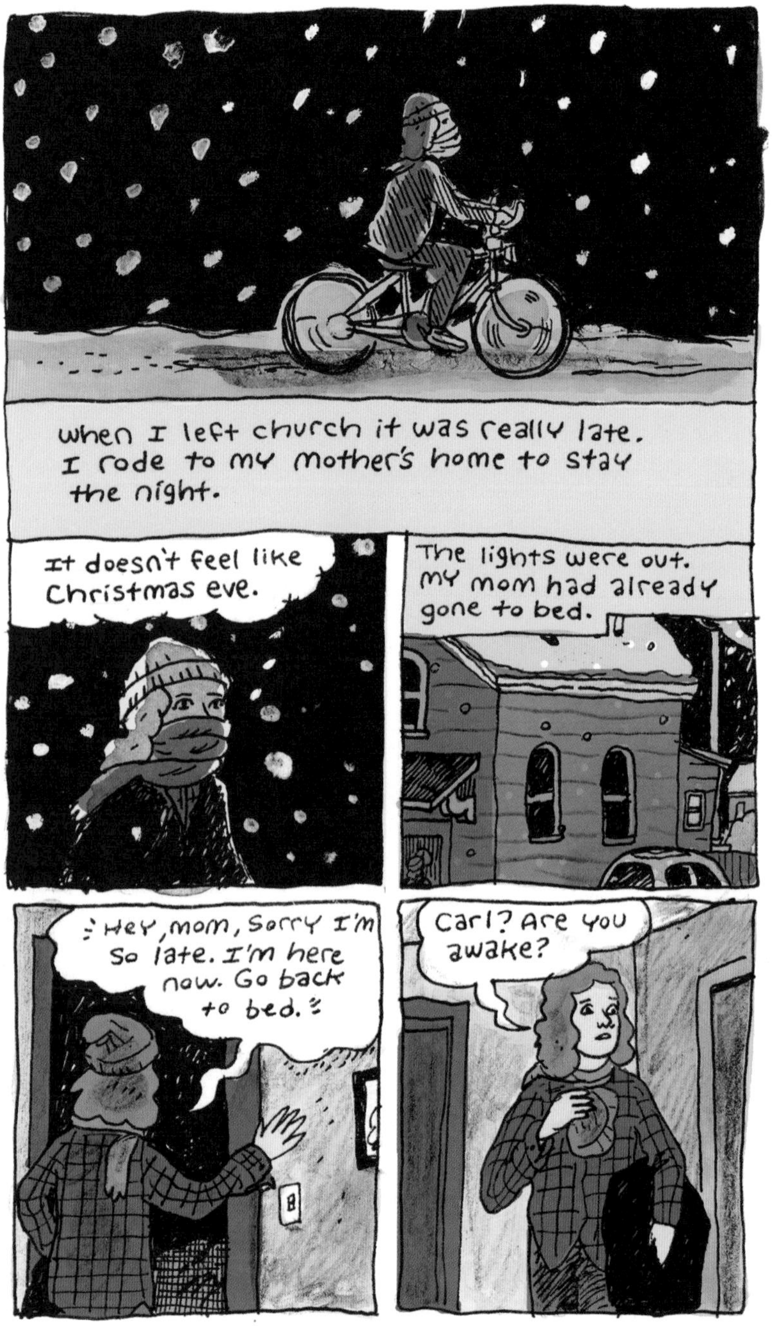
when I left church it was really late. I rode to my mother's home to stay the night.
It doesn't feel like Christmas eve.
The lights were out. My mom had already gone to bed.
Hey, mom, sorry I'm so late. I'm here now. Go back to bed.
Carl? Are you awake?

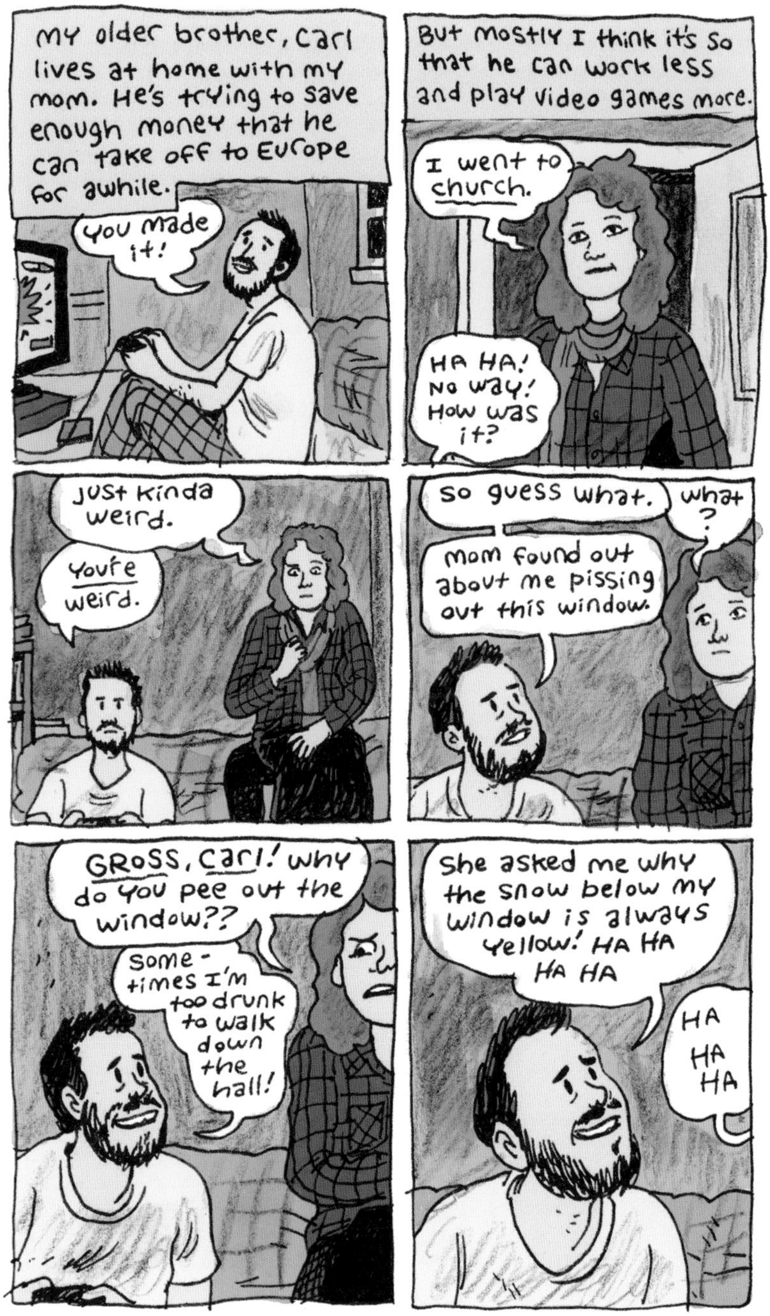
My older brother, Carl lives at home with my mom. He's trying to save enough money that he can take off to Europe for awhile.
You made it!
But mostly I think it's so that he can work less and play video games more.
I went to church.
HA HA! No way! How was it?
Just kinda weird.
You're weird.
So guess what.
What?
Mom found out about me pissing out this window.
GROSS, Carl! Why do you pee out the window??
Sometimes I'm too drunk to walk down the hall!
She asked me why the snow below my window is always yellow! HA HA HA HA
HA HA HA

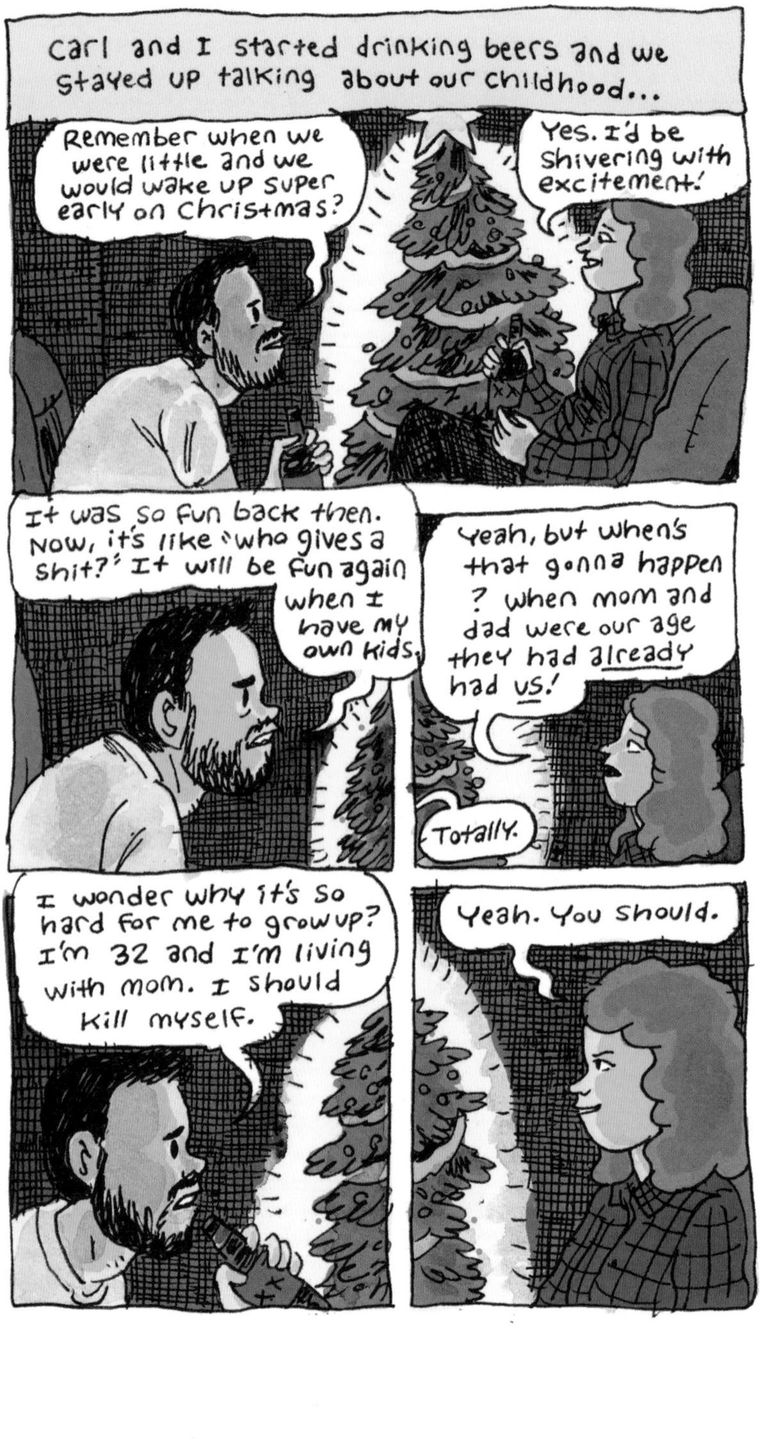
Carl and I started drinking beers and we stayed up talking about our childhood...
Remember when we were little and we would wake up super early on Christmas?
Yes. I'd be shivering with excitement!
It was so fun back then. Now, it's like "who gives a shit?" It will be fun again when I have my own kids.
Yeah, but when's that gonna happen? When mom and dad were our age they had already had us!
Totally.
I wonder why it's so hard for me to grow up? I'm 32 and I'm living with mom. I should kill myself.
Yeah. You should.

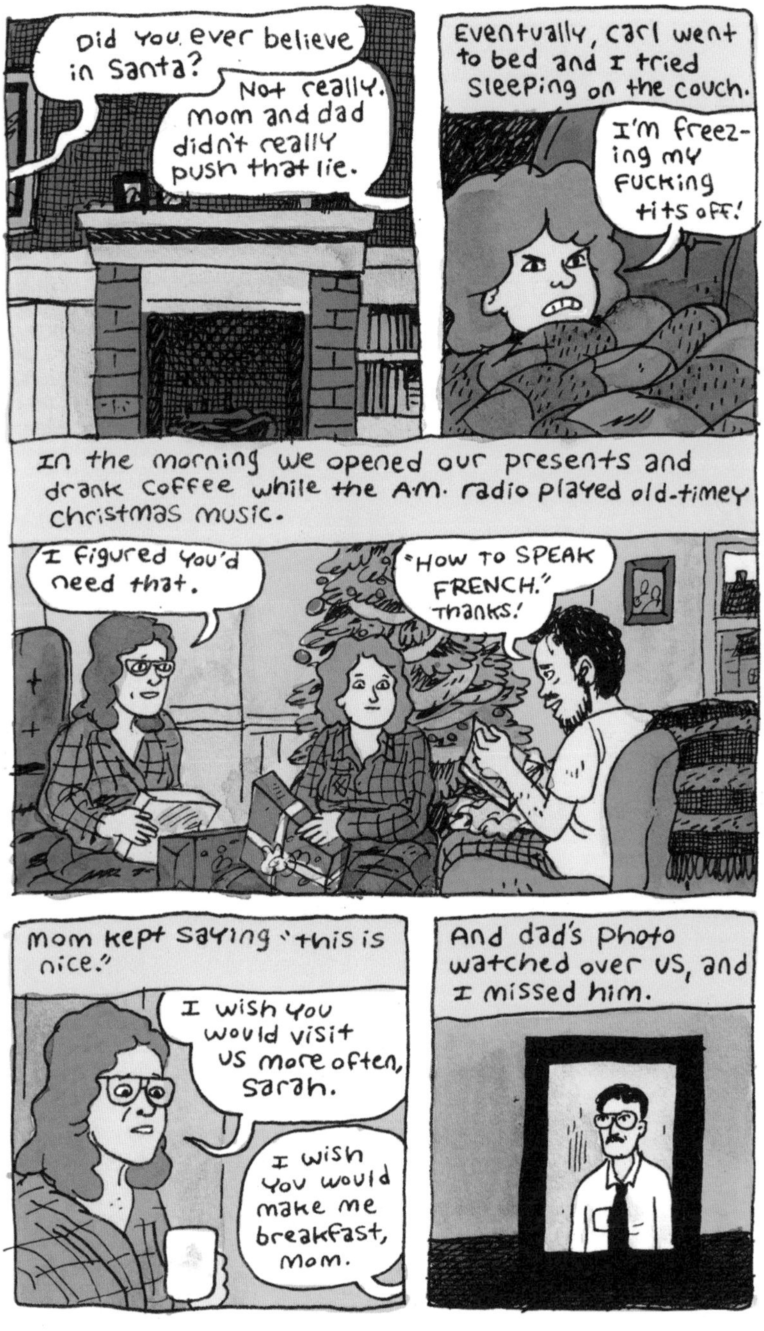
Did you ever believe in Santa?
Not really. Mom and dad didn't really push that lie.
Eventually, Carl went to bed and I tried sleeping on the couch.
I'm freezing my fucking tits off!
In the morning we opened our presents and drank coffee while the A.M. radio played old-timey christmas music.
I figured you'd need that.
"How to speak French." Thanks!
Mom kept saying "this is nice."
I wish you would visit us more often, Sarah.
I wish you would make me breakfast, Mom.
And dad's photo watched over us, and I missed him.

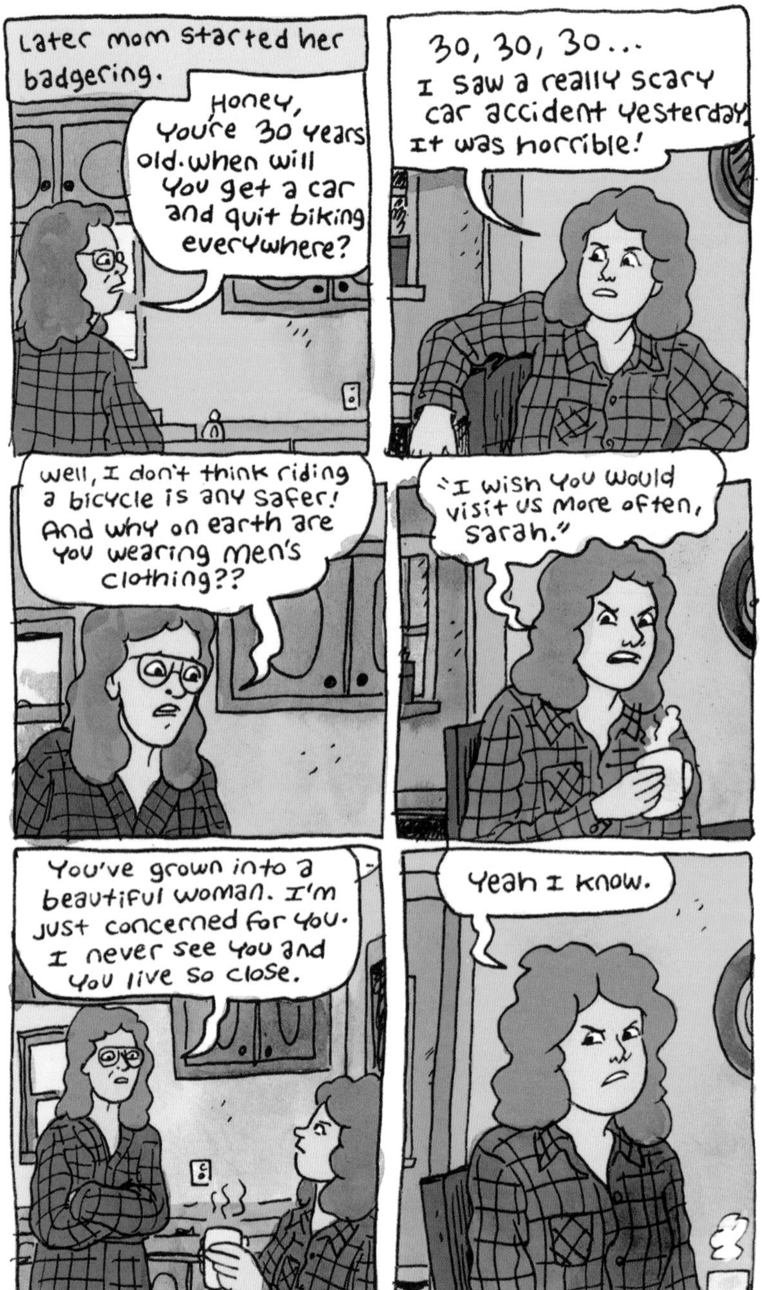
Later mom started her badgering.
Honey, You're 30 years old. When will you get a car and quit biking everywhere?
30, 30, 30...
I saw a really scary car accident yesterday. It was horrible!
Well, I don't think riding a bicycle is any safer! And why on earth are you wearing men's clothing??
"I wish you would visit us more often, Sarah."
You've grown into a beautiful woman. I'm just concerned for you. I never see you and you live so close.
Yeah I know.

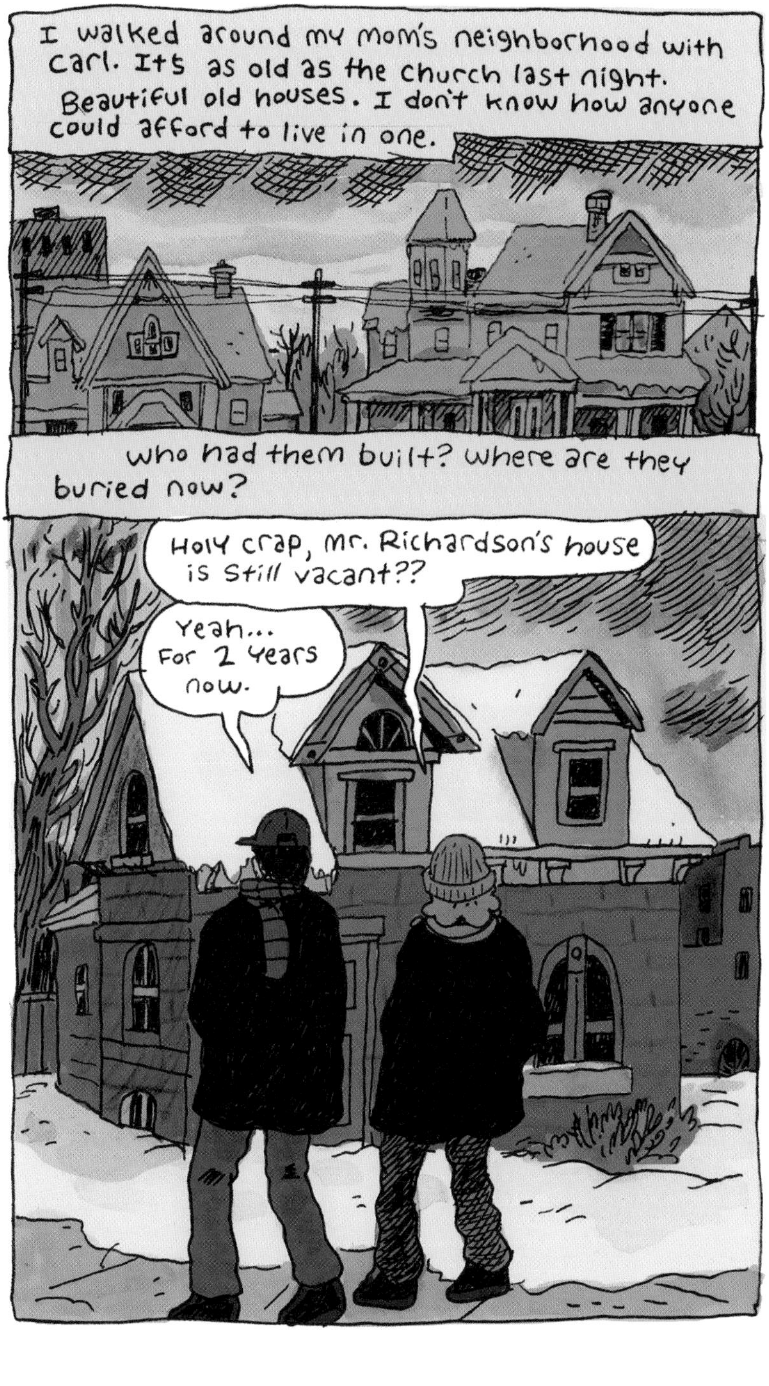
I walked around my mom's neighborhood with Carl. It's as old as the church last night. Beautiful old houses. I don't know how anyone could afford to live in one.
who had them built? where are they buried now?
Holy crap, Mr. Richardson's house is still vacant??
Yeah... For 2 years now.

Have you ever been inside?
The coast is clear.
Kind of creepy, isn't it?
Yeah, no shit.
Didn't Mr. Richardson die in his Lazyboy chair?
I think so.
I'll bet that his chair was right here.
Creepy...

I really hate it in here. I think it's haunted...
There's no such thing as ghosts.
SCRATCH SCRATCH
What was that??
Okay - Let's get out of here!
In the late afternoon we watched "A Christmas Story" on TV. I really wanted to go home but I felt like I should wait a little longer.
...
I was getting fidgety.
I wonder what my roommates are doing?

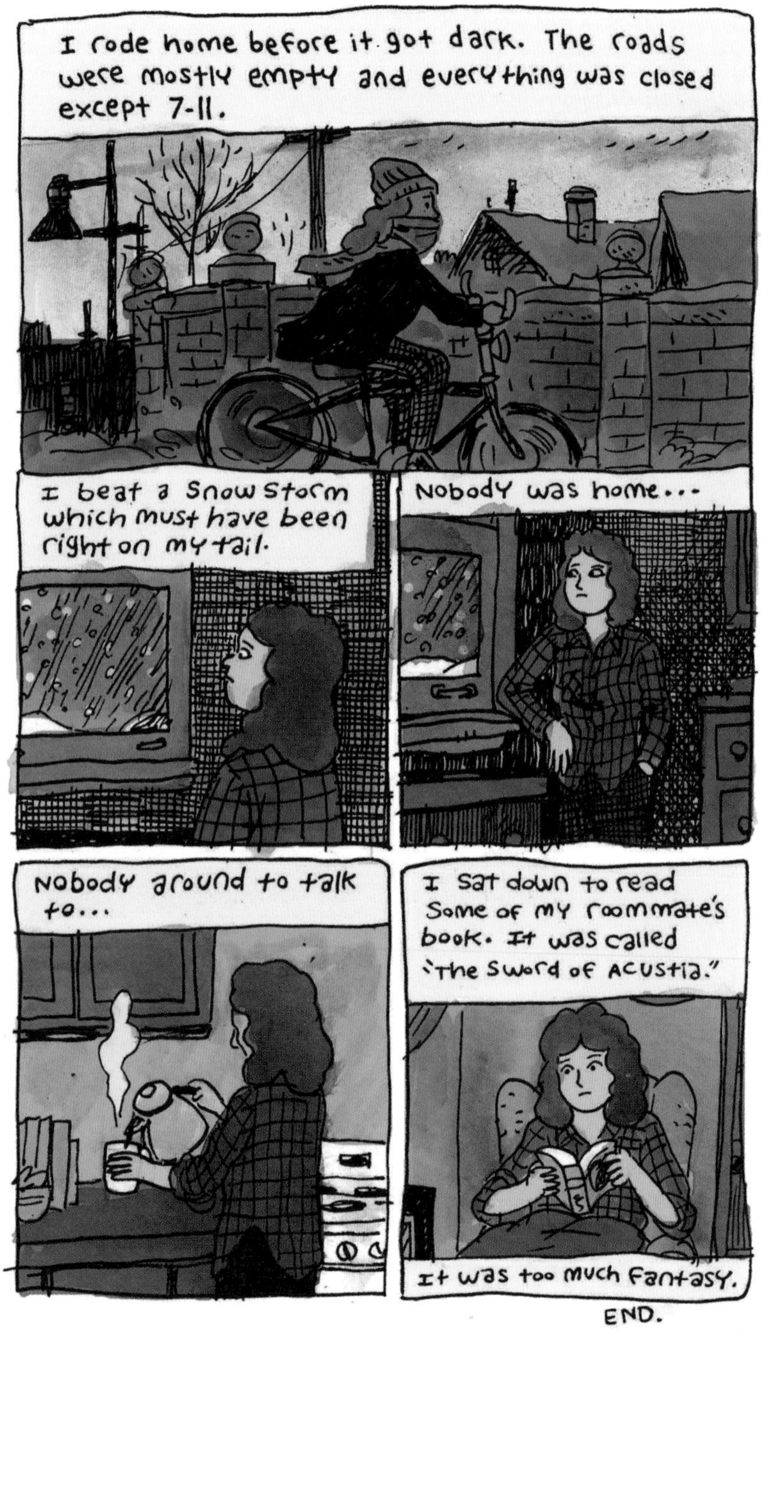
I rode home before it got dark. The roads were mostly empty and everything was closed except 7-11.
I beat a snow storm which must have been right on my tail.
Nobody was home...
Nobody around to talk to...
I sat down to read some of my roommate's book. It was called "The Sword of Acustia."
It was too much fantasy.
END.

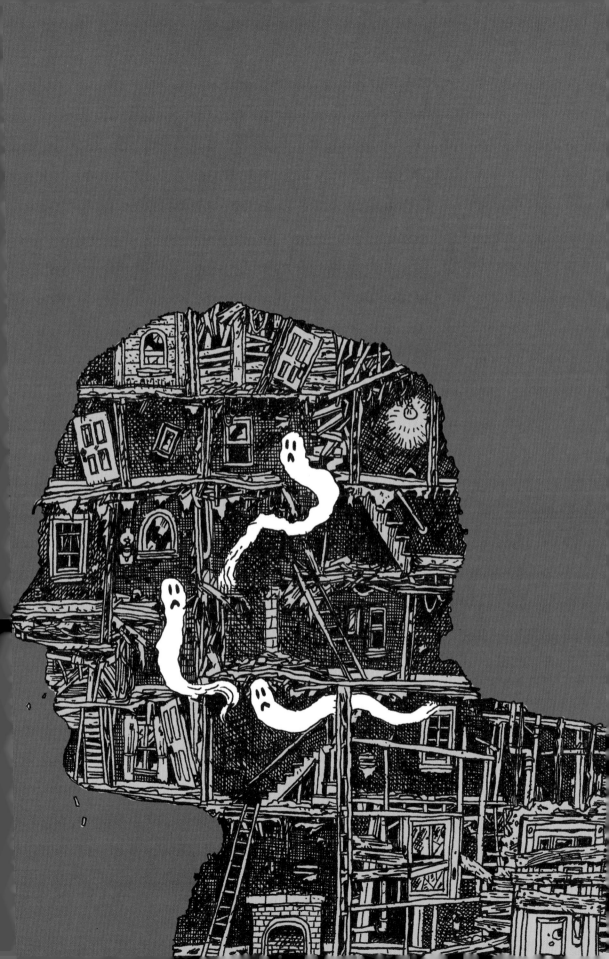

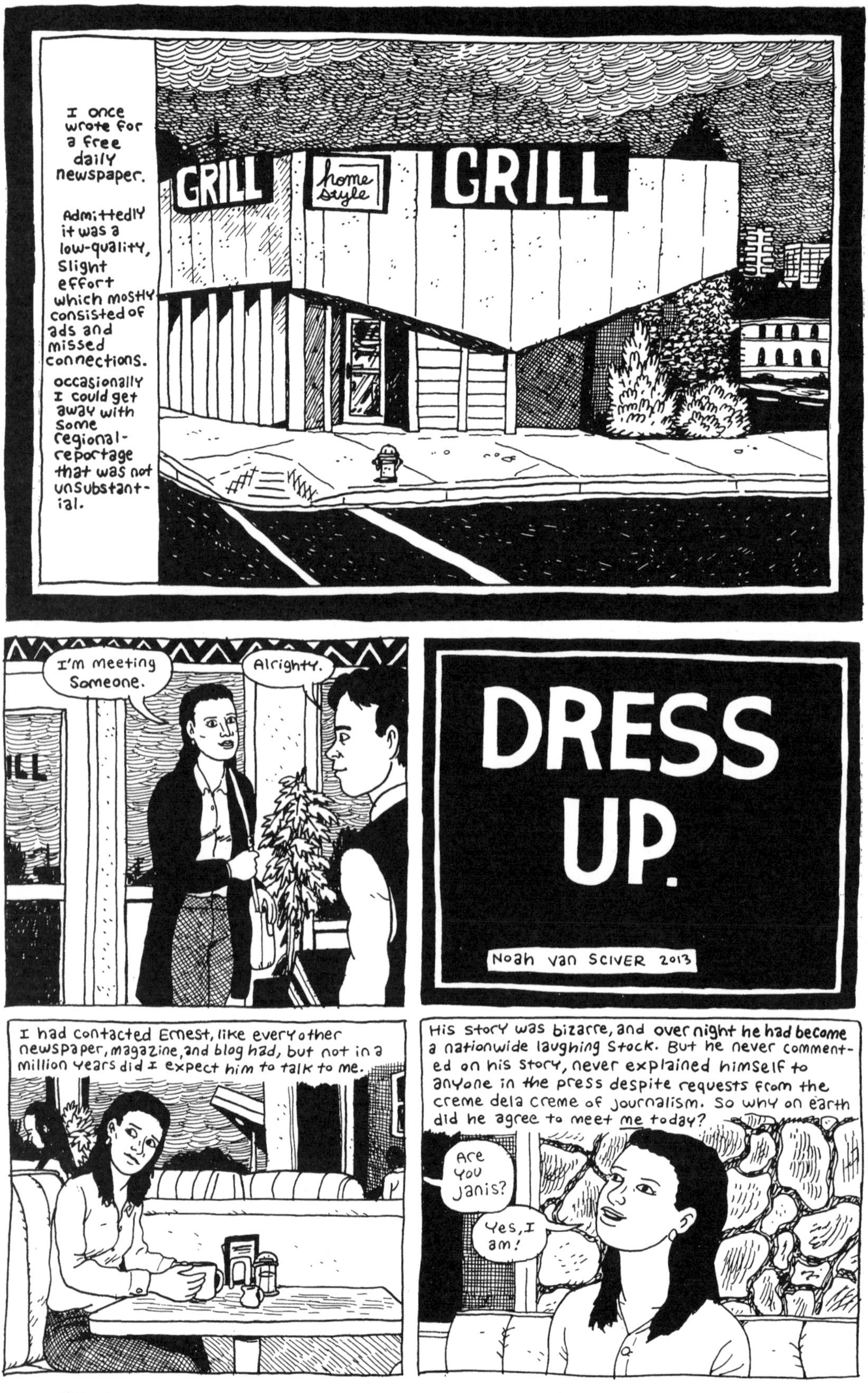
I once wrote for a free daily newspaper.
Admittedly it was a low-quality, slight effort which mostly consisted of ads and missed connections.
occasionally I could get away with some regional-reportage that was not unsubstant-ial.
GRILL
home style
GRILL
I'm meeting someone.
Alrighty.
DRESS UP.
Noah van SCIVER 2013
I had contacted Ernest, like every other newspaper, magazine, and blog had, but not in a million years did I expect him to talk to me.
His story was bizarre, and overnight he had become a nationwide laughing stock. But he never comment-ed on his story, never explained himself to anyone in the press despite requests from the creme dela creme of journalism. So why on earth did he agree to meet me today?
Are you Janis?
Yes, I am!

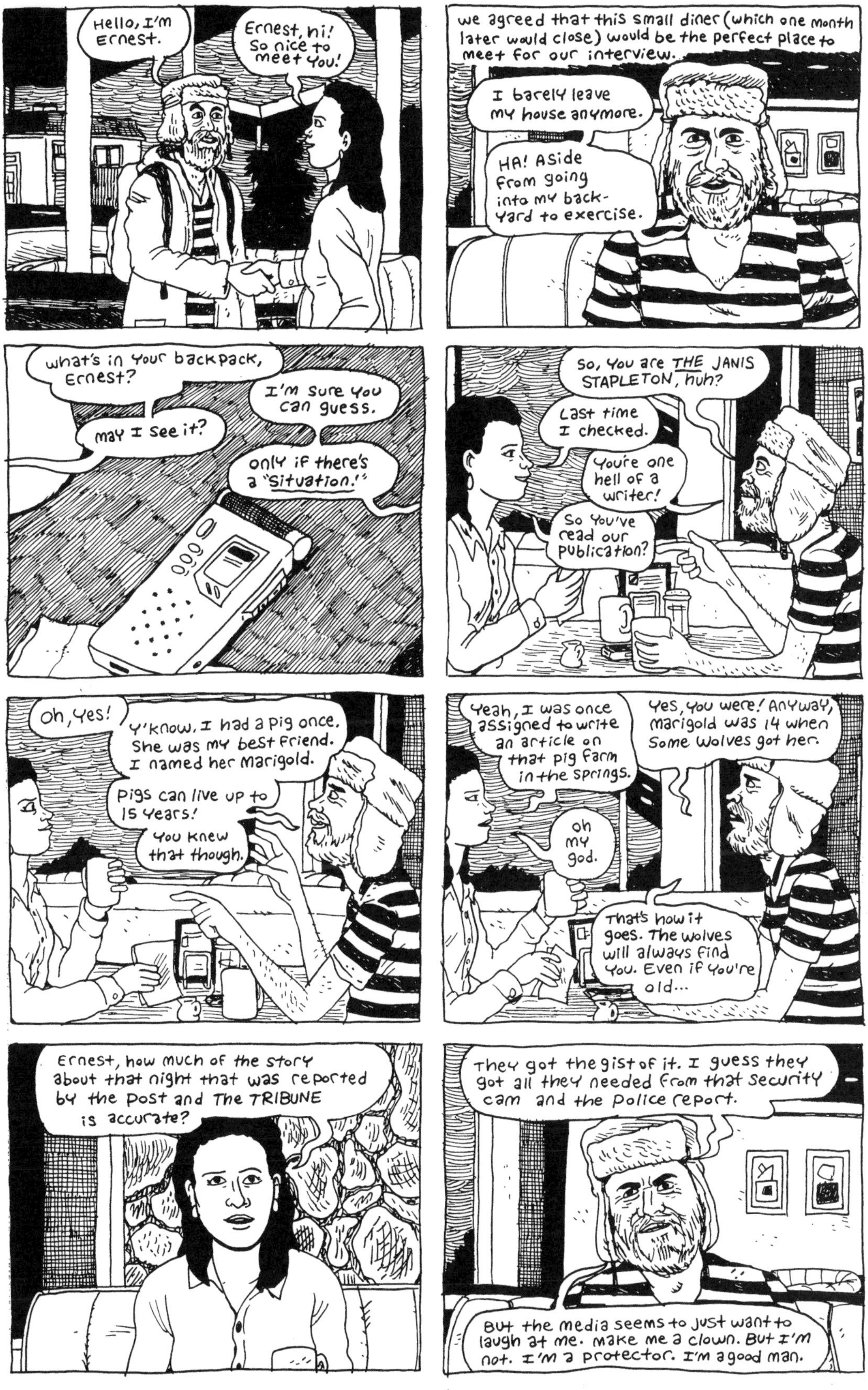
Hello, I'm Ernest.
Ernest, hi! So nice to meet you!
we agreed that this small diner (which one month later would close) would be the perfect place to meet for our interview.
I barely leave my house anymore.
HA! Aside from going into my back-yard to exercise.
what's in your backpack, Ernest?
I'm sure you can guess.
may I see it?
only if there's a "situation."
So, you are THE JANIS STAPLETON, huh?
Last time I checked.
You're one hell of a writer!
So you've read our publication?
Oh, yes!
Y'know, I had a pig once. She was my best friend. I named her Marigold.
Pigs can live up to 15 years!
You knew that though.
Yeah, I was once assigned to write an article on that pig farm in the springs.
Yes, you were! Anyway, Marigold was 14 when some wolves got her.
oh my god.
That's how it goes. The wolves will always find you. Even if you're old...
Ernest, how much of the story about that night that was reported by the Post and The TRIBUNE is accurate?
They got the gist of it. I guess they got all they needed from that security cam and the police report.
But the media seems to just want to laugh at me. Make me a clown. But I'm not. I'm a protector. I'm a good man.

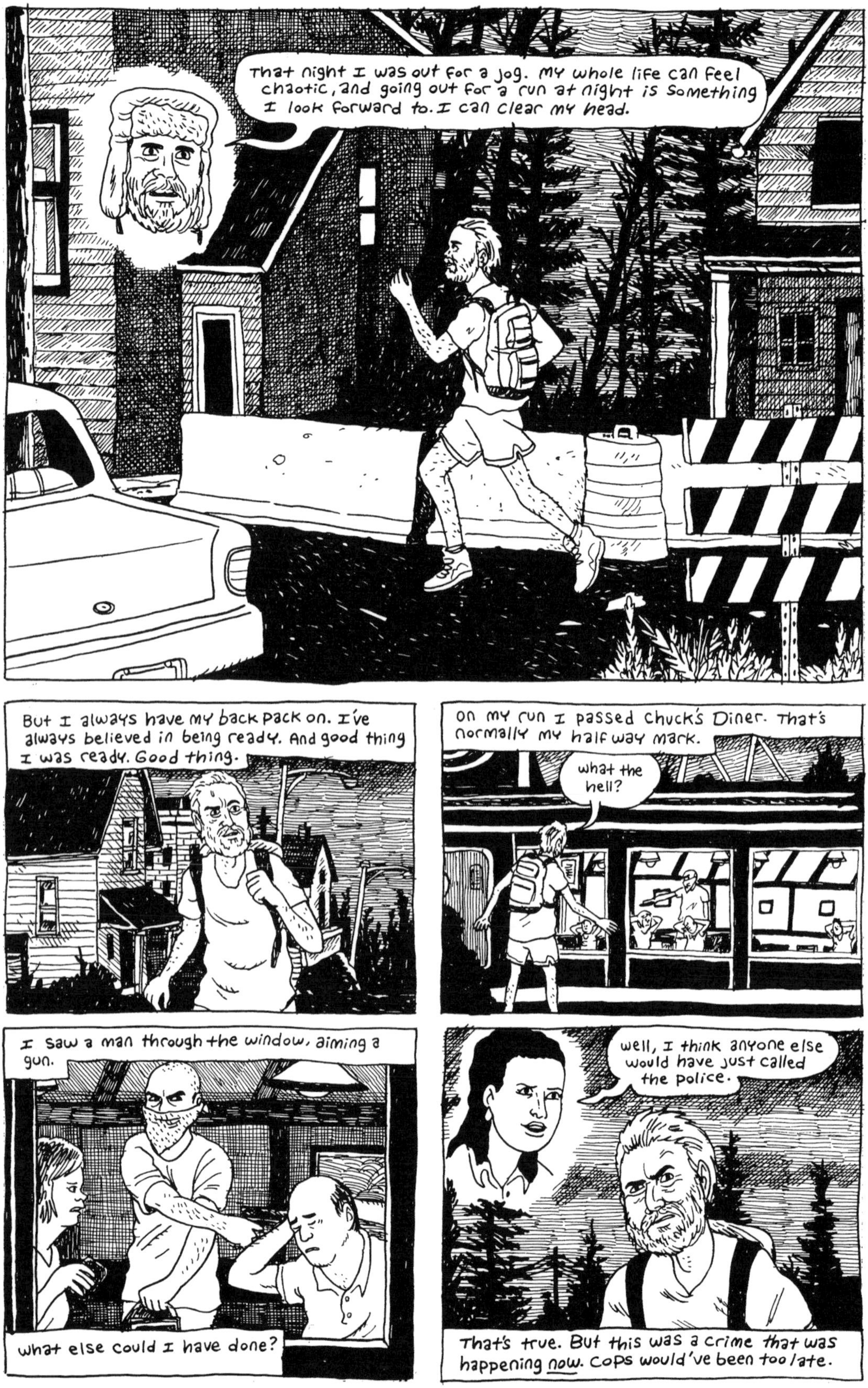
That night I was out for a jog. My whole life can feel chaotic, and going out for a run at night is something I look forward to. I can clear my head.
But I always have my back pack on. I've always believed in being ready. And good thing I was ready. Good thing.
On my run I passed Chuck's Diner. That's normally my half way mark.
what the hell?
I saw a man through the window, aiming a gun.
what else could I have done?
well, I think anyone else would have just called the police.
That's true. But this was a crime that was happening now. Cops would've been too late.

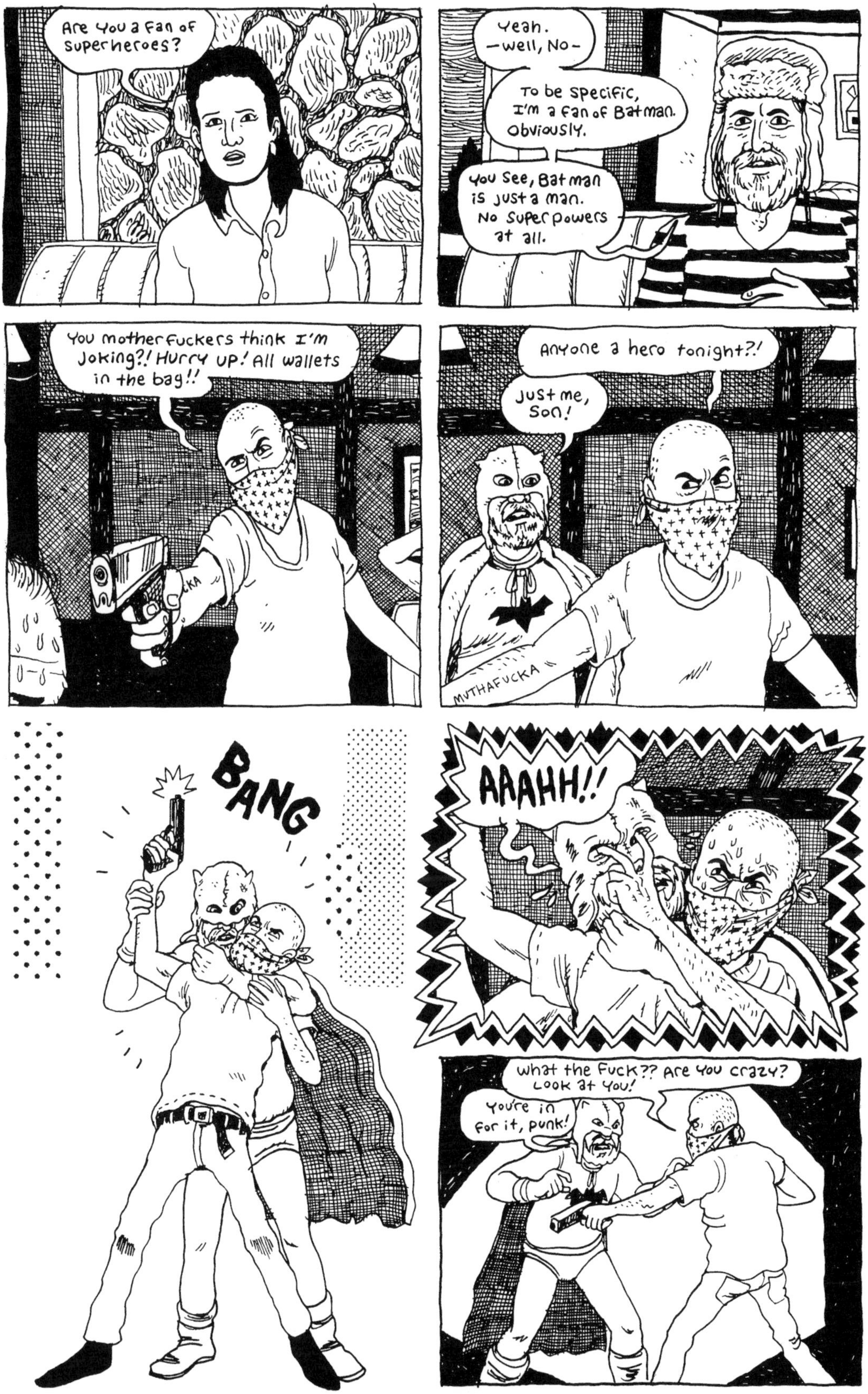
Are you a fan of superheroes?
Yeah. —well, No—
To be specific, I'm a fan of Batman. Obviously.
You see, Batman is just a man. No superpowers at all.
You motherfuckers think I'm joking?! Hurry up! All wallets in the bag!!
Anyone a hero tonight?!
Just me, Son!
MUTHAFUCKA
BANG
AAAHH!!
What the fuck?? Are you crazy? Look at you!
You're in for it, punk!

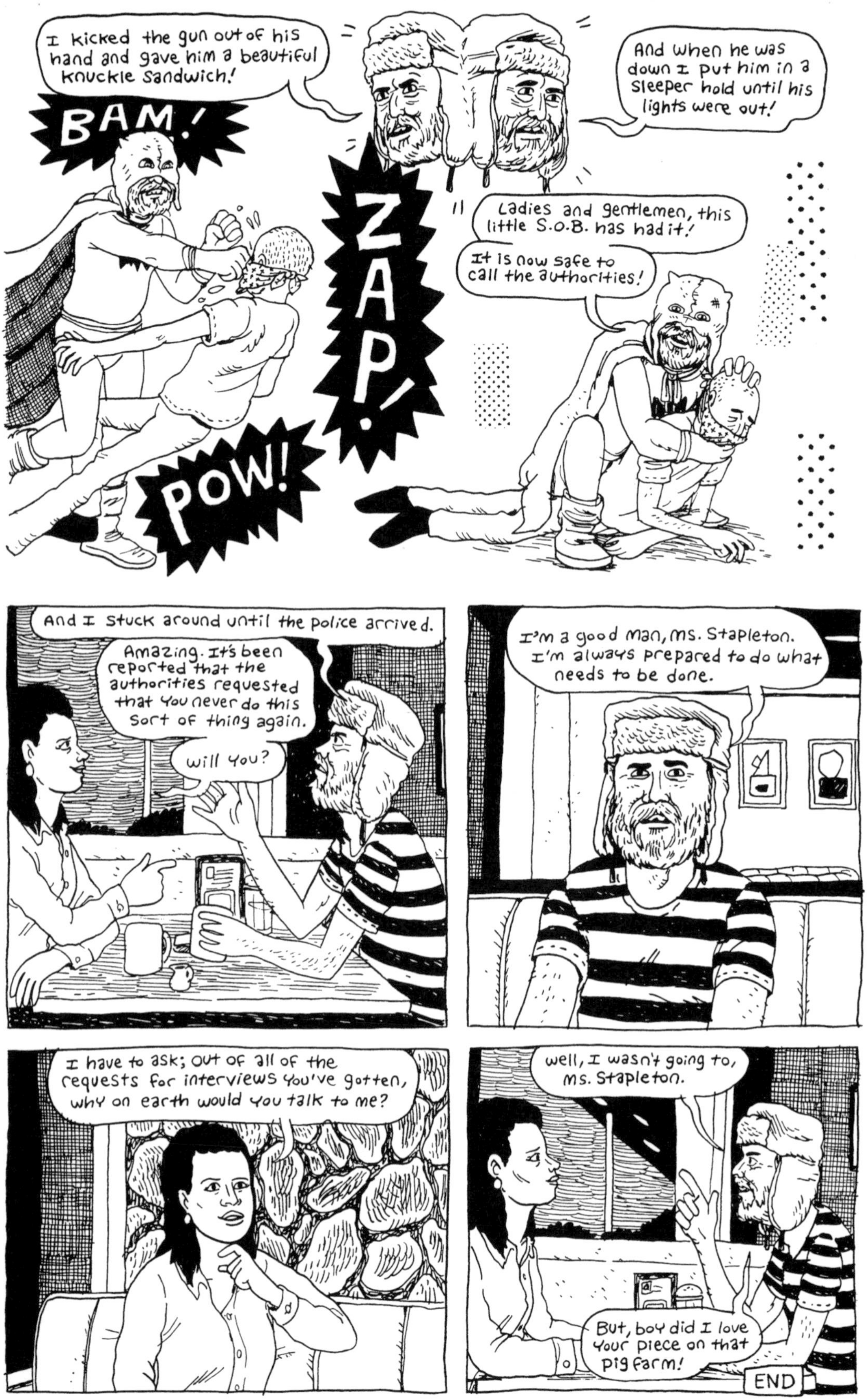
I kicked the gun out of his hand and gave him a beautiful knuckle sandwich!
BAM!
And when he was down I put him in a sleeper hold until his lights were out!
ZAP!
POW!
Ladies and gentlemen, this little S.O.B. has had it!
It is now safe to call the authorities!
And I stuck around until the police arrived.
Amazing. It's been reported that the authorities requested that you never do this sort of thing again.
Will you?
I'm a good man, Ms. Stapleton. I'm always prepared to do what needs to be done.
I have to ask; out of all of the requests for interviews you've gotten, why on earth would you talk to me?
Well, I wasn't going to, Ms. Stapleton.
But, boy did I love your piece on that pig farm!
END

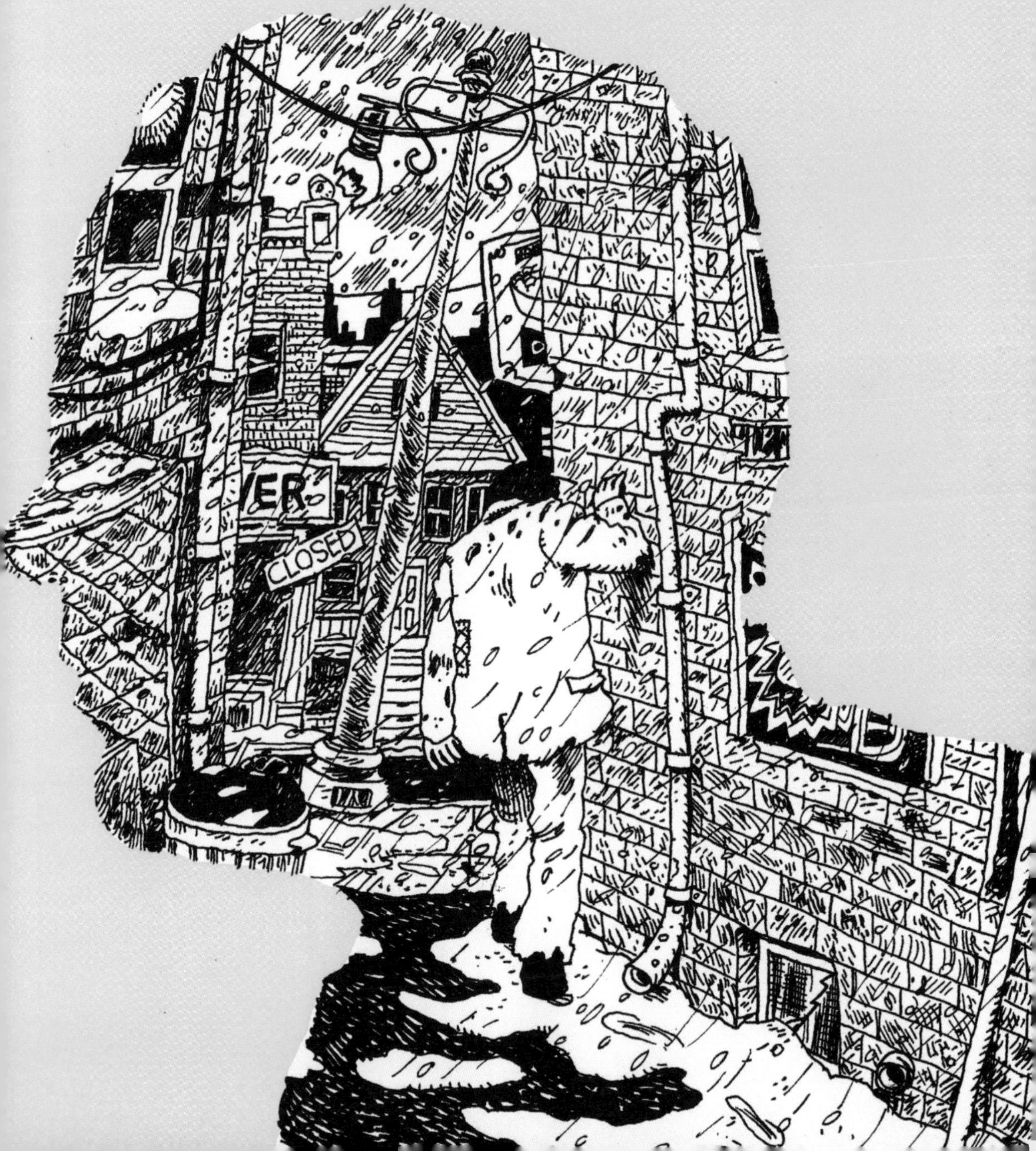
CLOSED

AN EVENING ALONE.

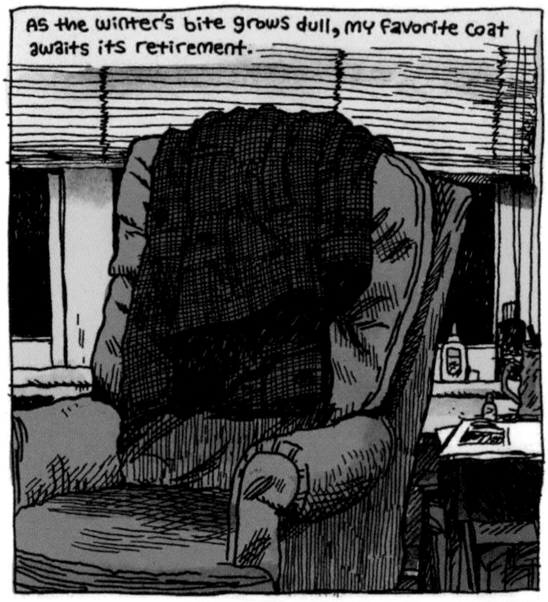
As the winter's bite grows dull, my favorite coat awaits its retirement.

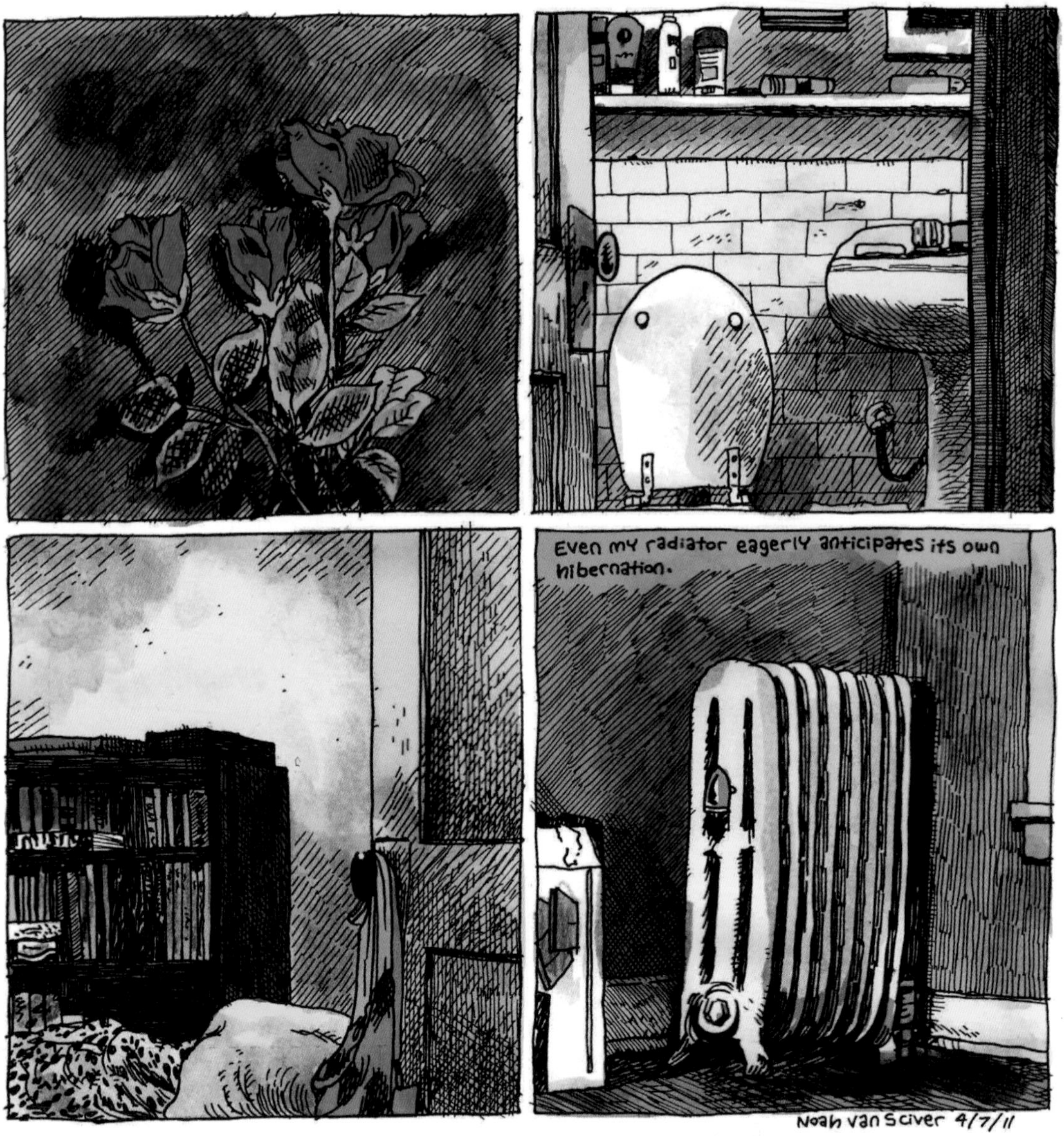
Even my radiator eagerly anticipates its own hibernation.
Noah van Sciver 4/7/11

WHEN YOU DISAPPEAR

Noah van Sciver

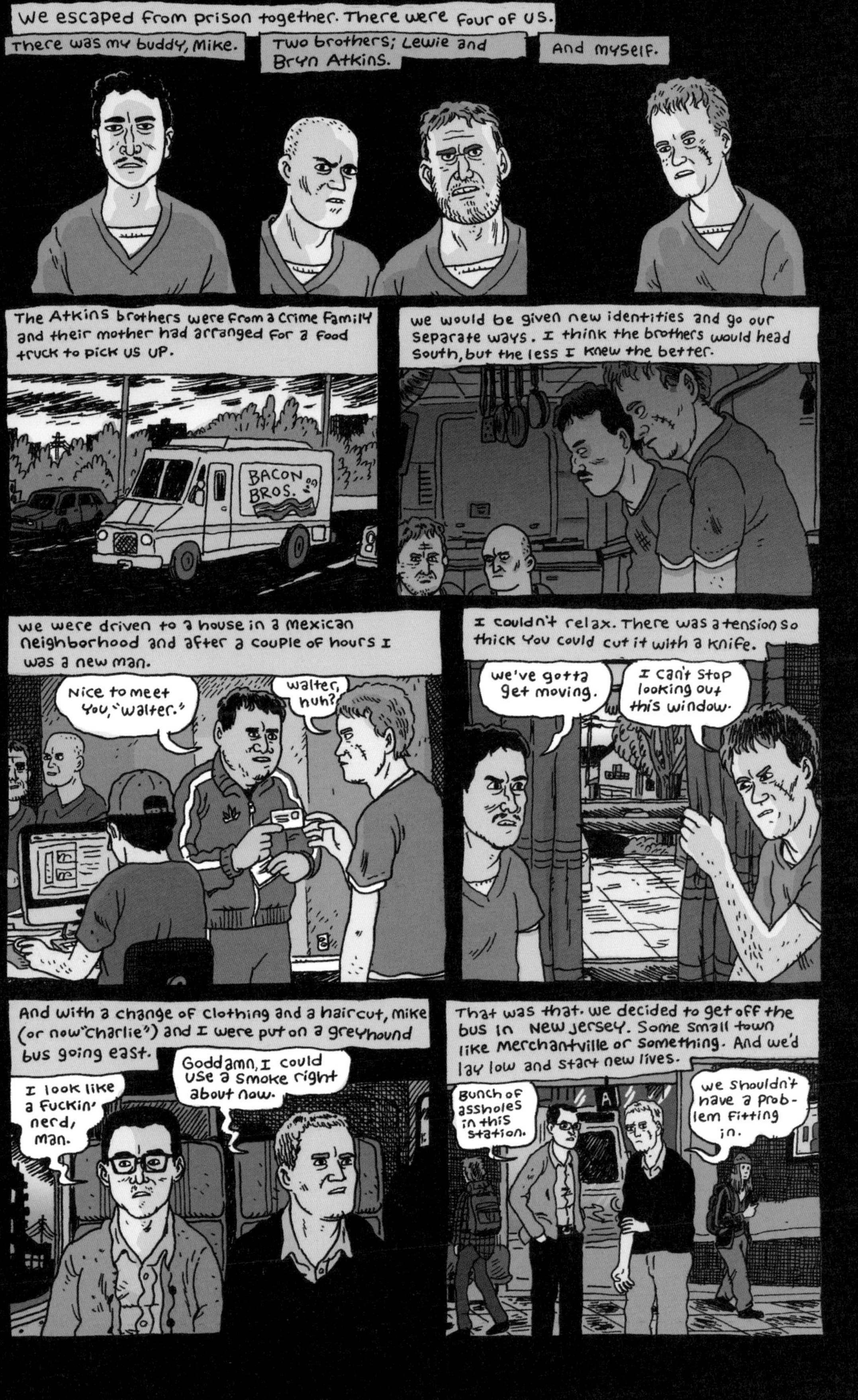

We escaped from prison together. There were four of us.
There was my buddy, Mike.
Two brothers; Lewie and Bryn Atkins.
And myself.
The Atkins brothers were from a crime family and their mother had arranged for a food truck to pick us up.
BACON BROS.
We would be given new identities and go our separate ways. I think the brothers would head south, but the less I knew the better.
We were driven to a house in a Mexican neighborhood and after a couple of hours I was a new man.
Nice to meet you, "Walter."
Walter, huh?
I couldn't relax. There was a tension so thick you could cut it with a knife.
We've gotta get moving.
I can't stop looking out this window.
And with a change of clothing and a haircut, Mike (or now "Charlie") and I were put on a greyhound bus going east.
I look like a fuckin' nerd, man.
Goddamn, I could use a smoke right about now.
That was that. We decided to get off the bus in New Jersey. Some small town like Merchantville or something. And we'd lay low and start new lives.
Bunch of assholes in this station.
We shouldn't have a prob-lem fitting in.

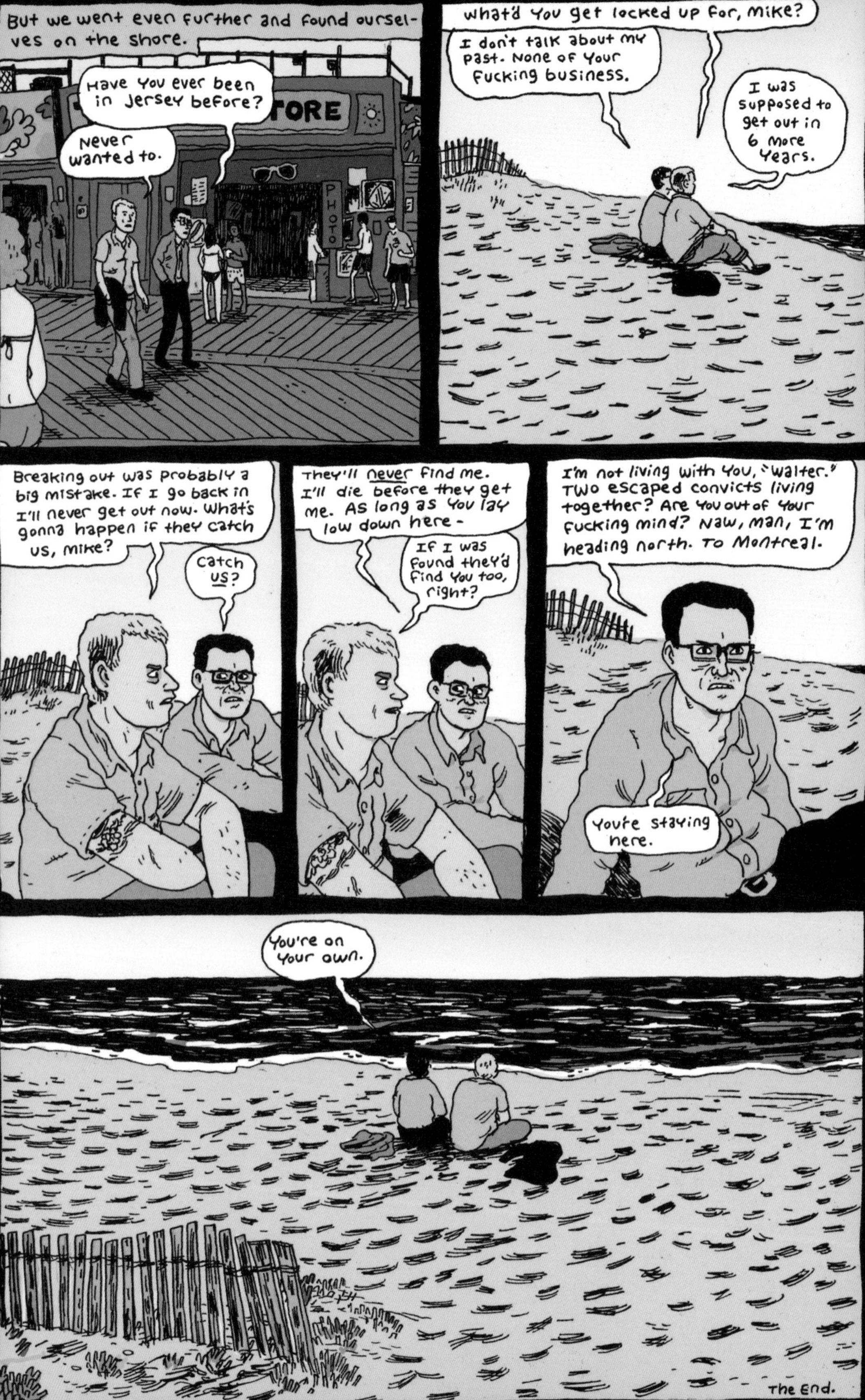
But we went even further and found ourselves on the shore.
Have you ever been in Jersey before?
Never wanted to.
TORE
PHOTO
What'd you get locked up for, Mike?
I don't talk about my past. None of your fucking business.
I was supposed to get out in 6 more years.
Breaking out was probably a big mistake. If I go back in I'll never get out now. What's gonna happen if they catch us, Mike?
Catch us?
They'll never find me. I'll die before they get me. As long as you lay low down here -
If I was found they'd find you too, right?
I'm not living with you, "Walter." Two escaped convicts living together? Are you out of your fucking mind? Naw, man, I'm heading north. To Montreal.
You're staying here.
You're on your own.
The End.

Dreamt 7/14/14

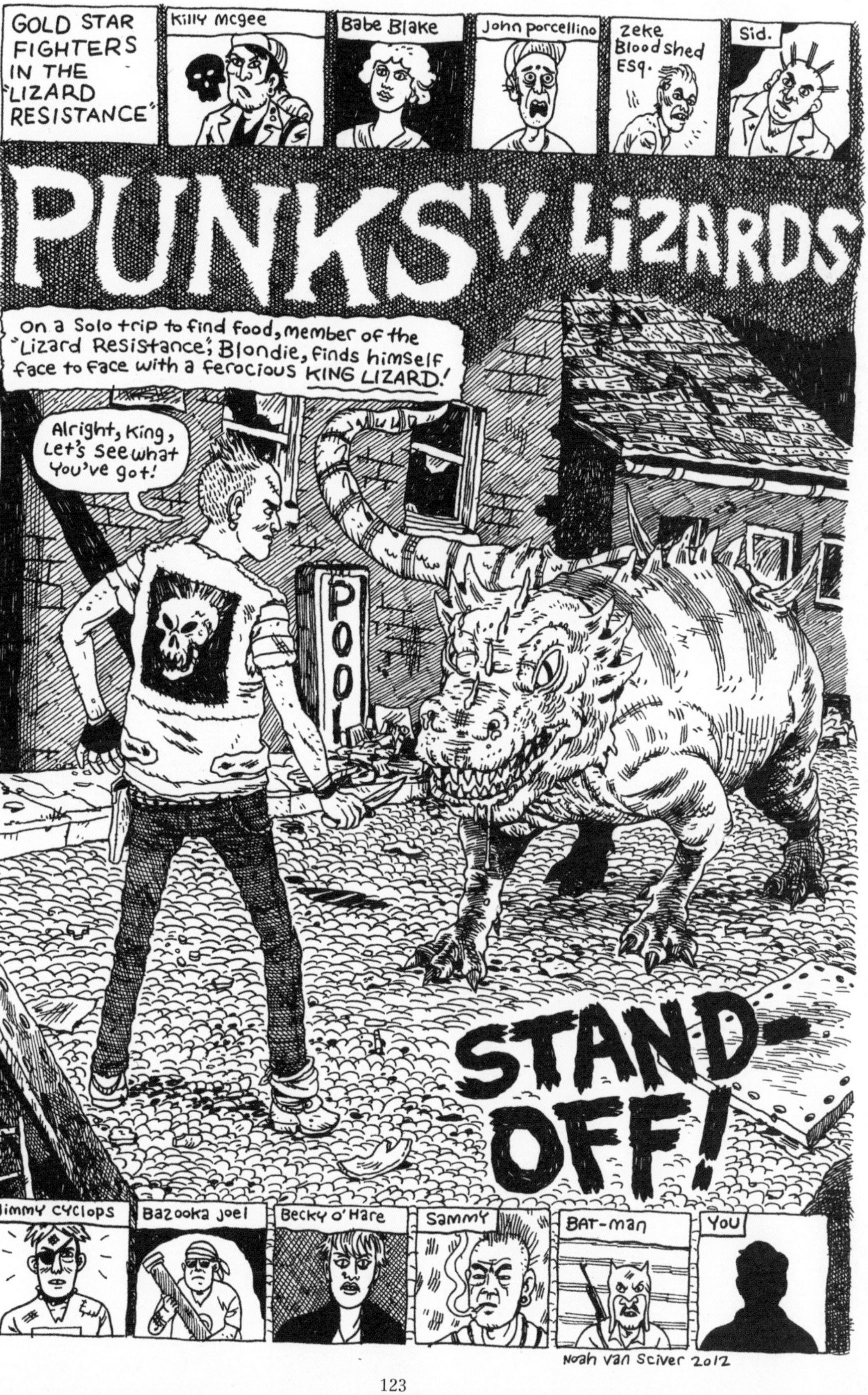
GOLD STAR FIGHTERS IN THE "LIZARD RESISTANCE"
Killy Mcgee
Babe Blake
John porcellino
Zeke Bloodshed Esq.
Sid.
PUNKS V. LiZARDS
On a Solo trip to find food, member of the "Lizard Resistance", Blondie, finds himself face to face with a ferocious KING LIZARD!
Alright, King, Let's see what You've got!
POOL
STAND-OFF!
Jimmy CYClops
Bazooka joel
Becky o' Hare
Sammy
BAT-man
YOU
Noah Van Sciver 2012

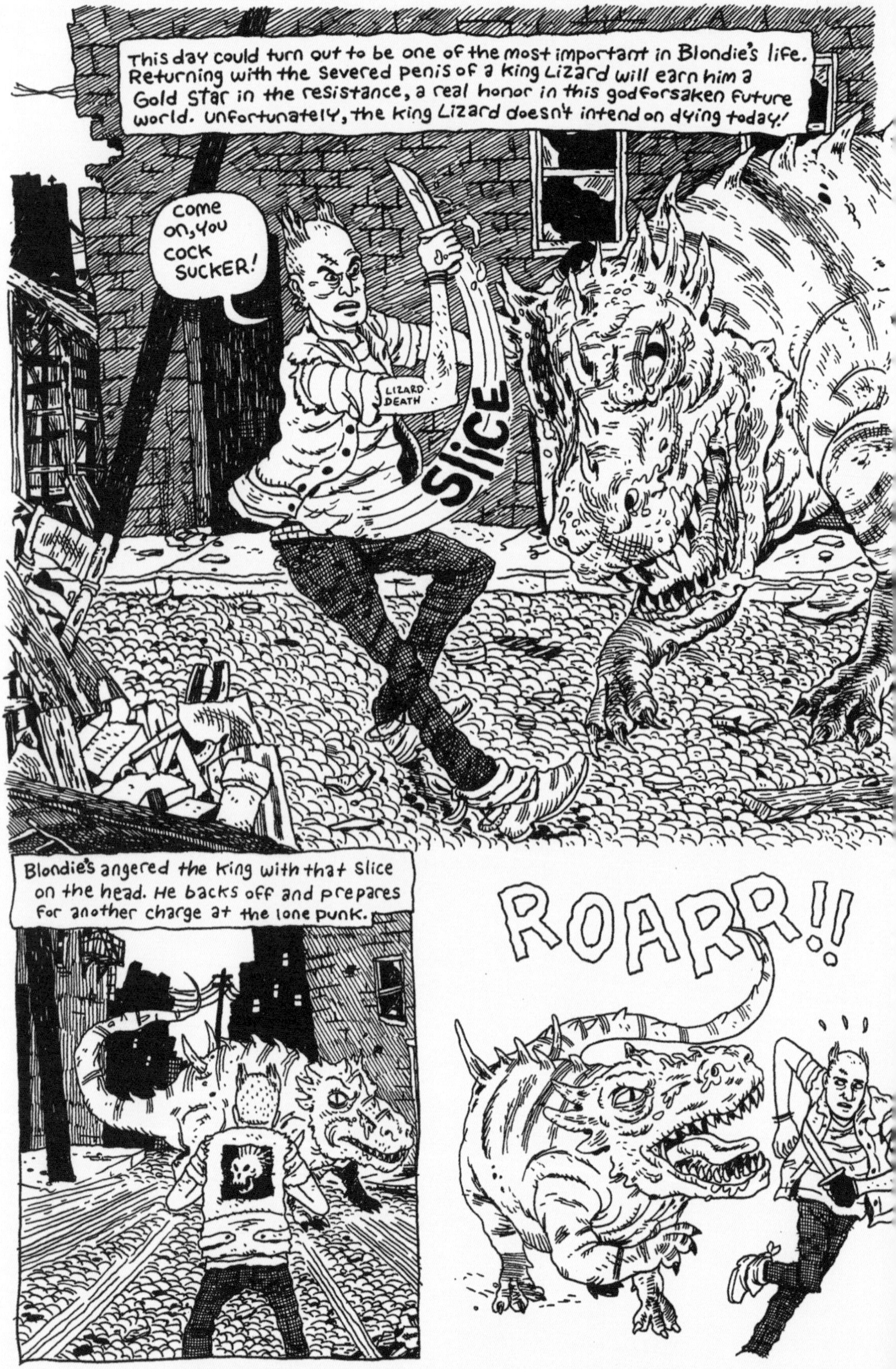
This day could turn out to be one of the most important in Blondie's life. Returning with the severed penis of a king Lizard will earn him a Gold Star in the resistance, a real honor in this godforsaken future world. Unfortunately, the king Lizard doesn't intend on dying today!
Come on, you cock sucker!
LIZARD DEATH
SLICE
Blondie's angered the king with that slice on the head. He backs off and prepares for another charge at the lone punk.
ROARR!!

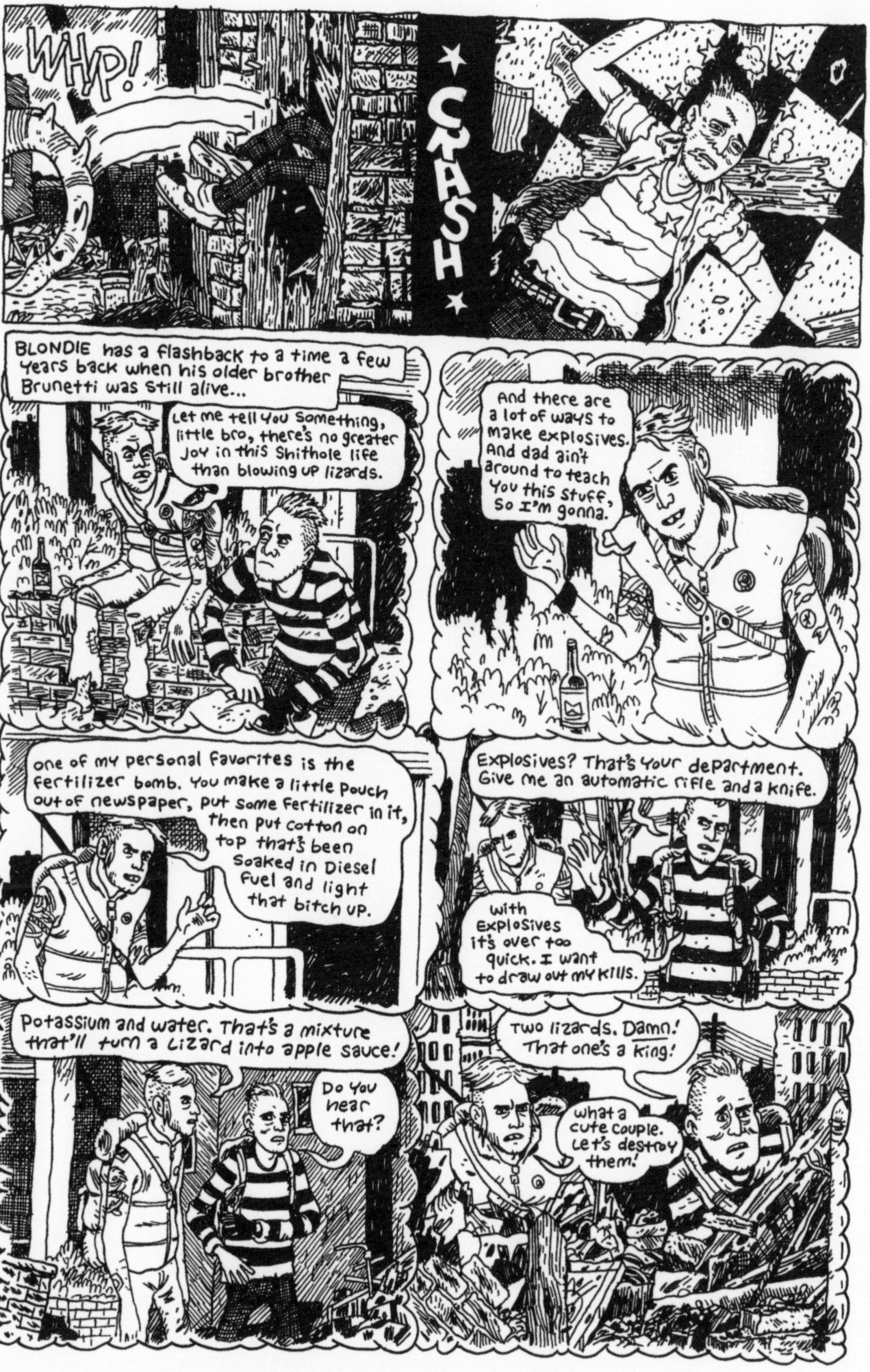
WHP!
CRASH
BLONDIE has a flashback to a time a few years back when his older brother Brunetti was still alive...
Let me tell you something, little bro, there's no greater joy in this shithole life than blowing up lizards.
And there are a lot of ways to make explosives. And dad ain't around to teach you this stuff, so I'm gonna.
One of my personal favorites is the fertilizer bomb. You make a little pouch out of newspaper, put some fertilizer in it, then put cotton on top that's been soaked in Diesel fuel and light that bitch up.
Explosives? That's your department. Give me an automatic rifle and a knife.
With explosives it's over too quick. I want to draw out my kills.
Potassium and water. That's a mixture that'll turn a lizard into apple sauce!
Do you hear that?
Two lizards. Damn! That one's a king!
What a cute couple. Let's destroy them!

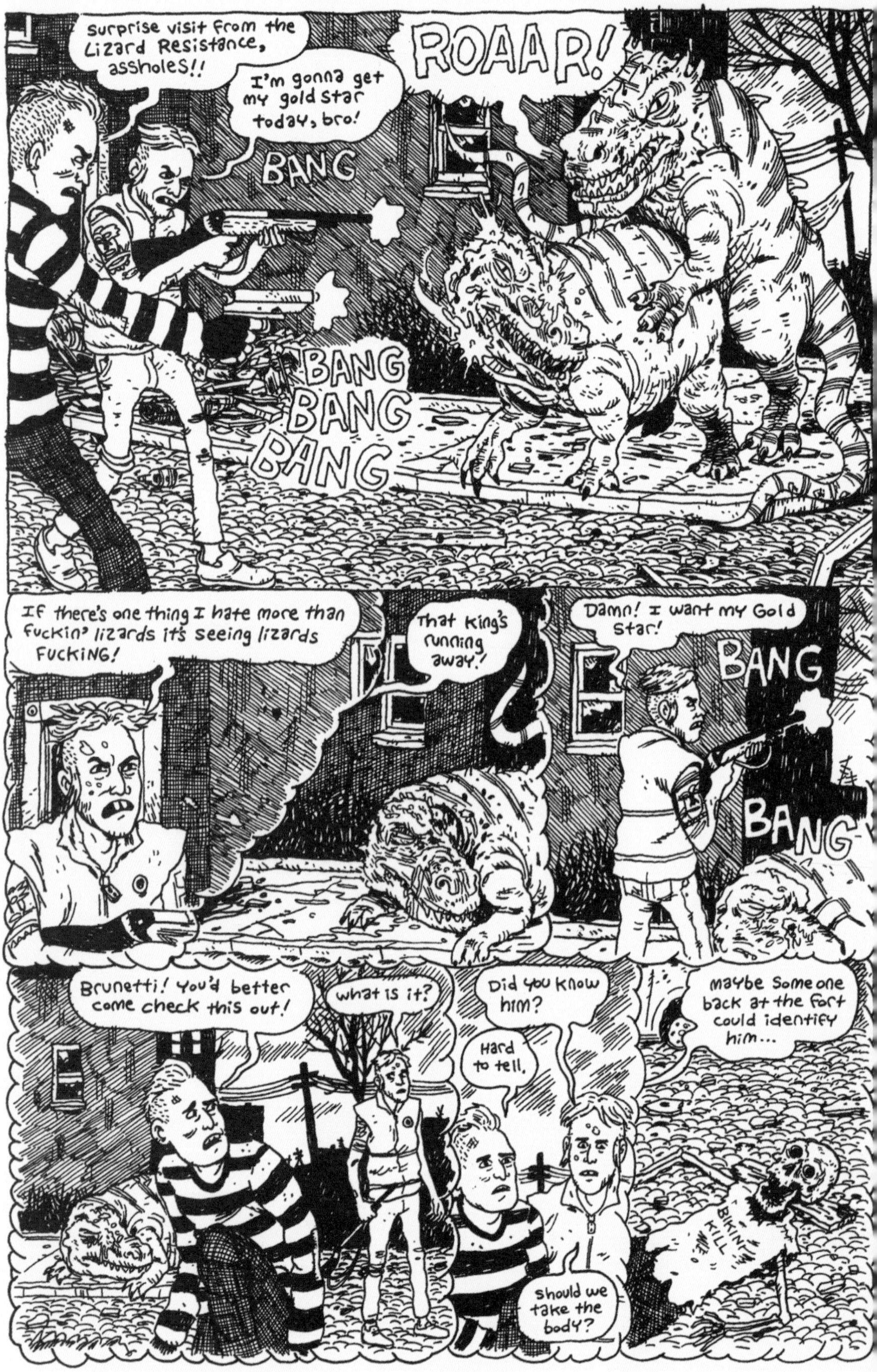
Surprise visit from the Lizard Resistance, assholes!!
I'm gonna get my gold star today, bro!
ROAAR!
BANG
BANG BANG BANG
If there's one thing I hate more than fuckin' lizards it's seeing lizards FUCKING!
That King's running away!
Damn! I want my Gold star!
BANG
BANG
Brunetti! You'd better come check this out!
what is it?
Did you know him?
Hard to tell.
maybe Some one back at the fort could identify him...
Should we take the body?
BIKINI KILL

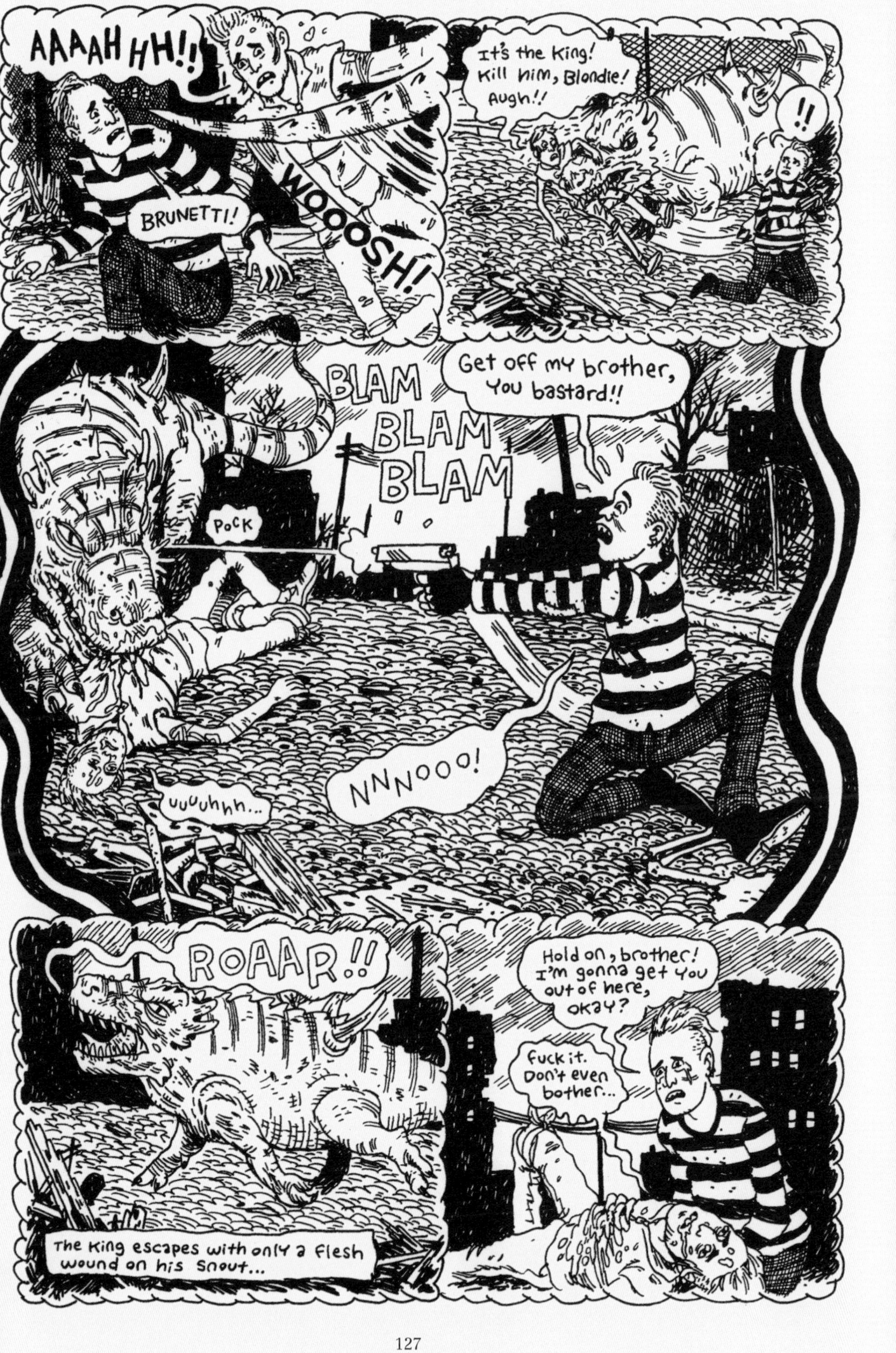
AAAAH HH!!
BRUNETTI!
WOOOOSH!
It's the King! Kill him, Blondie! Augh!!
!!
BLAM BLAM BLAM
Get off my brother, You bastard!!
POCK
NNNOOO!
uuuuhhh...
ROAAR!!
The King escapes with only a flesh wound on his snout...
Hold on, brother! I'm gonna get you out of here, okay?
fuck it. Don't even bother...

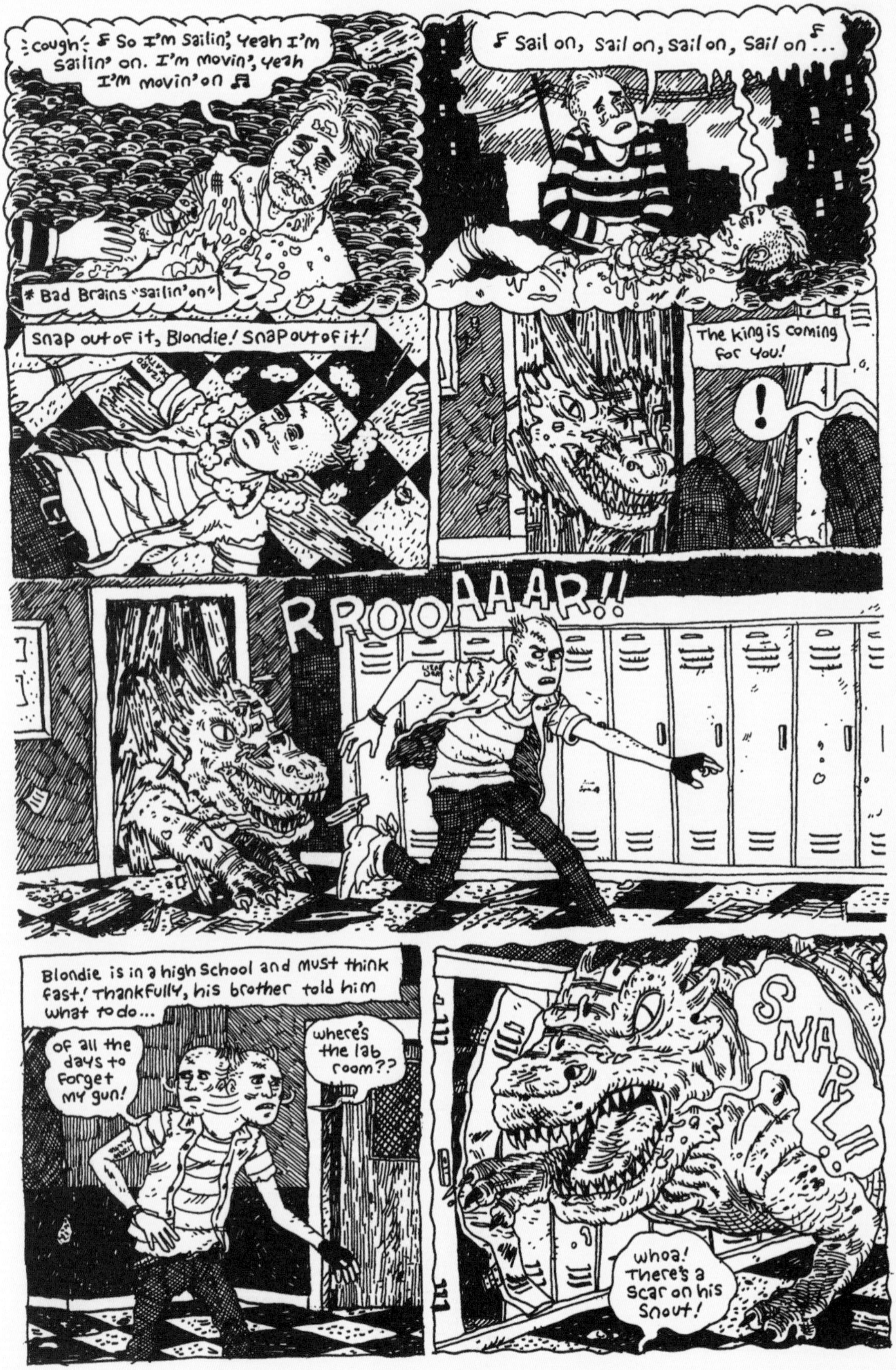
cough ♪ So I'm sailin', yeah I'm sailin' on. I'm movin', yeah I'm movin' on ♫
* Bad Brains "sailin' on"
♪ Sail on, sail on, sail on, sail on ♪ ...
Snap out of it, Blondie! Snap out of it!
The king is coming for you!
!
RROOAAAR!!
Blondie is in a high school and must think fast! Thankfully, his brother told him what to do...
of all the days to forget my gun!
where's the lab room??
SNARL!!
whoa! There's a scar on his snout!

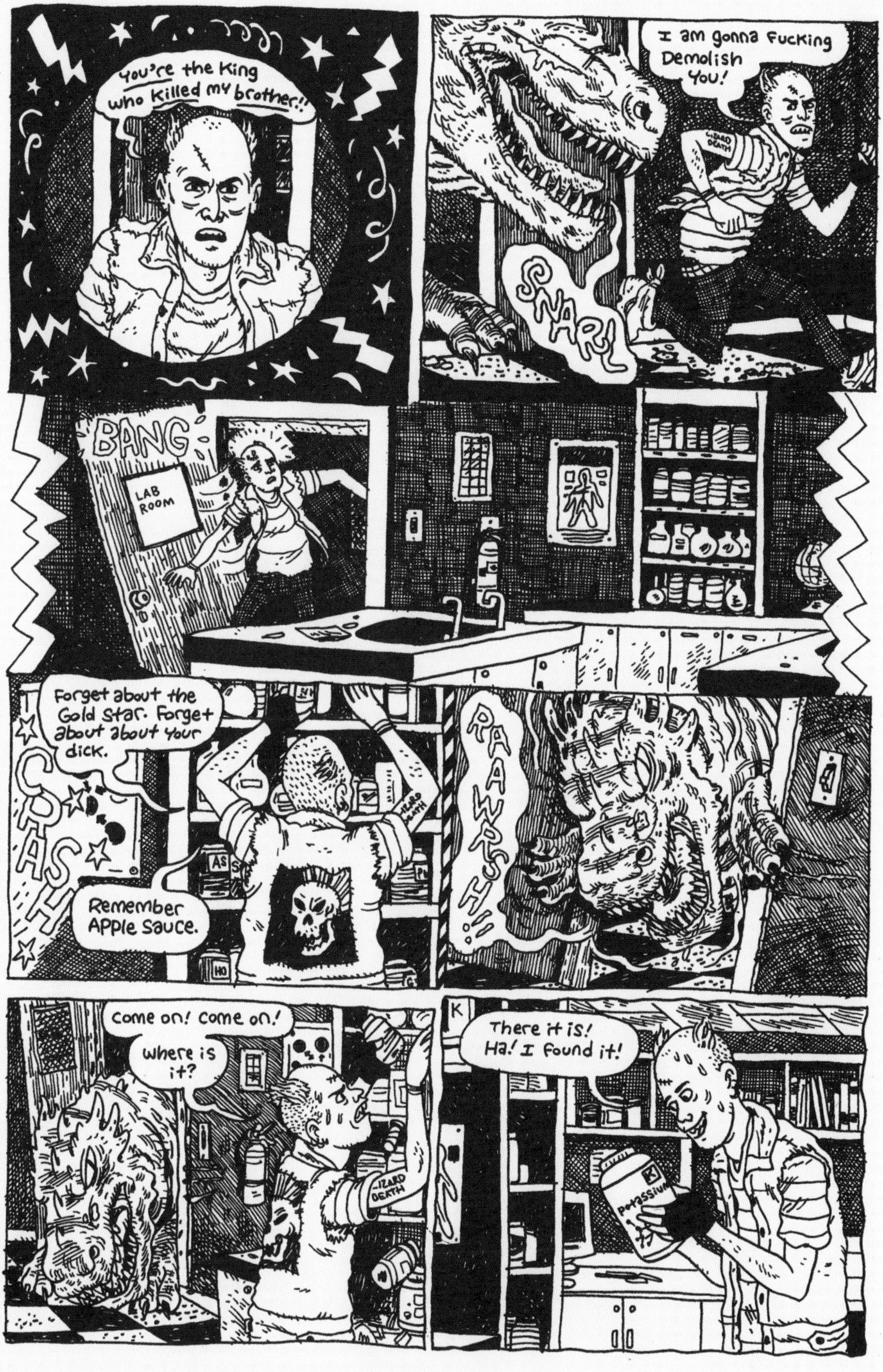
You're the King who killed my brother!!
I am gonna Fucking Demolish You!
LIZARD DEATH
SNARL
BANG
LAB ROOM
Forget about the Gold Star. Forget about about your dick.
Remember Apple Sauce.
CRASH
RAAWRSH!!
Come on! Come on!
Where is it?
LIZARD DEATH
There it is! Ha! I found it!
Potassium

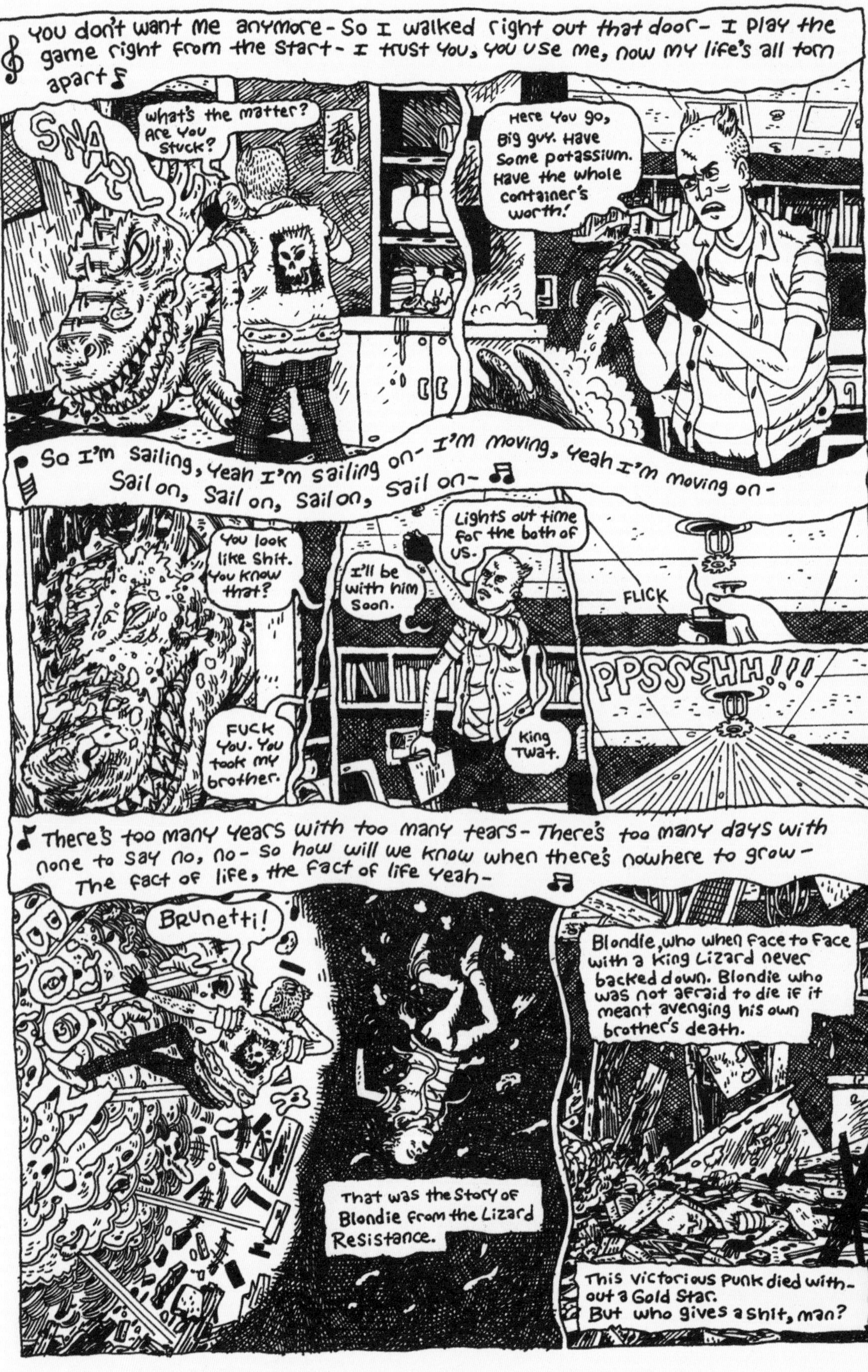
You don't want me anymore - So I walked right out that door - I play the game right from the start - I trust you, you use me, now my life's all torn apart
SNARL
What's the matter? Are you stuck?
Here you go, Big guy. Have some potassium. Have the whole container's worth!
So I'm sailing, yeah I'm sailing on - I'm moving, yeah I'm moving on - Sail on, Sail on, Sail on, Sail on -
You look like shit. You know that?
Fuck you. You took my brother.
Lights out time for the both of us.
I'll be with him soon.
King Twat.
FLICK
PPSSSHH!!!
There's too many years with too many tears - There's too many days with none to say no, no - So how will we know when there's nowhere to grow - The fact of life, the fact of life yeah -
Brunetti!
That was the story of Blondie from the Lizard Resistance.
Blondie, who when face to face with a King Lizard never backed down. Blondie who was not afraid to die if it meant avenging his own brother's death.
This victorious punk died without a Gold Star.
But who gives a shit, man?

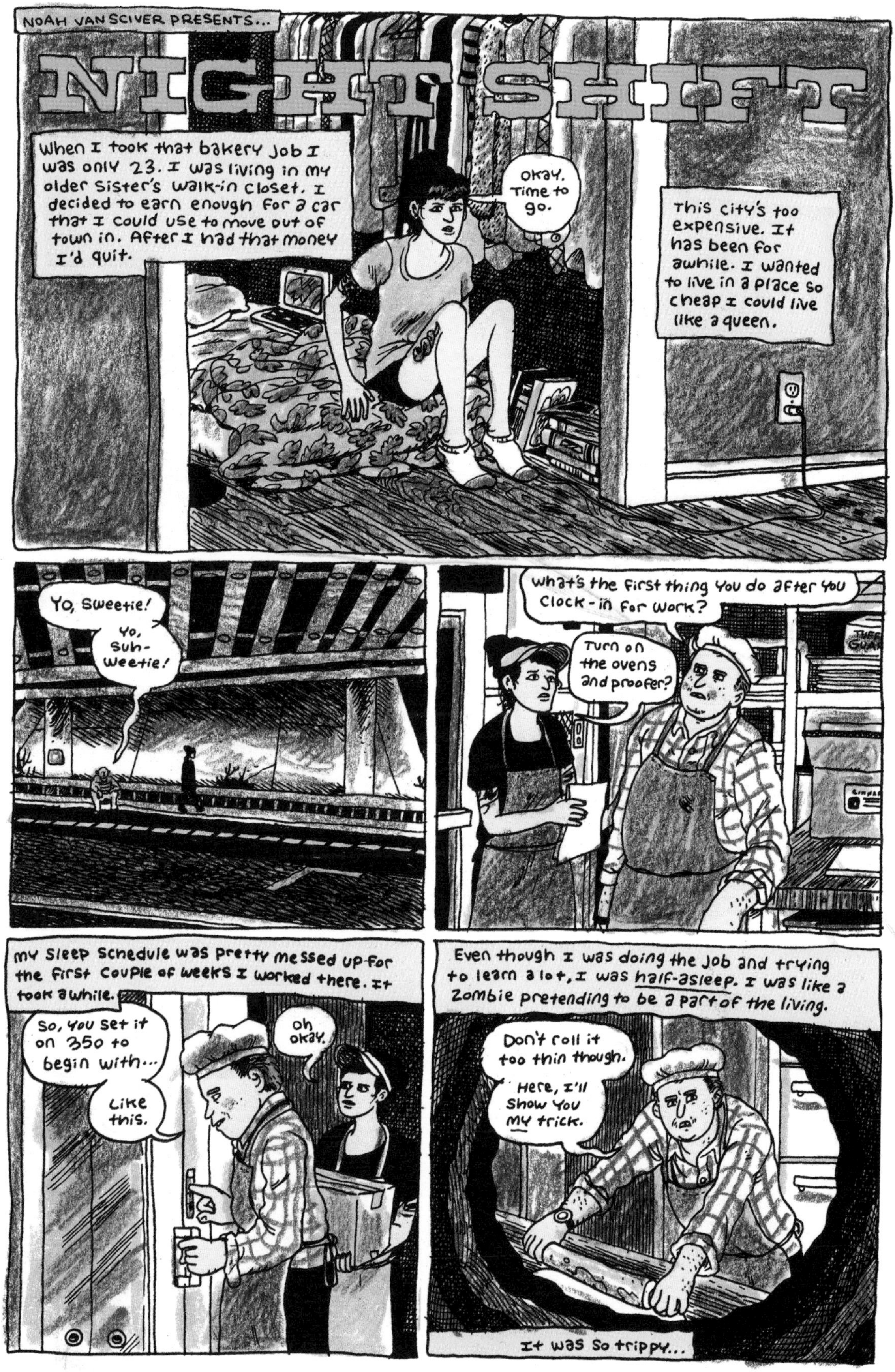
NOAH VAN SCIVER PRESENTS...
NIGHT SHIFT
When I took that bakery job I was only 23. I was living in my older sister's walk-in closet. I decided to earn enough for a car that I could use to move out of town in. After I had that money I'd quit.
Okay. Time to go.
This city's too expensive. It has been for awhile. I wanted to live in a place so cheap I could live like a queen.
Yo, sweetie!
Yo, suh-weetie!
What's the first thing you do after you clock-in for work?
Turn on the ovens and proofer?
My sleep schedule was pretty messed up for the first couple of weeks I worked there. It took awhile.
So, you set it on 350 to begin with...
Like this.
Oh okay.
Even though I was doing the job and trying to learn a lot, I was half-asleep. I was like a zombie pretending to be a part of the living.
Don't roll it too thin though.
Here, I'll show you my trick.
It was so trippy...

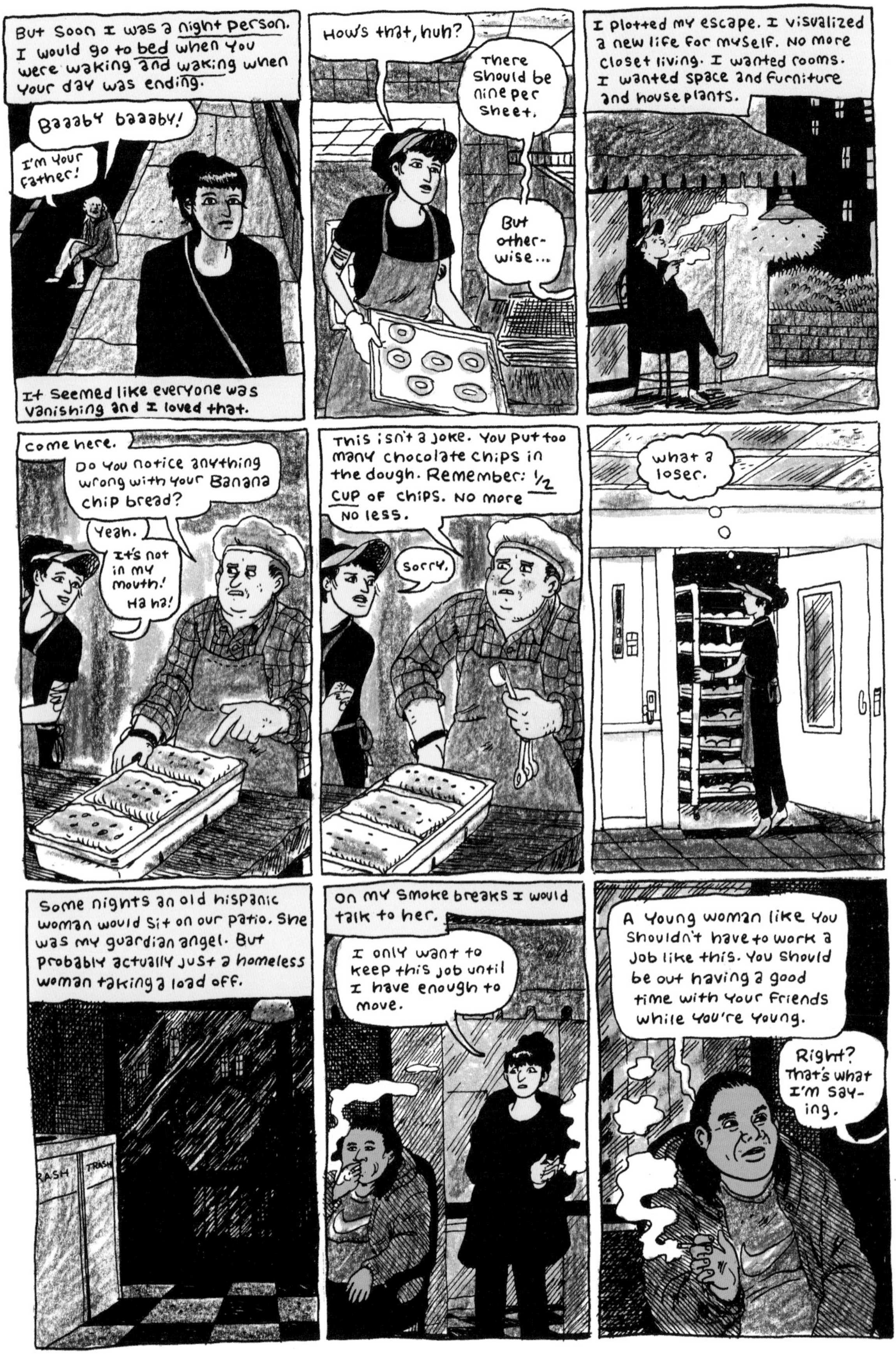
But soon I was a night person. I would go to bed when you were waking and waking when your day was ending.
Baaaby baaaby!
I'm your father!
It seemed like everyone was vanishing and I loved that.
How's that, huh?
There should be nine per sheet.
But otherwise...
I plotted my escape. I visualized a new life for myself. No more closet living. I wanted rooms. I wanted space and furniture and house plants.
Come here.
Do you notice anything wrong with your Banana chip bread?
Yeah.
It's not in my mouth! Ha ha!
This isn't a joke. You put too many chocolate chips in the dough. Remember: 1/2 cup of chips. No more no less.
Sorry.
What a loser.
Some nights an old hispanic woman would sit on our patio. She was my guardian angel. But probably actually just a homeless woman taking a load off.
TRASH
TRASH
On my smoke breaks I would talk to her.
I only want to keep this job until I have enough to move.
A young woman like you shouldn't have to work a job like this. You should be out having a good time with your friends while you're young.
Right? That's what I'm saying.

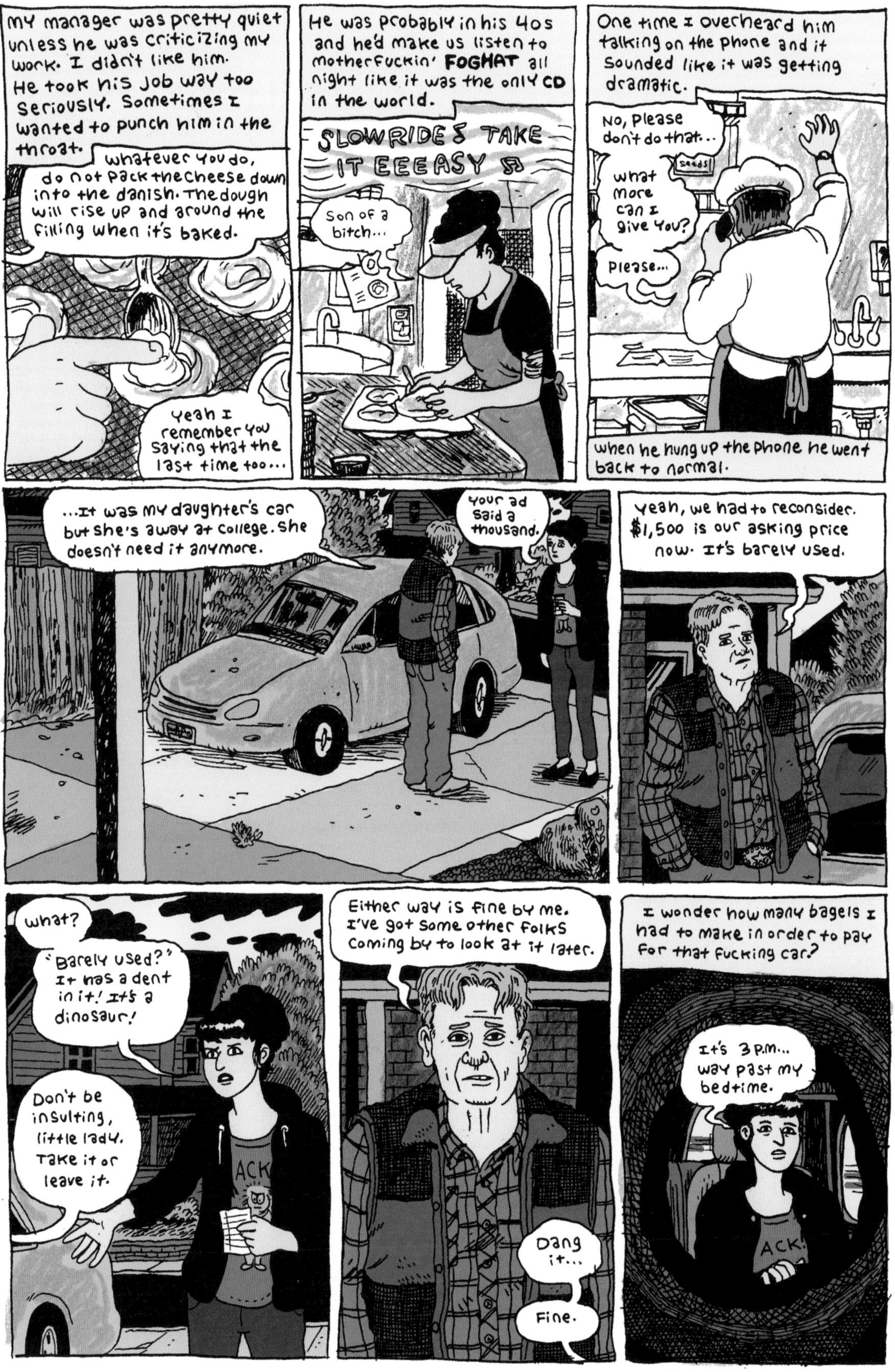
My manager was pretty quiet unless he was criticizing my work. I didn't like him. He took his job way too seriously. Sometimes I wanted to punch him in the throat.
Whatever you do, do not pack the cheese down into the danish. The dough will rise up and around the filling when it's baked.
Yeah I remember you saying that the last time too...
He was probably in his 40s and he'd make us listen to motherfuckin' FOGHAT all night like it was the only CD in the world.
SLOWRIDE TAKE IT EEEASY
Son of a bitch...
One time I overheard him talking on the phone and it sounded like it was getting dramatic.
No, please don't do that...
What more can I give you?
Please...
When he hung up the phone he went back to normal.
...It was my daughter's car but she's away at college. She doesn't need it anymore.
Your ad said a thousand.
Yeah, we had to reconsider. $1,500 is our asking price now. It's barely used.
What?
"Barely used?" It has a dent in it! It's a dinosaur!
Don't be insulting, little lady. Take it or leave it.
Either way is fine by me. I've got some other folks coming by to look at it later.
Dang it...
Fine.
I wonder how many bagels I had to make in order to pay for that fucking car?
It's 3 P.M... way past my bedtime.

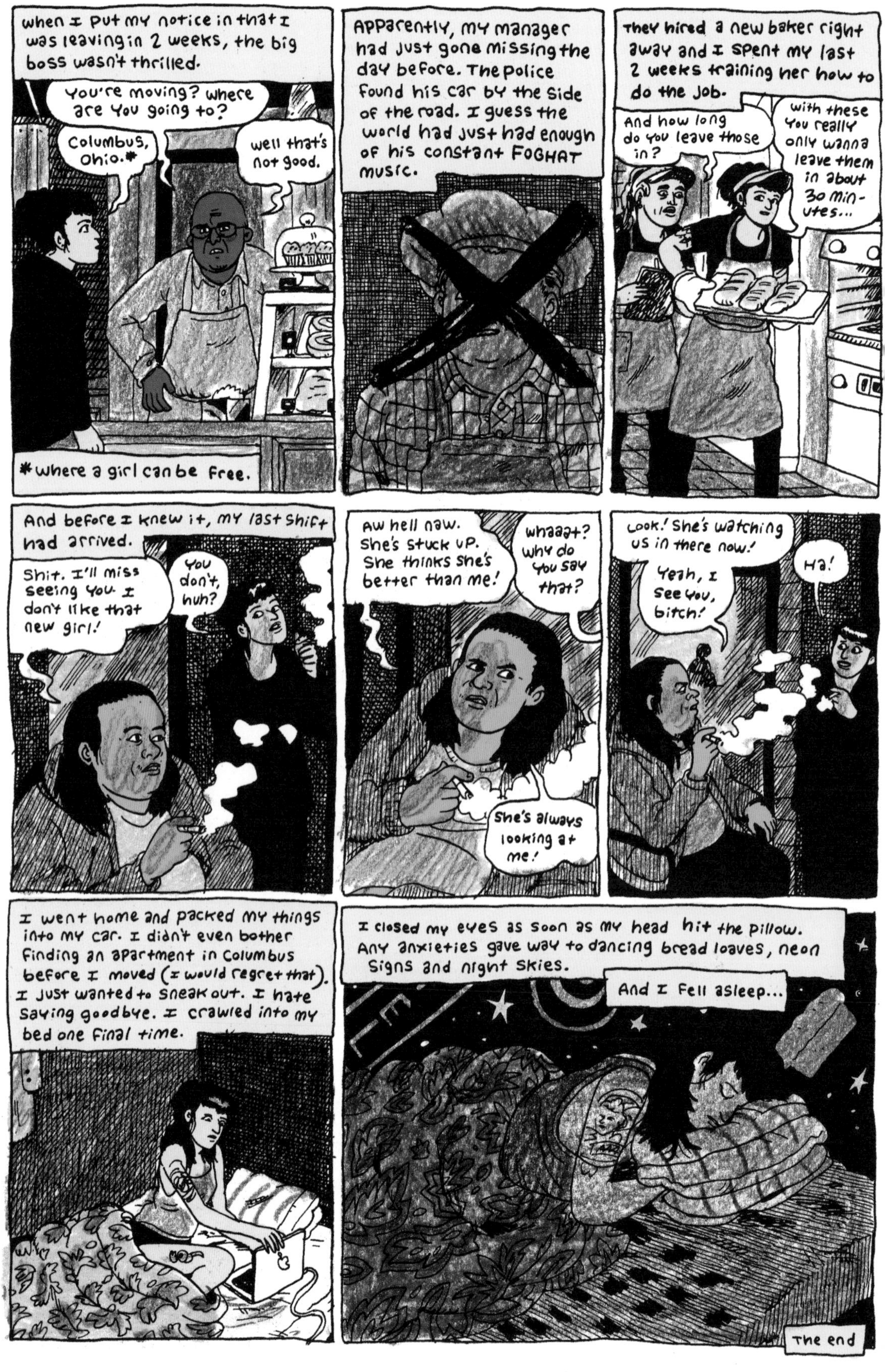
when I put my notice in that I was leaving in 2 weeks, the big boss wasn't thrilled.
You're moving? where are you going to?
Columbus, Ohio.*
well that's not good.
*where a girl can be free.
Apparently, my manager had just gone missing the day before. The police found his car by the side of the road. I guess the world had just had enough of his constant FOGHAT music.
They hired a new baker right away and I spent my last 2 weeks training her how to do the job.
And how long do you leave those in?
with these you really only wanna leave them in about 30 minutes...
And before I knew it, my last shift had arrived.
Shit. I'll miss seeing you. I don't like that new girl!
You don't, huh?
Aw hell naw. She's stuck up. She thinks she's better than me!
whaaat? why do you say that?
She's always looking at me!
Look! She's watching us in there now!
Yeah, I see you, bitch!
Ha!
I went home and packed my things into my car. I didn't even bother finding an apartment in Columbus before I moved (I would regret that). I just wanted to sneak out. I hate saying goodbye. I crawled into my bed one final time.
I closed my eyes as soon as my head hit the pillow. Any anxieties gave way to dancing bread loaves, neon signs and night skies.
And I fell asleep...
The end

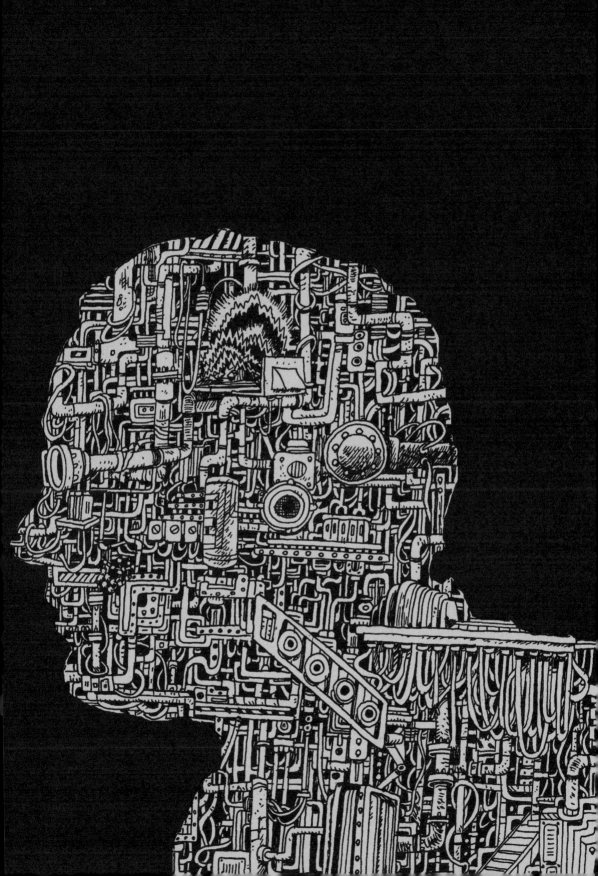

ABOUT THE ARTIST

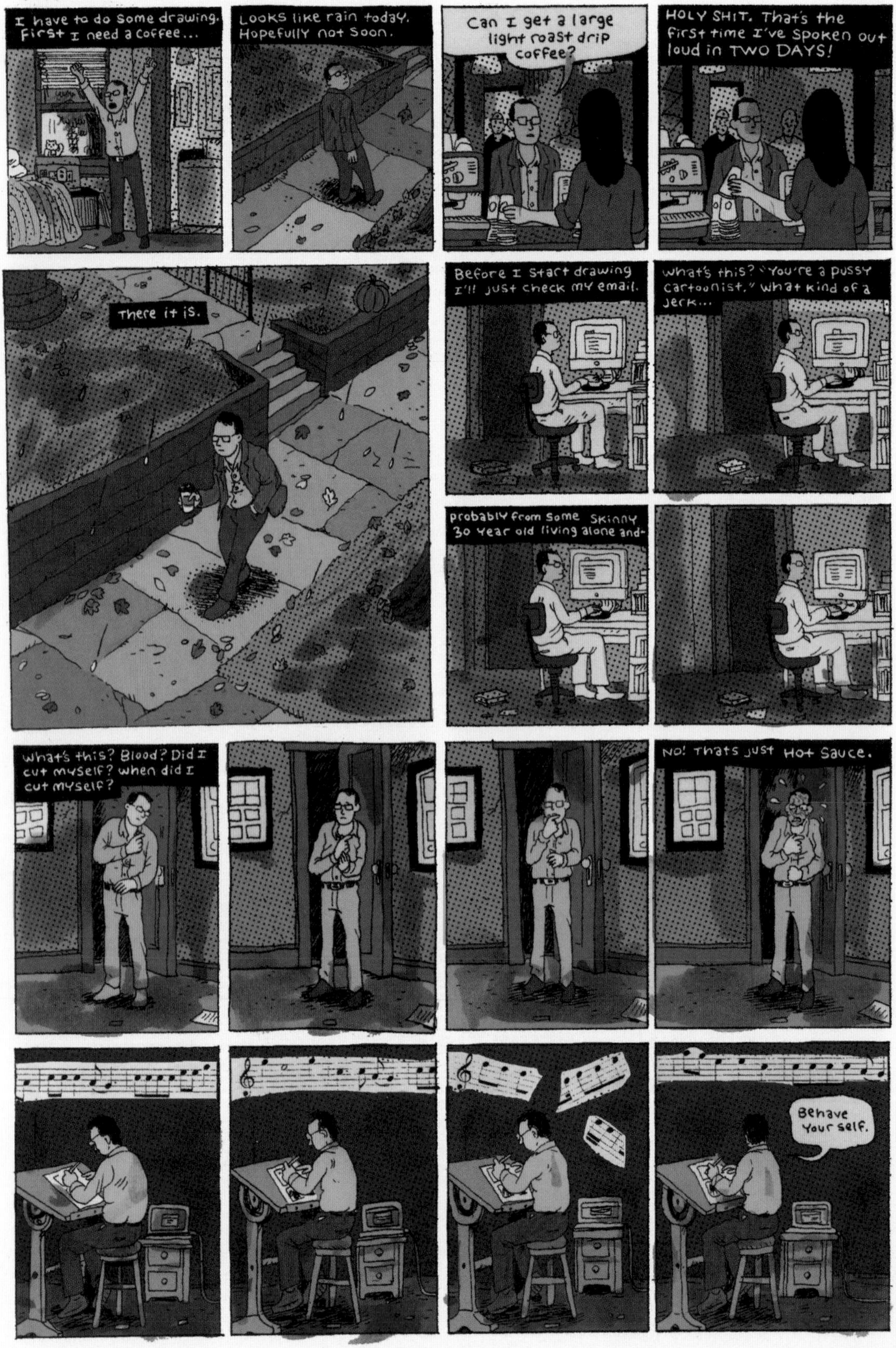
I have to do some drawing. First I need a coffee...
Looks like rain today. Hopefully not soon.
Can I get a large light roast drip coffee?
HOLY SHIT. That's the first time I've spoken out loud in TWO DAYS!
There it is.
Before I start drawing I'll just check my email.
What's this? "You're a pussy cartoonist." What kind of a jerk...
probably from some skinny 30 year old living alone and-
What's this? Blood? Did I cut myself? When did I cut myself?
No! Thats just Hot Sauce.
Behave Your self.

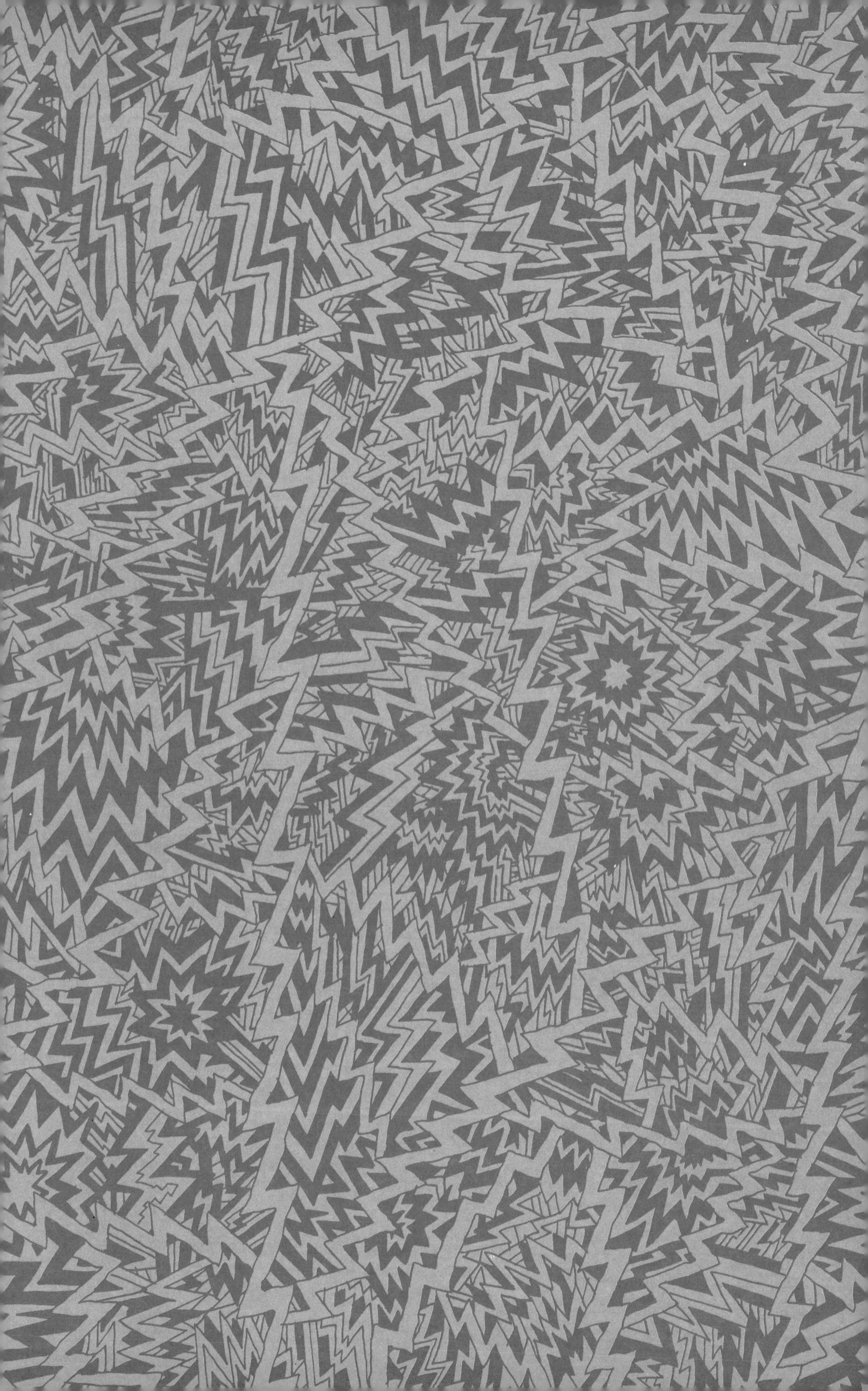